THE LAST TRIBE

DR. JOHN CLICK

To Jean a Friend but
more a Personel Friend.

John Click

ISBN: 1463584938
ISBN 13: 9781463584931
Library of Congress Control Number: 2011910225
CreateSpace, North Charleston, SC

Dedication

To Rubye, my beloved wife who has always believed me to be better than I am. To Curtis Lundgren, trusted friend and literary advisor par excellence for challenging me to make of this work a book rather than merely a writing exercise.

To Kathy Wall, novelist extraordinaire, friend and encourager, without whose counsel this novel would have remained nothing more than a protracted writing exercise and to Linda Arruza and Paula Duncan for their invaluable assistance in reviewing and editing the manuscript.

Finally, to the family of faith that is First Baptist Church of Hilton Head Island, South Carolina, and its pastor Dr. John Keller for their insights, encouragement and suggestions as the book neared completion.

Prologue

But there's a Tree, of many, one,
A single Field which I have looked upon,
Both of them speak of something that is gone

Intimations of Immortality ...   William Wordsworth

THE TWO ANIMALS LAY at the base of the tree, their fur bathed in light. For several moments, the man and woman stood silently pondering them before the man lifted one of the creatures' heads and stared quizzically into its vacant eyes. Its unblinking stare told him the shadows pressing in about them had taken something precious from the earth, something he found no words to describe.

Lava-like, the shadows oozed closer and closer toward the tree, compressing the light, until finally, as a diamond formed in the earth's dark depths, both tree and light blazed as a single beacon against the backdrop of invading gloom.

Suddenly the man's and woman's hands shot up to shield their eyes from a final radiant flash of protest as the tree and light were swallowed by the shadows. Now the man could see that nothing remained where the tree had stood except the pelts of the two animals and a small oblong stone nestled in the fur of one. Stooping, he picked it up and turned it slowly in his hands, letting his fingers trace the raised design on its surface. In its depths, he saw the light, which only moments before seemed extinguished by the shadows, still blazed brightly.

Bending again, he retrieved the skins. Draping one over the shoulders of the woman and the other around his own, he pointed toward the horizon and began walking. In the distance, dark clouds gathered, and a cold wind announced an approaching storm.

Clutching the stone tightly, he felt the warmth of its inner fire and with it a comforting conviction: *The storm will pass.* Assured by the thought, he smiled at the woman for the first time since they had entered the shadows. The storm drew closer, the wind colder, yet the stone's warmth remained constant. More, its heat was spreading—first up his arm, then, in what seemed only a moment, enfolded his whole body in the cocoon of its embrace. Reaching, he took the woman's hand, hoping her touch would confirm what he was feeling. It did. Her gentle squeeze and the wonder written on her face were all the assurance he needed the stone's warmth had reached her as well.

United by memories of what had been and was no more, they began walking toward the distant horizon, the stone's warmth infusing their hearts with certainty that somewhere beyond the storm lay a way of escape from the shadows.

CHAPTER 1

JERUSALEM, 70 AD

RESIGNED, THE OLD MAN embraced his fate, clutched his soiled robe tightly about him, and shuffled wearily along the corridor behind the young soldier. Light from the guard's torch painted flickering images on the passage's stonewalls, and a cool mustiness enveloped the pair when they opened the ancient oak door.

"Hurry, there's not much time," the old man muttered, more to himself than to the soldier, as he commanded his ancient body to move faster. From somewhere above them, the sounds of muffled cries and the clash of swords on shields announced that the final assault had begun.

Rome's legions have broken through. That thought, sharper than any Roman's blade, cut him to the heart. The Temple, like the rest of Jerusalem, was destined for destruction. That realization, coupled with the feeling of impending doom he'd first felt on sighting Titus's approaching legions months before, spurred him on through the tunnel beneath the Temple toward his final appointment with destiny.

The sun's journey across the heavens had just begun when he finished offering incense and prayers for the last time in the Temple's Holy Place. The bile rising in his throat brought with it the bitter taste of indescribable loss.

He had hardly said "amen" when, from beyond the veil of the Holy of Holies, he heard a chorus of voices shouting to one another, "Let us depart! Let us depart!"

Those voices, and the terrifying apprehension that God was abandoning them, confirmed his fears with sickening certainty when the altar fire flickered out and he felt the brush of angels' wings as they departed.

Ahead, the old man saw the guard had stopped at a stone barrier, one so skillfully fitted together the thinnest blade could not slide between its joints.

"Hold the light here."

Pointing to a corner where the barrier and the corridor joined, the Priest felt along its edge until his fingers found a slight indentation in one of the stones. Placing both hands there, he pressed with all of his fading strength, his effort rewarded by the sound of stone grinding against stone as the barrier pivoted back to reveal a stairway descending into the darkness.

"Lead and I will follow."

Reaching out unsteadily, he put a quivering hand on the guard's shoulder and for a moment watched the torch light flicker before beginning the slow descent. Shouts and cries from above grew fainter with each step so that by the time they reached the bottom of the stairs the surrounding bedrock had almost muffled the sounds completely.

Just beyond the stairs, the guard stood before a door.

"In here," the old man said breathlessly as he moved ahead to open it.

For a moment, both men stood transfixed at the entrance to a vault-like room carved from solid rock, its walls awash with torchlight reflecting off metal vessels of every description: golden pots, bowls, censers, knives, tongs, candlesticks, brass fittings for curtains—priceless objects whose disarray testified to the haste with which the Temple's custodians had hidden its treasures.

"Bring the torch, my son." The old man, now hidden in the shadows, had reached the far corner of the room." You must prepare yourself," he said with such sad resignation it brought tears to the young guard's eyes.

He's prepared me well already, he thought as he wiped them away. Many times, they had rehearsed the route he would take along the watercourse that led under the city wall and into the valley, and he knew by heart the path from there to the hiding place in the wilderness. But none of the high Priest's instructions had prepared him for his last, painful duty.

"They are here," he said softly.

The guard could see the Priest clearly now. As he raised the lid of an oblong chest, a brilliant flash of torchlight reflecting off its golden surface punctuated his announcement.

Carefully, he reached into the box and withdrew a small object wrapped in animal skin along with a scroll, tied with a leather thong.

"Take these to the place that has been prepared," he said, presenting the objects to the guard.

Beyond the chest, the guard could see the curtains on the far wall swaying gently. *A breeze from the hidden passage,* he realized, as he accepted his precious charges. *The master has opened the secret door.*

"Hide them well," the old man said as he turned and knelt before the chest. "They must not be found until the time comes around again. But now my son." The old man's voice broke under the weight of unspeakable sorrow. "You must perform this last service for me."

The guard laid his charges aside and placed his torch in a holder beside the chest, thankful his master could not see his face or the hot tears flowing down his cheeks. Drawing his sword, he raised it high above the nape of the old man's neck.

Make my stroke clean and merciful, he prayed, feeling his hands suddenly steadied by an ingrained sense of duty.

The old man was also praying—not as the high Priest over the Temple of God, but in the soft and humble voice of a supplicant seeking admission into a King's presence.

"God of Abraham, Isaac, and Jacob, receive the soul of your servant."

"And mine," the guard cried as his sword flashed, sharp steel found its mark, and the blood of the high Priest splattered on the golden lid of the chest.

In the passageway just above the crypt, the guard could hear the faint tramp of hob-nailed boots as he retrieved the two precious objects and disappeared into the darkness beyond the curtain.

CHAPTER 2

PALESTINE, 1291 AD

BALIAN, MASTER OF THE Fortress of Saint Jean, had always done his duty. Now only one remained. From the rocky escarpment above the Sea of Salt, he could see the end approaching. Jerusalem had fallen and with it the dream inspiring the Crusades. Soon the land of Christ would no longer be a protected province for Christian pilgrims as the Knights Templar had envisioned.

A message had just arrived confirming his worst fears. Terse in the extreme, it did not carry the slightest hint of the promised reinforcements or the launching of a counter-offensive. Instead, the words reeked of defeat.

"All Templars," it said, "still occupying outlying fortresses are ordered to fall back to Acre immediately."

The Pope's promises are not worth the price of his indulgences, Balian thought bitterly. As for the king's assurances… If reports are true, his treasury is as empty as our granary.

With sorrow akin to a lost love, he knew that when Acre fell, Christendom's last foothold in Palestine would be gone forever and Islam's crescent moon would at last have conquered the cross of Christ.

Light from a single lamp painted flickering shapes on the walls of the small room where Balian sat at a crude table. For a moment, the quill quivered in his hand above the parchment on which he had been writing. Then, with grim resolution, he willed himself to sign his name.

Done, he tipped the lamp bowl and let the hot wax drip on the parchment below his signature. Then, removing his signet ring, he pressed it into the wax, rolled up the letter, and put it in the leather pouch along with the ancient scroll and stone.

From a shelf above the table, he retrieved his personal journal and found his account of the Bedouin shepherd's story. The man reported he had come upon a cave while herding his sheep in the hills above the Sea of Salt. Entering, he was surprised to discover a stone jar, but after breaking its seal was disappointed to find it held nothing but a scroll and a translucent, oblong stone with queer raised markings wrapped in a piece of animal skin. Knowing the Christian warriors and their holy men's interest in such worthless things, he brought his discoveries to the fortress hoping for a reward.

The scroll's ancient language was a mystery to Balian. As for the stone, one look into its shimmering depths was enough to convince him the Bedouin's only reward must be a merciful death. What dark powers slept within its heart was a mystery, but he trembled at the thought of what might happen if evil men awakened them. With the end so near, he could not keep such a secret to himself. It was imperative that the scroll and stone be carried to Beaujeu, commander of the fortress at Acre. He would know how to protect them so that none but The Brotherhood would ever know of their existence.

Bracing his hands against the edge of the table, Balian pushed himself slowly to his feet, pausing for a moment before reaching down and rolling up his journal, and returning it to the shelf.

Then, picking up the leather pouch, he squared his shoulders, walked across the room, and retrieved his sword and helmet from a rack. A dozen steps brought him through the door and down the passageway to the cave's entrance where for a moment he paused, letting his eyes follow the Jordan River snaking through the valley below. Then, in a voice betraying resignation to his fate, he barked an order.

"Seal the cave! Prepare to form up! We ride to Acre!"

CHAPTER 3

ACRE, 1291 AD

THEY CAME AT SUNRISE. The dull thud of catapults and the thunder of boulders crashing against the crumbling walls suddenly stopped, leaving behind contrails of brooding silence that hovered over Acre, smothering any remaining hope for escape. Suddenly, drummers astride hundreds of lumbering camels began moving forward to the slow, staccato beat of kettledrums announcing the coming of the forces of Khalil and his Egyptian Mamluks.

Now the city will fall quickly. Beaujeu was sure of it. Through the windows of his tower chamber, he could hear the thunder of the drums growing louder by the moment. His eyes swept the plain and hills beyond the walls and for several moments, he saw nothing. Then, like disciplined columns of black ants, the Mamluks spilled over the crest of the hills until they stretched in unbroken, motionless lines around the north, south, and east sides of the city. As if cued by an invisible hand, the drumming suddenly stopped, and an ominous silence once again settled in.

Beaujeu eyed his knights positioned along the battlements as they nervously fingered their crossbows.

The enemy waits for fear to collect in their hearts, he thought, and their anxious glances told him it had. He felt it too, choking off any lingering hope of escape.

Just then the drumming began again, not in a slow beat as before but in quick-time, as thousands of black-robed warriors, their scimitars flashing, flooded down from the hills and out upon the plain, where they congealed into a swelling black tide surging toward the battered walls of Acre.

What fools we were to believe them, Beaujeu reflected bitterly, as the Mamluks' drums grew still louder. Like his brother knights, his vow to Pope and king had meant everything. By the grace of God and their sovereign's good pleasure, they had pledged to break the Moslem grip on the land of Christ. Now years of constant warfare and the growing indifference of both his sovereign and the Pope had robbed him, like many of his brothers, of his idealism and sense of holy purpose.

He had wanted to believe King Philip and the Holy Father when they promised reinforcements were coming. Now he realized their treasuries to fund more troops were as empty as their assurances and only death or slavery awaited every Christian that remained in the city. His last spark of idealism flickered out as he thought *I have but two remaining duties to fulfill: secreting away the stone and scroll and making one last stand for Christ and King.*

He heard the door open. Turning, he was relieved to see that his beloved friend and counselor Friar Ricoldo had arrived in answer to his summons. A lean, grave man with hawkish features and burning eyes, Ricoldo was Father Confessor to the Templars at Acre and the only person Beaujeu trusted completely. More importantly, Jacques de Molay, The Brotherhood's Grand Master, trusted him as well.

With a weak smile, he acknowledged his friend then went to his desk and finished the letter he had begun on a piece of fresh parchment. After sealing it, he placed it in Ricoldo's outstretched hand.

"See that his Holiness gets this message," he said, then, reached across his desk to retrieve the leather pouch Balian's knight had delivered two days ago.

As they approached Acre, Balian and his men were caught in an ambush and the messenger had been the only survivor.

"Master Balian's charge to me," the knight reported, was that I get this pouch to you at all costs. He said the letter inside would explain everything."

"This pouch must be delivered to Templar Commander de Molay on Cyprus," Beaujeu said, passing it to Ricoldo. "Guard it as you would the life of the Holy Father."

The report of Balian concerning the stone had read like the ravings of one overcome by desert heat. However, if true, none but the Templar's inner circle must ever see it. Only de Molay could ensure such secrecy.

He and the Priest walked to the window overlooking the harbor. It was filled with ships of every sort, some in the final stages of preparation to flee the doomed city, others already sailing out of the harbor.

"Your ship awaits, Ricoldo," Beaujeu said, putting his arm on the Priest's shoulder and drawing him close.

"Let me stay and die with you." His voice broke, and Beaujeu felt his friend's shoulders shaking.

"Sometimes more courage is needed to live than to die," Beaujeu said as he opened the door and gently led the Priest down the steep steps and out onto the street. "Your duty, my friend, is to deliver the pouch to de Molay and my letter to the Holy Father. Now go!" Steeling himself against any further display of emotion, he pushed the Priest away. "Fulfill your duty, as I must mine."

He turned and, without a backward glance, reentered the fortress, retraced his steps up the stairway, and joined his brother knights on the wall by the eastern gate.

Sensing nearness to the boundary between life and death, each knight was lost in thoughts of home and family, of lives lived well or fruitlessly. But most of all they pondered that moment, now so near, when each would stand before his God.

The drumbeats grew louder. Louder still a shout that shook each knight from his reverie and brought hands to chests in the sign of the cross as "Allah Akbar!" the war cry of the faithful, erupted from thousands of throats and echoed off the crumbling walls of Acre.

The avengers of blood had come.

Chapter 4

The baby that would be Ruth lay wrapped in a warm, embracing cocoon of darkness, a darkness that hid past and future and compressed her memories into a constant now. Darkness was her whole world, all she could perceive, except for the whisperers. She did not understand them, but even if she had, she could not have answered since her vocal chords were still unformed. All she could do was wait, silent and sightless, as tissue fused itself in place and bone joined to bone. Wait, comforted by a single thought: I am not alone in the darkness.

Lubbock, Texas,
Baptist Memorial Hospital
Christmas Eve

ON THE CHRISTMAS EVE night Ruth Starling was born, the icy fingers of a "Blue Norther" strummed shrill tunes on ten thousand miles of highline wires crisscrossing the West Texas plains. The weatherman on WOR-TV had been only partially right. The storm he predicted had arrived, but with a fury he did not expect. Winter had come, bringing with it bloated gray clouds, pregnant with the promise of a white Christmas.

Wind tore at the flashing and gutters of Lubbock's Baptist Memorial Hospital, sending wails of protest deep inside, reaching all the way back to delivery room 10A where Frank Starling had been keeping an anxious vigil beside his wife Diana for almost seven hours.

Frank left the house early to put out hay for the livestock. Upon returning, he found Diana waiting just inside the kitchen door, eyeing the lowering clouds. Their house leaned slightly, as an old man, bent under the weight of its years. The panes of its westward looking windows always flashed gold at sunset, as though scanning the horizon for rescue from the assault of time.

"I was getting worried." A hint of nervousness in Diana's voice caused Frank to glance at the outline of her swollen belly.

It won't be long, he thought, savoring the prospect of becoming a father just as a sudden shiver reminded him of how chilled and already bone-weary he was.

Like his father, farming was Frank's life, each row planted, an extension of himself, and every harvest a testimony to his cooperation with the Creator. The land, like a book, was understandable only to those who knew its language. Early on he had learned the vocabulary of the seasons with their numbing winters, sizzling dry summers. and in between, the frustration and disappointment that cloaked itself in the boiling clouds of springtime.

Frank looked over as Diana held out a brightly wrapped box.

"Honey, I'm afraid you won't be here to open this in the morning." Flashing Frank a knowing look, she held out the gift. "With the Norther blowing in, you might as well have the use of..."

She didn't bother finishing her sentence. Frank hadn't heard a word she'd said.

Slumping into a chair at the kitchen table, he began removing his boots.

"I'm sorry," he managed to say before she dropped the box in his lap and cupped her hands around the bulging presence of their child.

From the beginning of their marriage, he and Diana had wanted children, but after four years of waiting they had almost lost hope of having any. Her gynecologist was not encouraging, and a second opinion only confirmed the diagnosis: Diana could not conceive.

Their miracle began on a brisk Sunday morning the previous spring. Fog blanketed the fields like a delicate lace tapestry as they made the five-mile drive to Lone Oak Church, where they attended. Hardly a word passed between them during the drive, their thoughts as impenetrable as the gauzy whiteness around them.

They argued quietly last night, the subject a recurring theme of late –adoption. As always, there had been no resolution.

By the time they exited the church, the fog had lifted and the sky scrubbed clean of clouds, and the warm sun gave no hint winter had just passed. As usual, Pastor Travis Duncan was standing outside the door greeting each family with a smile, some small talk, and a warm handshake.

His demeanor changed, however, as they approached, and he led them aside, out of hearing of the rest of the congregation.

"I know how much you and Frank want a baby," he said without preamble.

Diana stiffened with surprise and then dropped her head as her eyes filled with tears.

Reverend Duncan gently cupped her chin in his hands, raised her head, and looked directly into her eyes. "Soon, Diana, very soon," he promised, "God will give you the baby you've prayed for."

The early morning cold had finally loosened its grip. Now Frank studied his wife with concern. He could see the perspiration beading on her forehead as her pale face registered discomfort. Then he spotted her overnight bag on the floor and her heavy winter coat hanging on the chair beside it.

Frank leaped to his feet, the forgotten Christmas present crushed in his hands. "It's time?"

"Yes." She smiled broadly, as she gently rescued the box from his trembling fingers, lifted the lid and held up the heavy wool shirt, measuring it against his broad shoulders.

She gasped as her belly tightened in the second contraction in less than an hour.

"Put this on and get me to the hospital," she groaned through gritted teeth, "unless you want to deliver this baby yourself!"

Frank grabbed the shirt and began buttoning it. "Couldn't have made a better pick myself," he said as his weathered face erupted into the same boyish grin that had first drawn Diana to him back in high school.

Frank's heart fluttered. He wondered if Diana could see it beating through his new shirt as he bent to grab her overnight bag. He hoped growing concern for his wife did not register on his face and that his tone of voice contained no hint of worry about their baby's welfare.

As they left the house, dark gray clouds blowing in from the west announced the approaching blizzard, but for Frank another storm was brewing, one that had blown open the door in his mind, exposing memories he had hidden away since the terrifying Sunday night nine months ago.

Frank and Diana had always enjoyed each other physically, and that night their passion had carried both of them to new heights.

Diana nestled into the curve of Frank's body, a faint smile touching her lips as she slept. He had been unable to go to sleep, his thoughts running over a sermon Pastor Duncan had preached several weeks before. It was about faith, and though he could not recall all of it, the pastor's definition had stuck with him.

"Faith," he had said, "is seeing the invisible, believing the incredible, and then doing the impossible."

He remembered looking over at Diana, asleep beside him, marveling at her simple faith in the pastor's words that morning.

She believes, he thought and suddenly realized that he did too. That simple affirmation was enough to buoy him up with certainty that, despite all the doctors' dire predictions, his wife had just conceived.

Around midnight, he finally willed his eyes to close. As they did, he imagined a curtain rising on a play in which his family would play a major part. *A divinely directed drama*, he reflected, wondering where such an odd thought had come from...

A low growl jerked him from his reverie, freezing his mind in mid-thought. He was sure the sound came from somewhere on the porch roof that extended below the windows along the front of the house. Silver moonlight filtered through the curtains, and his internal alarm was sounding. *Warning! Danger!*

Jumping out of bed, he flung on his robe and raced to the bedroom closet. Fumbling behind a rack of clothes, he found his twelve-gauge shotgun, quickly loaded it with double-aught buckshot, then bolted down the stairs and out into the front yard.

Sprinting to the corner of the house where the limbs of a large tree overhung the roof of the porch, he stopped. Out of breath, he looked down. For a moment, he could not process what he saw.

Paw prints. As large as a man's hands, they shimmered in the moonlight as if drawn in phosphorescent paint. His mind raced.

No animal he knew of from these parts could have made them. Amazingly, the prints had left no indentions in the soft earth. Hesitantly, he touched one with the toe of his slipper. It dissolved instantly, leaving not even disheveled grass to mark where it had been.

Frank shook as his gaze followed the ghostly trail up the trunk of the tree. *Some huge animal on the roof of the porch!*

With no time to reflect, near panic sent him racing farther out into the yard to get a better view of the roof.

Turning, he looked up.

Framed by moonlight, he saw the horror that had awakened him. It stood on its hind legs, its forepaws braced against a windowsill—the largest cougar he had ever seen…and the strangest!

Unlike the brown-coated ones that hunger sometimes drove out of the Davis Mountains, this cougar's fur was as black as obsidian and shimmered in the moonlight streaming through the trees.

The beast is clawing at our bedroom window trying to get in!

The horrifying realization hit him just as the cougar turned its great head, fixed him with its blazing eyes, bared its teeth in a wicked snarl then screamed like a woman in agony.

As the scream died away, Frank realized he had *felt* rather than *heard* it. Like a physical force, he sensed it had unleashed a vile contagion that was spreading throughout his body.

Sickening horror seized him as he visualized layers of his skin, the fat and muscle, peeling away to reveal his innards. The scream liquefied into a yellow tide of pus that, mingling with his blood, was invading every tissue, every organ, every— the house, the beast, everything suddenly swam before his eyes.

The monster is feeding on my fear! That certainty was enough to jolt him from his stupor. He braced his shotgun against his shoulder and fired.

He felt its kick, but heard no blast as the cougar exploded into thousands of luminous shards that drifted lazily to earth like black snowflakes, there scooped up by invisible hands and reformed again into the hellish beast.

It rose again on its hind legs, faced Frank, and pointed a taloned paw toward a forest that was now creeping toward the house. *Mine!* The beast clawed the unspoken word on Frank's brain just as brown-skinned men began filing out of the forest.

Glowing paw prints followed the cougar as it strode with regal detachment toward them at the edge of the yard. *The woman will never have them,* the beast snarled in Frank's mind as it placed a thorny paw on the back of a trembling man lying face down before it.

Frank raised the gun and fired again. But this time it was not a cougar that reformed but an enormous snake. With the girth of the tree by the porch and at least forty feet long, it glided fluidly toward the terrified men. *A leviathan straight out of a horror movie,* he thought as it fixed its agate eyes on the men standing frozen in place by fear while at least ten feet of its monstrous tail swayed lazily before them.

He fumbled in the pocket of his robe. *Out of shells.* He fingered the trigger of his gun helplessly just as the snake, in a sudden burst of energy, flung its scaly coils around the men and dragged them back into the forest.

Frank's mind raced, struggling to separate the real from what he knew must be the hellish spawn of a nightmare. Reason quickly surrendered, however, to what his eyes could not deny. The familiar fields beyond the house were slowly dissolving before a lush green tide of trees and vines that had almost reached the border of the yard when they suddenly vanished.

The familiar fields reappeared, the vision's spell was broken and Frank suddenly remembered: *Diana!*

Rushing into the house, he bounded up the stairs and into the bedroom.

"Diana, I ...!"

The sight of the man asleep in his bed cut his words short.

Me! The electrifying revelation of himself asleep in the bed jolted him awake and brought his hands to his eyes to shield them against the sunlight streaming through the windows.

Downstairs, he heard Diana singing and smelled bacon frying just like every other morning.

Sweating and emotionally exhausted he dragged himself out of bed and remembered thinking, *either I've completely lost my mind, or what I thought last night is true. The curtain has come up on a drama in which our family will play a leading part.*

CHAPTER 5

A Dark Presence heard the words whispered to the small creature and trembled.

OHOOOOOO. DIANA SQUEEZED FRANK's hand, jerking his mind back to the sterile whiteness of the delivery room as another contraction gripped her.

"Soon, love." He hoped his voice did not reveal his weariness.

Her contractions remained constant until about two hours ago – several minutes of pain then a half hour of blessed relief.

Through the rain-streaked windows, he watched the trees bending before the force of the wind. It was probably his own overworked imagination, Frank thought darkly, but the pain and length of Diana's contractions seemed to be growing as the storm built.

"Silent night…"

The wailing wind and the cracking sound of breaking limbs sang a discordant duet, jarring counterpoint to the soothing Christmas music piped into the delivery room. Just then Diana's cry signaled her contractions had returned.

Her delicate hand tightened, a low moan followed, quickly muted by the competing sounds of wind and music.

"All is calm…"

The contractions became longer, relief between them shorter.

"All is bright…"

Again, her eyes closed, her moaning stopped, and there was a momentary lull in her contractions. Had her hand not continued squeezing his, Frank would have thought she was asleep.

"Sleep in heavenly peace."

No peace for me tonight. For a moment the shrieking wind and sleet raking the windows diverted Frank's attention, his premonitions mirroring the darkness outside when he remembered the beast of his dream.

What if it wasn't a dream? He reached out and rested his hand lightly on the cold windowpane. *Was the fragile glass all that held the snarling beast at bay?*

Seized by another contraction, again Diana's hand tightened on his.

Her cries of pain, the baying wind, and the Christmas music, so starkly out of place, was creating a bedlam of sounds sending his imagination reeling and giving substance to his fears.

To Frank's jagged senses the window suddenly became the gaping mouth of a well. Searching its inky depths, he half expected to see taloned claws reach out and snatch Diana and their baby away.

"Westward leading, still proceeding, guide us to thy perfect light."

The windowpanes seemed to dissolve under the assault of the wind and sleet and he felt himself drawn outside into the darkness.

His perspective changed again and now from a great height he looked down on the hospital whose windows were now small portholes through which pinpoints of light were shining.

An ark, he brooded, his mind now captive to his morbid imagination; *an ark adrift on an empty sea, carrying Diana, our baby ... even God away from me?*

"*Joy to the world, the Lord is come.*"

The melodious carol smothered the wind, and Diana's cries reached into the darkness and drew Frank again to her bedside.

"*Let earth receive her King.*"

"I am here."

Frank whirled at the sound of a soft voice behind him.

No one was there.

The voice spoke again with the timbre of a great cathedral's antiphonal choirs.

"Frank, the storms will pass, the sun will rise again and your child will greet its rising."

Frank felt his anxiety drain away under the caress of the voice's reassuring promise.

Just then, Diana moaned again.

"Frank," she groaned between clenched teeth, "I think the baby's coming."

He gripped her hand and felt a burning pain as Diana dug her fingernails into his palm.

"Darling, I'm here," he said, ignoring the trickle of blood dripping from his hand onto the floor, secure in the certainty God had just reached out to him.

"And heaven, and heaven and nature sing."

Frank smiled at the sound of the invisible choir that now seemed so appropriate for the moment.

"Amen," he whispered.

"I see the baby's head," the doctor said. "Bear down hard, Diana."

Apprehension in the doctor's voice caused Frank to look up just as the old fear returned like a cold knife in his gut.

The voice promised the storm would pass, but now it had become a full-fledged blizzard. Sleet on its leading edge had given way to snow that swirled about the windows as moths attracted to the light.

He remembered as a boy there was a closet in his room across from the foot of his bed. Sometimes at night, he would lie awake and stare at the shadowy outlines of the clothes hanging there, imagining they were monsters ready to slip into the room the moment he closed his eyes.

Frank felt his eyes drawn again into the darkness outside as the momentary comfort of the voice slipped away. *What fearful thing is hiding somewhere in the shadows,* he wondered. Feeling a sudden chill, he remembered a line of scripture, *"We wrestle not with flesh and blood, but ... rulers of this present darkness."* The recollection was no comfort, but only reinforced the possibility his terrifying dream on the night of their baby's conception was a warning of things to come.

The doctor's voice jerked him from his morbid meanderings back to the delivery room.

"One more time, Diana. Push!"

Her nails dug painfully into Frank's palm, but still he clutched her hand.

As suddenly as they started, the contractions stopped, Diana's grip relaxed and she fell back, exhausted, on the bed.

Frank felt as if they were in the eye of a hurricane as a momentary hush settled over the delivery room. Through the window, he could see the snow had stopped; solid overcast had given way to high thin clouds and the wind was wheezing dying gasps signaling the storm had passed.

A lusty cry shattered the quiet.

Diana's lips trembled and tears glistened on her cheeks as the doctor placed their baby on her stomach. "She's a beautiful little girl," he said, his own relief evident in his voice.

"God bless you, little girl," Frank whispered, looking down at the tiny, squawling bundle.

One of the attending nurses lifted the baby and whisked her away for cleaning and weighing just as Diana's eyes fluttered closed.

Overcome with gratitude for Diana's safe delivery, Frank slipped out the door and leaned against the hall wall, his body limp with exhaustion. A nurse bustling by stopped abruptly in front of him.

"Sir? Is everything all right?" she asked as Frank looked up.

"What?"

"Your hand, sir. You should get that looked at."

He glanced down at the streaks of dried blood where, in pain, Diana had driven her nails into his skin. He felt a tremor run through his body. The lines ran vertically from the base of his fingers nearly to his wrist and resembled nothing so much as ... *claw marks!*

He shuddered as the memory of the beast superimposed itself over the images of his innocent wife and daughter.

Mine! the cat hissed inside his head.

"No!" Frank's mind recoiled as he spun on his heel and sprinted toward the exit, leaving the nurse with a puzzled stare.

Outside, he skidded on the icy concrete, his breath wreathing around him in the freezing night air. The wind had died completely, and even the high, thin clouds had fled to reveal a brightly shining moon.

The calm won't last. Deep in his soul he knew that the struggle had just begun. His eyes swept across the empty parking lot to the plain that stretched in unbroken monotony to the horizon. Again, he glanced at his wounded hand. Just then, from somewhere far out on the moon-drenched plain he heard the high, shrill scream of a cougar.

Chapter 6

Yanoako territory, the Amazon jungle

Akhu, Shaman of the Yanoako, tossed in his hammock undisturbed by a baby's first cry in a far away place called Texas. Instead, his mind echoed with the nightmare of his own terrified screams as he relived his struggle to break the hold of the swirling water sucking his small body deeper and deeper into its green depths. He beat his arms wildly, knowing as he did, he was losing the battle. Looking up through the swirling column, he could see the sun shining dimly.

Suddenly, the whirlpool relaxed its grip, and he felt himself shoot toward the surface. Clearing the water, he heard the murmur of voices reaching out, tugging insistently at his eyelids until they pulled them open.

The dream again, he thought, remembering how, as a small boy he was caught in the tug of a whirlpool and would have drowned had an older boy not swum to his rescue.

He rolled and perched on the edge of his hammock. Through his hut's entrance, he saw the sun had already cleared the trees surrounding the village. Some of the men had gathered in the courtyard, busy stringing their bows and putting curare-tipped darts into their corn-shuck quivers in preparation for the day's hunt.

I won't join them today, he thought.

As Shaman, he could choose his own path and needed only the gods' approval for his actions. He let his body fall back into the hammock, closed his eyes and smiled, remembering last night and the boys' curiosity. He could see their faces, framed in firelight as they huddled together and watched him expectantly.

Waiting for another story, he had thought as he reached up and untied his necklace holding the sacred Stone of Memories, his badge of office. Locked within its shimmering depths was the trail the tribe's Shaman had taken into their peoples past for as long as any could remember. They held sacred these memories, believing as long as they remembered them the tribe would live on.

Like many times before, the boys' gasps of awe greeted his actions as he took the Stone, held it toward the fire, and watched it draw rainbow bands of light into its depths.

To the boys, moments spent waiting for Akhu to begin his storytelling moved as slowly as a three-toed sloth. *So impatient and curious,* Akhu thought as the hint of a smile formed on his lips and he began turning the Stone slowly in his hands.

Curiosity was a trait Akhu understood very well. If it had been a disease, it would have killed him the morning nine flood times ago when it brought him uninvited into then Shaman Twanke's hut in search of this very Stone.

How quickly the seasons have passed since Twanke's path into the stone became my own, he thought.

That morning, only the sun breaking above the trees saw him slip into Twanke's hut fired by his burning desire to *know*.

The night before he and the other boys had gathered around the fire with Twanke. As usual, Akhu, like the others, sat spellbound as the old man spun stories from the Yanoako's past.

Twanke remained by the fire for a long time after telling his tale, staring silently at his Stone of Memories. The boys waited patiently for his permission to leave the circle. Finally, realizing none would come, all but Akhu left the fire for their hammocks in the long house.

Looking across the fire at his teacher, he thought, *I must see what he sees,* and vowed, *some day I will.* At times like these, he always hoped if he sat quietly and waited patiently long enough Twanke would finally let him look into the Stone and experience its mysteries for himself. However, just like all the other nights, his patience went unrewarded, weariness finally overcame his curiosity, and he, too, left the fire to join the other boys.

Sleep that night was slow in coming. When it finally did, it brought with it the familiar dream of whirling water sucking at his thrashing body.

Just like today, he awakened the next morning to the sound of the men preparing for the day's hunt. From the edge of his hammock he watched as they picked up their blowguns and quivers of darts and filed out of the long house, their freshly oiled bodies glistening in the sun as they walked past the communal garden before disappearing into the jungle.

However, that morning he had seen something else, something that broke the grip of caution and jerked him from his hammock. Twanke was with the hunters, and he was not wearing his necklace!

Once he had seen him secret the stone away in the folds of his hammock and was sure it must be there. Sprinting to the outer edge of the poles supporting the long house, he ran across the village courtyard and in a moment reached Twanke's hut and quickly slipped inside. Cool night air still lingered within its shadows, its thick thatched walls muffling the sounds of the awakening village.

Several times before, he had crept into Twanke's empty hut and had always enjoyed the freedom he felt there. Everywhere else, others surrounded him: their smells, their voices, their moans in the darkness, were all part of the fabric that was his life. The press of their presence was a constant reminder only the Shaman was a complete and solitary person. He and the others were only small parts of the whole…the tribe.

Hardly daring to breathe, he went to Twanke's hammock and nervously reached his hand into its folds. Sure enough, just as he suspected, the necklace was there … he could feel it. Drawing it from its hiding place, he eagerly grasped the large center Stone and held it out amazed, how even in the hut's faint light it came alive with bands of shimmering colors.

As he watched, the colors transfigured into translucent blackness that slowly peeled away to reveal a small opening in the stone. In only a moment it widened to become the yawning mouth of a cave that swallowed first the stone that birthed it, then the hut itself.

Akhu felt a current, stronger than the great river at flood time, as it swept him into its gaping mouth. *It's happening again,* he realized, as his curiosity surrendered to helplessness that quickly gave way to panic as the current became the whirlpool of his nightmare sucking him into the stone's dark depths.

In a moment, the sounds of the awakening village with its cacophony of laughter, barking dogs, and screech of quarrelsome monkeys fell silent.

He was moving faster and faster through a corridor ablaze with a whirlpool of stars vanishing as quickly as they appeared, leaving him to plummet on in darkness that seemed to throb with hidden life. *Trapped in the gullet of a great beast ... swallowed alive*, he thought as frantic seized him!

Still faster he flew. Ahead he spotted a pinpoint of light that growing brighter dissolved the darkness into gray half-light. Clinging about him like a fog, it slowly lifted to reveal strange and frightening things: Metal birds flew about spitting fire from their wings. Boiling mountains of fire, whipped into waves as if by a strong wind, rolled toward him, leaving in their wake the charred bodies of men and animals.

As he raced along the passage, he glimpsed high stone walls with men rushing about bracing ladders against them. Warriors with long knives slashed away at their enemies, who were falling in bloody heaps about them. Painted on the shields of some were crossed red lines, on others a small sliver of the moon and a star. Arrows rained down from the walls on the warriors below, their howls of pain following him as he careened still deeper into the Stone.

As the light grew still brighter, the scene changed again. He saw an ax raised high then driven down. A head, its face frozen by death in a look of disbelief, fell from its jerking body, rolled toward him, finally stopped, and fixed him with a sightless stare.

The stench of burning flesh filled the tunnel as he sped past a blur of bodies cast into a blazing fire. He glimpsed a woman holding the limp body of a baby, its life dripping away into a pool of red at her feet, her wail of unbearable sorrow following him as he careened on ... faster ... faster.

Suddenly, surrounding him were swaying bodies and the babble of voices as women sang and danced before a metal god whose belly billowed smoke. He felt a blast of heat from its red-hot hands, held out impassively to receive a screaming child.

Still, faster he shot through the tunnel.

Everything was a blur now. Only the dissonant shouts and screams, the roar of beasts and cries of their prey continued to remind him of the terrifying vistas he could no longer see.

As quickly as it began, the bedlam died away, the tug on his body relaxed, and he felt himself slowing.

Slower and slower, he moved forward until finally he felt solid earth under his feet. Relief replaced panic when he realized he was no longer in the cave but on a trail bordered by a jungle so still only his beating heart broke the silence. In the distance, he saw a bright light spilling between two soaring stones standing sentinel on either side of an opening in a wall blocking the path.

A woman, unlike any he had ever seen was standing beside the stones. Her skin was white like milk, her hair the color of melted gold; about her flowed a garment the color of lilies, that rippled across her body like still water disturbed by a sudden breeze. Around her neck, she wore a golden charm and in her hand, she held something dark and edged in gold.

She smiled and raised a hand in welcome.

"Have you been sent to guide me," he asked the smiling woman.

"Not yet," she said, "but soon."

"Not ever!" A deep drumbeat of a voice echoed from the tunnel, stirring again the screams and babble that had followed him on his descent into the stone.

From somewhere, beyond the reach of the light, he heard a low guttural snarl. Hardly had it died away when a black jaguar crept from the darkness and fixed burning eyes of undiluted hate on him.

It's about to spring, he thought, feeling his body stiffen, *and I have no weapon*!

The snarl erased the woman's smile and instantly replaced it with the glare of a determined hunter.

At that moment the beast sprang.

Akhu felt its hot breath on his face just as the woman stepped between them. Reaching out, she touched the cat with the black, gold-edged thing she held, and when she did, the creature shattered like a clay pot at her feet.

"Soon I *will* come to guide you, Akhu," the woman said, turning and facing him. "Soon," she repeated the word with a calm assurance that betrayed neither fear nor notice of the beast that had just threatened them.

"Shi will send me to you." She smiled again as she backed into the light still spilling between the stones. "You must follow no one into the forbidden land until I am sent to lead you.

I will come soon…soon…"

Her voice trailed away to a whisper then was gone as she disappeared into the light.

"Akhu!" A demanding voice called for his attention. "Look away from the stone! Look away now!"

Somehow, he knew the voice must be obeyed and willed his eyes to look away from the light into which the woman had vanished. Immediately he felt himself shoot upward through the tunnel even faster than his descent.

"Look at me, Akhu."

Twanke's voice, he realized as he felt the Stone relax its grip.

"Look at me."

He felt his head being shaken from side to side.

As his vision slowly cleared, he realized he still stood near Twanke's hammock except now Twanke stood beside him. Familiar sounds of the village had replaced the awful cries and sights of the tunnel—he was once again among the living.

"My Stone", Twanke said as he gripped his shoulder and gently reached out his hand. "Have I not told you curiosity baits many traps?"

"I saw strange things, Father," he remembered saying. "They frightened me."

"I know, my son." Twanke cupped his upturned face in his hands. "I, too, have seen those terrible things, sights more frightening than the charge of a wounded jaguar."

Even nine passing flood times could not erase from Akhu's memory how Twanke stared into his eyes, as if searching for something he had lost, before asking, "and did you see anything else?"

"I saw a beautiful woman standing in the light beside great stones on the path."

"And?" There had been a hint of excitement in Twanke's voice.

"I asked if she was sent to guide me."

"And how did she reply?"

"She said, 'Not yet, Akhu, but soon Shi will send me to guide you.'"

"She called your name, my son?" Akhu remembered he saw tears in the old man's eyes and finding no words to explain, could only nod in reply.

"I too have seen the woman," Twanke whispered so softly his words seemed meant only for himself, "but she never called my name."

Pulling himself up, Akhu sat on the edge of his hammock and through the hut's entrance could see the last of the hunters as they disappeared into the jungle.

He remembered again his boyhood vision in Twanke's hut and his first journey into the Stone of Memory. *Will this be just another day or the day the beautiful woman keeps her promise?*

At the edge of the courtyard, he saw mothers gathering their children together preparing to go work in the village garden or to collect firewood.

Will it be just another day for them as well? He left his hut and walked wearily into the village's ceremonial area.

Since that morning many flood times ago when he first looked into Twanke's Stone of Memory one word had followed him through his days and into his dreams. *When?*

CHAPTER 7

NEAR SUNDOWN, THE HUNTERS returned and after cleaning their game joined the other villagers in a common meal. Full stomachs soon made the Elders' eyes heavy, so one by one they left the fire for their hammocks in the long house until finally, only Akhu and the older boys remained.

They want to hear another story, he thought, letting his eyes sweep the circle of anxious faces.

"The great god Wanadi speaks with many voices," he finally said, gesturing for the boys to lean closer. "It was his voice that called the wild pig and tapir to our hunters today." He looked at the boy sitting beside him and playfully patted his bulging stomach. "And aren't you glad he did?"

The other boys laughed their agreement but quickly grew serious as he once again untied his necklace. Their eyes followed his fingers as they felt each stone along the strand, growing wide with anticipation when he finally grasped his Stone of Memory, and held it to the light.

He fixed his eyes on the Stone, now shimmering in the firelight and as if reminded of things the boys would face said, "sometimes Wanadi speaks to us through pain."

Akhu recalled his teacher, Twanke, once spoke those very words while cradling a dying hunter in his arms. The man had stumbled into the village, mortally wounded by an outsider's fire stick. As the man cried out in pain, Twanke looked up and seemed to search until he found Akhu's face among the other boys gathered around. His teacher's words, like darts from a blowgun, were pinned to his memory. "Through the pain of your Marake test, Akhu, you will hear the gods speak clearly, and you will never forget their words," he had said solemnly.

Tonight, gazing at the sacred Stone, Akhu could see the hunter's bloody wound and hear his cries. *The outsiders have brought much pain to the Yanoako*, he reflected bitterly as he looked more deeply into the Stone and began his story.

His tale took wings, carrying the boys back to a time long ago. Sunrises and sunsets flashed like lightning across the sky. Seasons, dry and wet, became blurs as old age overtook youth with an arrow's speed.

Back they sped and like the first time in Twanke's hut, the pale-skinned woman waited for him at the two great stones beside the trail. Again, her command to come no farther brought the familiar sadness he felt each time he came so near to learning the secrets of the taboo land.

But like so many times before, he dared not resist her order. Turning, he retraced his steps up the pathway of the seasons. As he did, the Stone's grip loosened, the journey ended, and once again he found himself with the boys beside the campfire. They watched him anxiously, waiting for some sign he might reveal the rest of the story concerning their tribe's beginning; but as always, he could not.

How can I tell them things Twanke did not teach me, or the Stone of Memory has not revealed? Sensing the boys' disappointment, he dismissed them with a gesture and retired to his hut.

Recalling his own life's journey, beginning with his first terrifying experience with Twanke's Stone of Memory until now as Shaman of the Yanoako was a different matter. When he returned from his first journey into the Stone, he remembered particularly Twanke's tears when he described his vision of the lovely woman. *Those tears,* he mused just before sleep overtook him, *should have warned me my life would soon change forever.*

That change was not long in coming.

Soon after Akhu's first boyhood experience with the Stone, Twanke took him into the jungle to search for healing plants. The sun had barely risen above the trees surrounding the village when they entered the forest and for a long time they concentrated on their search in silence. Twanke instructed him that seeking the sacred plants required the same skill and stealth that allowed a hunter to follow the trail of the wild pig and creep up for the kill.

"Your voice," he said, "will draw demons that will suck away the healing powers of the plants you seek."

The sun was high overhead when Akhu finally broke his silence and called to Twanke. But there was no answer. Standing, he looked about but could not see him.

"Master!" he shouted again.

Twanke must have heard fear in his voice because he answered quickly.

"I am here."

At first, Akhu could not tell the direction of the disembodied voice. Then he glimpsed the sun reflecting off Twanke's necklace.

Drawing close, he found Twanke sitting, his back against the trunk of a large mahogany tree. With a slight gesture of his hand, he invited Akhu to join him.

For a long time neither spoke, the rustle of the wind in the canopy overhead and the occasional scream of a howler monkey were the only sounds disturbing the silence.

"We are joined at the heart, my son." Twanke's eyes never shifted as he spoke but seemed fixed on something only he could see. "Hedu Ka Misti, the place of spirits, awaits me. The voices of the Fathers are calling and soon I must go." The old man's wrinkled hands lightly brushed his chest as if confirming his body's existence, then he continued. "This body will be burned, its bones ground to powder, mixed with water and drunk by our people. Then Akhu, I, like all others before me, will be only a memory."

Gradually, his eyes lost their faraway stare and he turned and looked at Akhu. "You must prepare yourself for that day," he said.

Again, the veil of silence fell between them and like those nights beside the fire Akhu sat patiently waiting for Twanke to explain, but he did not.

As dusk fell, the cool breeze caressed their naked bodies and seemed to revive Twanke from his reverie.

"Darkness is coming and soon the jaguar will awaken," he said.

The old Shaman stretched, stood, and without another word, turned and started retracing their path back to the village.

You must prepare yourself. Twanke's words echoed in Akhu's mind with every step. *You must prepare…prepare…*

Just after dawn the next morning, a village Elder awakened Akhu. "Twanke calls," he said. "You must come." *Hedu Ka Misti awaits me.* Twanke's words from the day before still echoed in his mind as he neared the Shaman's hut. At its entrance, he paused. Though the light was dim, he could see Twanke in the far corner wrapped in shadows sitting on his jaguar bench. His dark eyes, undimmed by age, followed as he entered then stood before him.

"Here, my son." He gestured to a place beside him on the bench. "Sit here."

Akhu felt a rush of excitement, and hesitated. *None but the Shaman is allowed to sit on the sacred seat.*

Sensing Akhu's hesitation, Twanke reached out a gnarled hand and drew him down beside him. "It is fitting you sit here," he said solemnly.

For several moments, only the sounds of the awakening village broke the morning stillness.

"We have traveled many days together," Twanke finally said. "You have learned much. Soon it will be time for your last lesson."

As Akhu struggled to understand what Twanke meant, the old man laid his hand on a newly painted design on his chest. "Inside this body," he said, "lays a hidden world of rivers, mountains, and forests. Here, my spirit helpers, my Hekuras, have lived since Shi chose me to sit on the jaguar bench many flood-times ago. The Hekuras have been my guides. They have shown me the trails to enemy camps, the paths of the pigs and deer through the forest, and the hidden places where the healing plants grow."

Twanke leaned forward and placed his hands on his knees. "But now this body grows weary."

Akhu felt as if he was seeing his beloved teacher for the first time after many seasons of separation. Like a rushing river, time's passing had carved deep gullies into Twanke's weathered face.

"Trees in my hidden world have lost their leaves," he continued. "My streams are dry, and the earth of my garden yields no corn. Even the poles of my long house are rotten, and soon its roof will fall."

He paused and looked into Akhu's eyes. "My Hekuras grow restless. Soon they must find another home."

"Akhu, your body will be their home," he finally said.

Like flint striking flint, Twanke's words instantly lit a torch in his mind. Now he understood where his teacher's words yesterday in the forest had been leading.

He had no time to think about the implication of Twanke's revelation before he continued.

"I have planted and cultivated your hidden garden, Akhu. Now your streams are alive with fish and your forests filled with game. Soon your inner world will be ready to receive the Hekuras. Welcome them. They will help you understand the secrets of the forest and guide you to everything the Yanoako need."

Akhu struggled to understand the enormity of his teacher's revelation, especially his cryptic words as they left the forest. "Father, yesterday you said soon it would be time for my last lesson. What did you mean?"

"Yes, it will soon be time my son." He touched the strange designs again on his body. Sacred paintings like these and the beauty of your feathered halo will call the Hekuras to you. But..."

Again, Twanke paused and seemed to be searching Akhu's face for signs of understanding.

"A much stronger power will be needed to keep them with you."

"What is that, Father?" He trembled with anticipation, certain he teetered on the edge of a great discovery.

Twanke grasped Akhu's shoulders, drew him close and dug his nails into his flesh. "A power only sacrifice and pain can give," he said, looking directly into his eyes.

Apparently energized by these words, Twanke barked a command. "Beginning today you will learn the lesson of sacrifice. For one season, you will eat only once each third rising of the sun. And then, at your Marake test it will be time to learn the lessons only pain can teach you."

He felt a gnawing fear of what awaited him at that mysterious ceremony marking his passage into manhood.

"When you complete the test," Twanke continued, "you will sit on the jaguar bench as Shaman of the Yanoako. It is Shi who wills it."

Shi, the god above all other gods, wills it. Twanke naming the unknowable god frightened Akhu. From earliest childhood, he was taught that although Shi created all things, he soon lost interest in this world and left it in the care of the lesser god, Wanadi. However, even Wanadi was far away and spoke only to Mado, the jaguar, and to the tribe's Shaman. Now Twanke was telling him it was Shi rather than Wanadi that had willed he become Shaman.

Akhu remembered again the beautiful woman in his vision.

Shi will send me to you, she had promised.

Akhu's mind whirled as he tried to understand the meaning of these strange and confusing revelations. First, the woman had spoken to him of Shi, the unknowable god, and now Twanke said that Shi decreed he would one day be Shaman.

Twanke had also spoken of the god, Wanadi, and his servant, Mado the jaguar, many times. When he had, Akhu trembled at the memory of the springing beast in his vision, how, like a clay pot, it shattered at the touch of the woman. Had that jaguar been Mado? How could it have been if the jaguar was Wanadi's servant and both were chosen by Shi to care for and protect the Yanoako?

Twanke began speaking again, damming back Akhu's stream of questions.

"Akhu, you will lead our people because only you, besides myself, have journeyed into the Stone of Memory and seen the pale-skinned woman and because only you, has she called by name."

For the first time since Twanke began speaking, Akhu saw the hint of a smile on the old man's face.

"She called you by name," he repeated as he reached out and clasped Akhu's hand. "Shi will lead her to you when it is time to go into the forbidden land."

Twanke paused again as if listening to a voice only he could hear.

"Wait for her to come to you Akhu. Wait for Shi to say it is time. And remember this, my son. Remember well." Twanke turned his head away and peered into the shadows about him. "Wanadi may not be what he seems," he whispered, as if to himself. "Listen only to Shi or the woman he will send; only to Shi or the woman."

As Akhu walked away from Twanke's hut, one word echoed in his mind: *When, when, when? When will she come?*

CHAPTER 8

OXFORD UNIVERSITY
SAME TIME

HALF A WORLD AWAY, low clouds promising rain, clutched at the spires of Trinity College as Frederick Neisen hurried toward Brighton Hall for his first lecture. According to the seminar's syllabus, the subject for the afternoon was cultural correspondence and focused on similarities between the dream walks of Australian aborigines and the time journeys of the Yanoako, an Amazonian Indian tribe.

He slid into his seat, eagerly anticipating his teacher, Dr. Francis Abelard's, presentation, but found himself gazing instead through the window at the stately and quiet beauty of Oxford's spires and gables cloaked in mist. As if from somewhere far away, he heard the muffled voice of Dr. Abelard as he began lecturing.

"Though widely separated geographically, the planet's so-called 'primitives' have intuitively sensed what we in our more advanced societies have either forgotten or chosen to ignore."

The beautiful scene outside the window so captured Frederick's attention that for several moments he was unaware Abelard had stopped speaking. The room's silence finally alerted him, and turning, he was embarrassed to find his teacher and fellow classmates staring at him.

"And how do you account for this, Mr. Neisen?"

"I'm not sure I…" Frederick stammered to a halt, unsure what the professor meant by *this*.

Abelard fixed him with an annoyed glare. "Their sense of direction, Mr. Neisen. Di-rec-tion." He massaged the word, milking each syllable for its maximum dramatic impact.

Draped in a black academic gown, Abelard's great bulk overpowered his small head, especially small, some thought, for such a ponderous intellect. Crowned by a patch of unruly hair, it sat upon an elongated neck swathed in sagging skin. As he spoke, it jutted in and out of his collar, reminding Frederick of a large buzzard pecking away at carrion. The way his deep-set eyes probed with emotionless detachment the faces of each student, added to the impression.

"Since the Tower of Babel," Abelard continued, "when man first reached for the stars, human progress, or its lack, has been measured in terms of direction.

"Advanced societies believe the human race rides on a swift running river of time that is carrying us forward toward a future growing brighter with each challenge overcome along the way.

"I believe you have a saying in America…" He glanced at Frederick again. "Something about 'going with the flow'?"

Frederick nodded an acknowledgment, relieved Abelard had apparently forgiven him for his inattention.

"'Going with the flow.' That about sums up so-called enlightened societies' views of progress.

"By the way," he added, "this flow is always forward. And if a society fails to go forward?" He paused again, as if for dramatic effect, and looked about the room. "That's the reason primitives remain primitive."

Now totally absorbed with his subject, the class' attention was riveted on Abelard as he strode to the chalkboard. Frederick had never heard a teacher lecture with such obvious passion.

As he spoke, he scrawled barely legible words on the board. "Salvation. Happiness. City of God. Valhalla. Paradise. Whatever name you choose to describe the ultimate good, it is always somewhere just beyond our reach."

He stopped again and scanned the students' faces for their reaction, then continued.

"Regardless of religious or political philosophies, all advanced societies believe the perfect world lies ahead of us. Some believe we will reach it after a climactic battle between good and evil; others, after the final step in societal evolution; still others, following an ultimate medical or scientific breakthrough."

He paused again and let his gaze drift from face to face until it settled again on Frederick. "Only the more enlightened among us know better," he said.

"This drive forward toward a utopian goal is what inspired nearly all the great explorers to set out on their journeys. Consumed by a spirit of exploration and discovery, they did not accept the opinions of ancient cartographers who wrote 'Nothing Beyond' at the borders of their maps where knowledge of the known world ended."

Frederick swallowed, unnerved to find Abelard still staring at him. The thought flashed into his head: *He's talking directly to me!*

There was more than a trace of sarcasm in the professor's voice as he peered over his glasses, his long, turkey-like neck extended in Frederick's direction. "Those of you raised in a strong Christian tradition know your religion teaches that Jesus Christ came into the world to bring redemption to humanity. But His mission is incomplete. Your credo states that our planet, the cosmos, and all living things still await the final redemption, which will come only when Christ returns to make the world a Paradise again."

A thin smile creased Abelard's face as he studied Frederick for a reaction to what he was saying. It was as if Abelard was reading his expression to judge whether he was able to rattle him with his obvious mockery of centuries of Christian belief. Frederick returned the stare, his eyes unwavering. Far from shocking him, Abelard's lecture only fertilized thoughts that had germinated in his mind ever since his break with traditional religion when he was just out of high school.

Frederick leaned forward, eagerly absorbing Abelard's words as he closed his lecture.

"Think of it," he said. "All religions, all philosophies look to the future for deliverance. But what if the primitives have it right? What if, through their dream journeys and time walks, they have tapped a racial memory as old as mankind itself, one repressed in more civilized societies by centuries of so-called progress?"

Frederick's heart thumped in his chest as Abelard seemed about to verbalize his most privately held thoughts, ideas he had not fully articulated even to himself.

"Perhaps the old mapmakers were wiser than they knew when they said there was nothing beyond the Gates of Hercules. Perhaps primitives are the truly blessed not to be living in a world filled with a carnival of competing ideas and deafened by the barkers of religion, philosophy, and science who promise a future paradise. Could it be that, unlike us, they have heard the roar of the falls ahead and know intuitively they drop off the edge of the world into oblivion?"

However, it was Abelard's last words that brought Frederick forward to speak to him after the lecture and won for him an invitation to Abelard's apartment that evening.

"What if the path to Paradise, to the fulfillment of all our dreams, lies behind us rather than ahead," Abelard had said softly, almost as a benediction.

Frederick stared into the fire on the hearth, Abelard's afternoon lecture still echoing in his mind. *Not a lecture, more like a revelation*, he reflected, as he thumbed nervously at the serpentine carvings on the arms of the ancient leather-backed chair. The room was in disarray, a wild hodgepodge of books and scholarly journals scattered about. The smell of stale pipe smoke clung to everything, confirming his first impression that his host was an unrepentant bachelor. The great broadsword hung above the mantle, and a full suit of body armor on a rack in the corner testified to his teacher's fascination with all things medieval.

"...and so, Mr. Neisen, toward what end do you plan to focus your considerable gifts?"

Dr. Abelard's blunt inquiry signaled an end to the social pleasantries that until now marked their evening together. The question of his life's purpose now lay like a deep gulf between him and the widely published and internationally acclaimed Chairman of Oxford's Department of Social Anthropology. Abelard, best known for his groundbreaking, often controversial, research into relationships between ancient myths and modern man's social and moral development held the department's prestigious Ragsdale Chair of Anthropology.

Though his views put him at odds theologically with traditional Christianity, theologians respected him for demonstrating some

Biblical narratives, believed by liberal scholars to be myths, actually were rooted in historically verifiable events.

Frederick knew he must bridge the chasm just created by Abelard's question of his life's purpose with a satisfactory answer if the budding relationship with his teacher was to blossom into a lasting one.

He knew Abelard's hawkish eyes were on him, taking note of every word, weighing critically his every nuance or change of tone.

"Dr. Abelard, it's like I indicated in my letter and like you stated so brilliantly today in your critical assessment of Christianity's impact on the human species, western society has had two thousand years to build a better world, modeled at least in part after the Christian ethic and ..."

He paused and glanced at his teacher, trying to gauge his response. Except for an impassive stare, he saw none. He recalled that afternoon his first impression of the great man had been that of a buzzard, hovering over fresh kills. Watching…waiting.

"And ...," Abelard interjected, priming Frederick to continue with his thought.

"And ..." Frederick nervously cleared his throat. "In my opinion Christianity has failed." Then, in a transparent effort to curry Abelard's favor added, "from what I've read in your books and heard today in your lecture you feel it has fallen short as well."

"Fallen short, but not totally," Abelard added cryptically, before shepherding the conversation down a more personal path.

"In your letter, Mr. Neisen, you said you had witnessed Christianity's failure first hand."

"That's right. I saw it fail my father."

"Oh?" Abelard gave his student his steely-eyed attention. "And how was that?"

"If you recall, sir, I stated on my application for admission that my father was a minister."

"Yes, I remember."

"Well, he had been preaching for some time before I came along, and spoke to me only once about his early years in the ministry." Frederick paused, glancing quickly to see if he still had the great man's attention. "A deacon told my dad that I had written obscene words on a restroom wall in his church. The actual perpetrator laid the blame on me, and a prominent member chose to believe him. He told my father he should punish me and make me clean up the mess."

"And?" Abelard looked quizzically over the top of his glasses.

"To dad's credit, he believed me when I told him I did not do it. However, when I asked him why the other boy, one my father had baptized only a year before, would do such an un-Christian thing, he said something I've never forgotten."

"What was that?"

"He said he'd given up believing God ever really changes human nature."

"That was when he described his early years as a preacher." For a moment, there was a far-away look in Frederick's eyes as he exhumed long buried memories.

"He told me that when he began in the ministry his faith had been very simplistic. For instance, he believed human history started in a literal Garden of Eden with a man and woman whose disobedience cost them Paradise. He believed the Bible described how God had worked throughout history to return humankind to that idyllic place. In those early years, he said all his sermons centered on Christ and His power to forgive sin and change human nature. They always ended with a plea, or 'altar call' as he called it,' for people to come forward to affirm their trust in Him."

"Continue," Abelard leaned forward in his chair.

"However, Dad said his sermons seemed to make no lasting difference in people's lives, so he finally stopped giving his 'altar calls' altogether. When some like-minded ministers gained prominence in his denomination, he began working with them, focusing his energy and messages on peace, love, and the importance of working for social justice rather than seeking converts for Christ.

"Several years after that talk with my dad, I attended a Billy Graham crusade. It struck me that Graham's passionate sermon was probably much like one Dad would have preached in his early years.

"When Graham gave his invitation, I had the strangest feeling." Frederick hesitated before dredging up still another unpleasant memory from the past. "Suddenly, I saw my dad on the platform instead of Billy Graham and, instead of inviting people to give their lives to Christ like Graham, he was looking directly at me and saying, 'I've given up on God.'

"After leaving home for college I never attended another church service or felt any inclination to do so."

Again, Frederick paused, gauging his story's impact on this man whose opinion mattered so much to him.

"It's like I said, Dr. Abelard. Christianity failed my father and a lot of others. Including me."

"And I also," Abelard murmured bitterly under his breath. In his mind's eye, he glimpsed a mother, far too young to die, and her little boy beside her bed. *Please God don't let my mother die,* he remembered praying with a fervency and sincerity reserved only for children. *But heaven was silent.* For a moment he felt the acidic hurt return, one that for years he had hidden under a carefully crafted veneer of intellectualism.

"What about his church's work for social justice?" Abelard asked.

"With all due respect, sir, look around at our society."

Abelard's gaze seemed to soften, but still Frederick had no idea what he was thinking. *My last chance to impress him,* he thought, judging by Abelard's tepid responses that all he had said up to now had failed to do so.

Desperately he fired his last salvo.

"Your lecture today Dr. Abelard, resonated with truth."

"Oh?" Abelard's eyes widened slightly as he resettled his large frame in the chair.

"You see I'm not like my father who, as a Texan might say, sometimes throws the baby out with the bath water."

Abelard's expression betrayed his complete befuddlement.

"What I mean, Doctor, is that my dad came to the place where he not only believed Christ had no interest in changing people, but discounted the Bible as just a collection of fables handed down from generation to generation. I'm not willing to go that far."

"Tell me then, Mr. Neisen…" Abelard's buzzard-like eyes settled on Frederick with surgical scrutiny. "Exactly how far *are* you willing to go and what are you willing to do?"

Here was the crux of Frederick's whole argument, and he answered quickly. "Unlike my dad, I believe there is a kernel of truth in the Bible."

"And what is that?" For the first time, there was a hint of excitement in Abelard's voice.

"I believe the Garden of Eden may be a real place and that it may be possible to regain it. Just because Christianity has not found the way back doesn't mean one may not exist."

The conviction Abelard heard in Frederick's voice brought a thin smile to his lips.

"You said 'may,' dear boy." For what seemed an eternity, he studied Frederick with an appraising stare, only the ticking of a clock somewhere breaking the silence.

"My young friend," he finally said softly, "I believe a way *does* exist."

Frederick sensed his life had reached a turning point and willed that his eyes remain focused on his teacher. As an undergraduate at Evangel University, Abelard's book, *Paradise Regained*, first sparked his interest in studying under him. That book opened his mind to the possibility that a way to regain Paradise might exist, but one that did not insult the mind by requiring blind faith in what he considered theological gobbledygook.

Here was the opportunity Frederick had been awaiting. He forced his voice to exude a confidence he was far from feeling.

"Then you have answered the question you asked me earlier, Dr. Abelard, about my life's purpose. If you will allow me, the focus of my life will be to help you find man's lost Paradise."

It was half past ten when Frederick finally left Abelard's flat and began the mile walk back to his digs at Trinity College. Light fog had settled over the city, its wispy fingers mingling with the light streaming from street lamps along Broad Street, diluting their glow from bright to pale yellow. Ahead, the ancient stone mountain that was the Everett Craig Museum loomed out of the mist.

When he arrived at Oxford two months ago, it was one of the first places he visited. He entered the museum for the first time and stood before the bust of Sir Norton Collins-Ragsdale with a feeling akin to reverential awe.

Though long dead, Ragsdale's designation as the world's leading authority in the field of social anthropology went unchallenged. More than any other writer on the subject, he helped Frederick realize Christianity was not the key to human progress. Instead, Ragsdale insisted the utopian dream of a better world would only come when humanity shed itself of what he called "Christianity's contagious illusion."

A barking dog somewhere nearby alerted him to his surroundings and he quickened his steps toward home, eying the saw-toothed, silhouetted shapes of medieval towers, gabled roofs, and belfries that hovered above the edge of the narrow street. His late hour weariness conspired with his imagination to produce the impression ancient buildings looming out of the fog were derelict schooners, grounded and doomed to rot away on some uncharted bar.

He loved Oxford, its history, its quirkiness. He still could hardly believe his good fortune. A graduate of a lackluster college with no powerful friends to endorse him, yet here he was at one of the most prestigious universities in the world with a full scholarship, studying under Ragsdale's successor, Dr. Francis Abelard.

Over a hundred had applied for the five graduate openings in the department of anthropology. His undergraduate counselor had warned him his chance of being among the few selected was poor.

Nevertheless, he filled out his application, feeling about as much confidence as one would have in picking a winning lottery number. Like most of the other applications, his would probably receive no more than a cursory glance by some administrative underling.

However, just as he was about to seal the envelope, a thought occurred to him. He was asking only for admission to the department of anthropology. Why not send a copy of his application directly to Dr. Abelard, along with a letter expressing his desire to study directly under him. Perhaps initiative and daring would count for something, he reasoned.

So, he wrote the letter and bared his soul to the man he so admired. Tonight his private visit with Abelard confirmed his conviction that the letter had opened the door. But now, he sensed his commitment to join his professor's quest for a way back to Eden had forged an unbreakable bond between them.

Back at his digs, he undressed, sat down at the desk, but found himself unable to concentrate on the reading for tomorrow's classes. He pondered Abelard's question: To what end do you plan to focus your considerable gifts?

The professor thought him *gifted*.

A brief flicker of self-doubt drew his eyes to his reflection in the mirror above his desk. Had Abelard meant just gifted enough to get by, or was he being typically British and understating his appraisal? Frederick spent a moment admiring the determined look he saw staring back at him. *Highly gifted*, he decided as he gave himself a knowing wink, closed his book, and made his way to bed.

CHAPTER 9

THE STARLING FARM NEAR LUBBOCK, TEXAS
TWELVE YEARS LATER

FRANK STARLING WATCHED HIS daughter, Ruth, with the keen eye of a man who knew his horses and a good rider when he saw one. *She's learning.* He nodded at his twelve-year old approvingly as she guided her little mare toward him.

For Frank, spring was always a busy time of year. That morning, he planned to haul one of the combines into town for repairs. With wheat harvest only a few months away, he knew all his equipment needed to be in top shape.

"Daddy, please don't go yet," Ruth, pleaded as she watched Frank hitch his pickup to the flatbed trailer that carried the combine. "Come out to the corral and watch me ride for a little while? You're such a good rider, Daddy," she purred sweetly. "I know you can give me some great pointers. Pleeeese!"

Her little-girl voice was warm enough to melt butter and quickly dissolved Frank's resolve to take care of business. He had promised his daughter that she could ride in Lubbock's annual rodeo parade when she turned twelve. Nudged by the fact the event was less than three weeks away, he held out his hand and let her lead him to the corral. Frank understood his priorities.

Ruth and Gypsy made their first circuit of the ring and trotted toward him. Smiling as she passed, he realized she didn't need his advice. His daughter just wanted to show off a little. He felt the familiar sadness. She was growing up so fast. Soon she would be a young woman with no time for mornings like this.

Frank was one-quarter Cherokee and, like his father, seldom displayed emotion. But what always brought a quick tear to his eyes were his memories of the strange happenings surrounding Ruth's birth. The fear that the beast-vision might have been an omen, a warning of danger to come, could still kick his heart rate up a few notches.

He tried to let the joy of holding her in his arms for the first time, then the wonder of watching her grow, crowd out his anxiety about her future. True, the sharp edge of the horror he witnessed on the night Diana conceived had dulled a bit with time. But the feeling Ruth somehow threatened Satan's plans and was in his crosshairs had never left him.

Ruth trotted Gypsy by again. In the bright sunlight, her hair shone with the gleam of pale gold with hints of burnished copper. Frank's eyes swept the fields beyond the corral. Sprigs of green poking through the earth announced nature had awakened. Though the sun was warm, he felt a sudden chill heralding the return of his dark premonitions even the promise of new life could not repress.

He tried to refocus his attention on Ruth. She sat ramrod-straight in the saddle, her reins held lightly in one hand. Frank noticed she had discarded her old scuffed riding boots in favor of the new Lacousis he and Diana bought her for Christmas. He did a quick double take – blue jeans, denim shirt and jacket, bright blue ribbon tying back her hair in a ponytail. And the gleaming new boots. *She's giving me a preview of how she'll look in the parade,* he realized smiling.

Glancing his way, she nudged Gypsy into a canter.

If only things could stay like this. A well-honed impulse caused Frank to glance at the palm of his right hand. The thin white lines of the scars were still visible. A reminder…but of what? Of the creature in his dream? The terror hidden in the storm the night of her birth? Or was it some divine purpose for his daughter not yet revealed?

The soulless thing hidden in the grass did not wonder about anything. Incapable of thought, ruled only by instinct, it lay in its hiding place as the warm sun revived it.

It had lain listless, imprisoned by the cold in its burrow for over three months, but the growing warmth finally freed it and drew it to the tall grass beside the fence of the corral.

The sun's energy was recharging its power, drained by the long winter's cold, sparking from cell to cell along the length of its scaly body. Fully awake, it felt the slight shaking of the earth and sensed the body heat of the enemy as it drew closer. Aware of the danger, its stillness only masked its deadly speed if threatened.

Later, Frank would curse himself for not noticing Gypsy's growing edginess each time she passed one particular spot near the corral fence where the waving grass provided the perfect cover.

As Ruth cantered by again, except for a quick sideways glance to judge her father's reaction, she looked straight ahead.

He forced a smile and nodded. "Looking good, honey," he called a moment before he felt the tug on his pants leg.

"Daddy, tell Ruth to let me ride with her." Tim, Frank's seven year-old, spoke with his usual command, certain the world had organized itself just for him.

Frank masked a laugh with his hand when he saw the casual stance the boy had taken. Just like his, a boot heel braced against the bottom rung of the fence, his new Stetson pulled low on his forehead.

Tim had wanted a western hat like his dad's, so for a Christmas gift Frank and Diana allowed him to select one of his own choosing. He picked a tan, five-x beaver Stetson from Sheplers in Lubbock and when Diana saw the price tag, she almost balked.

"One thing's for sure," she remarked as she handed over their credit card, "our son's got expensive tastes."

"Please, Daddy, tell Ruth to stop and let me ride with her."

Frank had forbidden him to ride alone, but did allow him up behind Ruth from time to time. "All right, son," he said and raised his hand to signal Ruth, who finished her circuit of the corral and brought Gypsy to a stop in front of them.

"Honey, take your brother for a few turns," he said, as he picked Tim up and placed him behind his sister. "Remember, not too fast, just a slow trot. And son, you be sure to hold on tight, hear?"

Ruth relaxed the reins and gave the mare a gentle nudge with her heel as she smiled at Tim over her shoulder.

She had always felt close to her little brother. Even though he was five years younger, she tried to include him whenever she could. Ruth had taught him how to tie his shoes and held his hand when he got on the school bus for the first time. At a PTA meeting the previous year, his kindergarten teacher, Mrs. Kilmer, remarked to Diana how impressed she was with the way Ruth looked after her brother.

From the back porch, Diana had a clear view of the children as they circled the corral. Tim's hands were around his sister's waist, and he squealed with delight when she relaxed the reins a bit and gave Gypsy her head.

"Not too fast," she heard Frank warn, as they went round and round in a widening circle that brought them closer and closer to the tall grass at the edge of the corral.

Sensitive cells on the creature's underbelly felt the vibrations growing stronger as the enemy drew closer. Nerve endings along its head and in its tongue registered increasing heat as the alien body approached.

As the vibrations increased, its response was instinctive. Muscles rippled to life, then flexed as six feet of deadly power coiled into a tight muscular knot.

The vibrations were shaking the earth beneath the creature. In a moment, the enemy would be upon it. Suddenly, its beady eyes saw the offending presence as it loomed high above…about to descend…about to crush it!

The creature's strike was a blur of motion as six feet of lethal Diamondback fury shot from the grass and buried its fangs in the horse's leg.

From the back porch, Diana saw Gypsy rear and heard the children scream. She watched, horrified, as time crawled and Tim floated toward the fence, his arms and legs thrashing, as if trying to swim on a sea of air.

In that brief moment, Frank glimpsed his son's face as his head jerked wildly about, frantically looking for someone to help him.

Diana saw Tim hit the fence headfirst, but Frank felt the full impact of the horror when he heard the crack of his son's slender neck.

Unbelievably, the Stetson was still perched on his head, only now its tan band was slowly turning red while, several feet away, Ruth lay unconscious, a thin rivulet of blood trickling from her right ear.

CHAPTER 10

THE FLOWERS FARM
SAME DAY, EARLY MORNING

MISS MINNIE FLOWERS FELT a little under the weather, but at eighty-two felt entitled to a few aches and pains. She had been awake since four-thirty, but no amount of coaxing could convince her body to leave the comfort of her feather bed before six a.m.

She remembered she had promised Frank Starling she would send her farm hand, Jeddah, over this morning to help him load his combine on a flat bed trailer. *Jeddah always gets here about seven. Plenty of time for him to scoot over to Frank's and be back in time to do his chores.*

So she lay there, mulling over things and watching for the first hint of light through her bedroom window, trying to figure out how to deal with an itch that since last Christmas she had been unable to scratch.

Seeing Ruth Starling last Sunday night in the church library reading that book again brought the matter to a head in Minnie's mind. *I really should talk to Diana about her daughter and that book*, she had thought.

Several months before last year's Christmas program, Ruth discovered it in the adventure section. It was an old book passed along with a number of others by a retired preacher as a gift to the library.

To Minnie it seemed the child hadn't put it down since; she was either checking it out or pulling it from the shelf and reading it at the library table on Sunday evenings before church.

She had intended to give in to her inclination Sunday when she met Ruth's mother in the church hallway, but got sidetracked when Diana began going on about how excited Ruth was about getting to ride her horse in the Lubbock parade.

She was almost sure Diana could be trusted with what she wanted to tell her ... but ... if the story ever got out... *Well, it would not be good for folks to think I am getting senile,* she reflected.

Maybe it's time for someone else to take over the library anyway, she mumbled to herself as she moved her considerable bulk to a less indented spot on the mattress. *After all, just because it was my idea to have a church library doesn't mean it belongs to me ... doesn't mean others can't take on the responsibility of managing things.*

Well maybe not my idea exactly, she thought, remembering the day at Gladys Haggard's funeral, *more like a revelation.*

Minnie had been the bookkeeper at her brother's grain elevator until her retirement twenty years ago. But being in her eighties had not dulled her brain a bit as she glanced around the funeral parlor calculating the cost of all the floral tributes to her friend.

What a waste. Once placed on the grave, they'll just dry up and blow away.

That was when she had her *revelation.* Why not start a church library and ask folks to give books in memory of the departed instead of sending flowers?

Minnie was on the phone to Pastor Duncan the next morning. He loved the idea and so did the deacons. The rest was history. The church converted a storeroom into a library and elected Minnie its librarian. In the ten years since, it had grown from a few books on temporary shelves to a large room stocked with volumes on topics ranging from theology to adventure.

It was a particular title, *Beyond the Far Horizon,* that drew Ruth's interest like iron filings to a magnet last December on the night of the children's Christmas program.

She had discovered the book several months before, so it seemed then by accident, though in retrospect she wasn't so sure, Her dad was in a committee meeting at the church and had left her in the office reception area. Seeing her sitting, obviously bored, the church secretary suggested she might like her to open the library so that she could browse the books while she waited.

She was a regular visitor to the children's books arranged on low shelves in the corner of the library. She especially liked the books of Bible stories that Miss Flowers, the librarian, described as "dressed up in modern clothes."

However, that afternoon she skirted around the children's books and headed for the adventure section, an area she had never visited before. She had no idea what it was she was looking for, but strangely felt she recognized it was when she spotted it even though its plain brown cover made it indistinguishable from all the other travel books pressing in around it.

But for whatever reason, though the same size as the others, it was not aligned with the other books, but extended out beyond them on the shelf as if to say, so Ruth imagined, *"here I am take me."* And she did. And stranger still, the book was warm to her touch as though someone had held it tightly for some time and only just now put it down.

And when she opened it, there, tucked away toward the book's middle, as if waiting just for her ... her fingers found him, his dark eyes seeking hers ... the Shaman.

That night at church she was aware Miss Flowers, the librarian, had walked over and was looking over her shoulder as she began thumbing through the book. It chronicled the travels of a globetrotting photographer in the early nineteen thirties. Written by his wife, it recounted their journeys through Africa, up crocodile-infested rivers in New Guinea, and deep into the Amazon rain forest. It also contained a large number of photographs of the strange people they encountered along the way. She felt her eyes strangely drawn to one of them, that of an Amazonian tribesman. With small sticks protruding from his lips and a halo of bird feathers crowning his head, he seemed to stare directly at her. A black stone hung from a cord around his neck, and he was very nearly naked. He sat regally on a long bench with strange symbols carved along its edges. A caption beneath the picture read: "Amazonian Shaman, seated on his jaguar bench."

"Honey, it's time to close up and go to church," she heard Minnie say as she tapped her on the shoulder. Ruth could hear the organ in the church auditorium down the hall begin the prelude announcing the beginning of the Christmas program as she began tracing the design pictured on the bench with her finger.

Her chin rested in her hands, her gaze fixed on the picture of the tribesman, but she raised her head when Minnie tapped her.

"Miss Flowers, why is the man so unhappy?" she asked, turning to Minnie who adjusted her bifocals to look more closely at the picture.

"Maybe he's lost and is looking for the way back," Ruth heard Minnie say, and wondered why she had said such a thing just as the room slowly dissolved and vanished: The books, racks, tables, floors, walls, ceiling—everything but Minnie!

Ruth's question and her own oblique answer ignited in Minnie's mind the memory of the terrifying vision. The grip of it had been too strong to break. Even the organ music, loud moments before, faded away and, except for seeing Ruth's questioning eyes staring into hers, she felt suspended in emptiness and surrounded by silence.

I had to have imagined it, she told herself for the umpteenth time as she remembered the vision. Feeling a sudden chill, she pulled the covers more tightly around her shoulders. But she couldn't shake Ruth's question as to why the man appeared so sad or her curious answer that perhaps it was because he was lost and looking for a way back. *Back to where?*

All she knew for sure was that as Ruth suddenly closed the book, the spell was broken, the building, library, and furnishings reappeared, and she could hear the surge of the organ signal the program had started.

As if awaking from a nap and unaware of what had happened, Ruth pushed back her chair and started for the door. "You'd better hurry," she said teasingly to Minnie as she exited, "or you'll be late for the Christmas program."

Minnie heaved herself to a sitting position on the edge of the bed and tried to drive the unsettling memories of the night of the Christmas program from her mind. She assured herself the whole library episode had just been a case of an overactive imagination. Still, she remembered checking the library card for *Beyond the Far Horizon,* and not being surprised to find that Ruth had checked the book out no fewer than seven times, not including this past Sunday. She should not procrastinate any longer. Even if all she did was mention the book to Ruth's mother, even if she didn't bring up her strange fantasy last Christmas, at least she'd feel she'd done her duty.

She looked out her sparkling windows to the sunlight shining on the dawn of spring. *Not today,* she mused. *Why spoil such a beautiful morning with thoughts of dark visions?* Willing her body out of bed, she put on her robe and house shoes and shuffled into the kitchen.

After putting on the coffee, she got out a mixing bowl and the ingredients for the cake she wanted to make for the upcoming church dinner. Through the window above the sink, she saw the crocuses beginning to push their yellow heads through the soil in her flower box.

"Get goin'," she murmured to herself. "This is no time to be feeling poorly."

She rubbed absently at her chest, telling the dull pain in there to go away.

She smiled at the crocuses. She always planted them for early blooming, her wake-up call for spring. *Resurrection time,* she'd always called it. She added sugar to the shortening in the bowl and reached for a mixing spoon to cream them together.

"Resurrection time," Minnie said aloud to the nodding heads of the yellow crocuses as the spoon dropped from her hand. Slowly she slumped to the floor, the warmth of her smile never fading.

Chapter 11

Ruth heard the terrified whinny of her horse, her mother scream, then felt herself vault forward, drifting on a sea of darkness toward a blue spot light focused on a platform in the distance.

Drifting nearer, she realized it was the platform of the Lone Oak Church and that except for her the church was empty. Arranged to stage left were Papier-mâché hills and Styrofoam rocks while a manger scene complete with sheep, lamb, and donkey cutouts commanded center stage – *just like the night of the Christmas program,* Ruth thought, *except …*

She felt confused, disoriented, like she had just walked into a familiar room and knew something was out of place, but wasn't quite sure what it was.

From behind closed eyelids, she gazed into the blank darkness around her then glanced back toward the platform and saw them—two tall shapes standing in the shadows just beyond the ring of light on the right side of the platform. *Funny,* she thought dreamily, *I don't remember any props like those.*

Was she at the Christmas program? She was almost sure she'd been in the library just before coming into the auditorium that night. At least it was her habit to go there and read before evening services. Now she had no memory of leaving Miss Flowers' wonderful collection of books in the library or of feeling her way in the darkness to the auditorium's front row where she now sat.

Where was Timmy? She searched the dream-stage for her little brother, remembering his excitement at the prospect of being in the Christmas play.

They came to church early so Tim could put on the costume Diana made him from a blue and white striped bathrobe Ruth had outgrown. Tim was the youngest of the boys asked to play a shepherd and given only four words to say. His cue came when another shepherd said, "Let us go even unto Bethlehem and see this thing which the Lord hath made known unto us." At this cue, Tim was to step forward, gesture to the other shepherds, and say, "Come on, let's go!" But if this was the children's Christmas program, where were he and the others?

A bedlam of sounds and a kaleidoscope of frightening images suddenly assaulted her senses – Gypsy rearing, Timmy screaming in panic, her father's terrified face and herself falling, falling into darkness.

A scene materialized then cleared as its wild osculation steadied. Ruth was again in the library. As usual, Miss Flowers was busy with her records and did not even look up when she walked over to the shelf of adventure books, found her favorite, sat, and began to read.

And then, as if she had needed this enforced unconsciousness to dredge up the memory, she saw herself staring trance-like at the picture of a brown-skinned man seated on what the book called "his jaguar bench." She watched, as if from a great height, as her own finger lazily traced the design on the bench.

Faintly, she thought she heard Miss Flowers announce that it was time to close the library. In the background, organ music drifted just on the edges of the strange silence.

And then her whole being was aware of only two things: the rapid beating of her own heart and the sad, dark eyes of the brown-skinned man staring into hers. She had no idea how long she hung there, between reality and vision, but at some point she became aware of Miss Flowers' voice suggesting the man in the picture was looking for God.

Then, gradually, as she lifted her finger from its tracing of the marks on the Shaman's bench, the organ music penetrated, and once again, she felt the dreamscape shifting…

Ruth floated in the darkness until she came to rest again in the auditorium, back in her seat. But this time the room was no longer empty. Shadowy forms sat all around. She recognized her father's profile next to her, his attention focused on the stage where one of the older shepherds had just given Tim his cue…

Let us go even unto Bethlehem and see this thing …"

After a painful pause, during which Tim remained mute beside him, the boy repeated his line, glancing nervously at the other children on the stage. Still, her little brother did not speak but stood stiffly, shifting his weight from one foot to the other. His head moved in jerky starts and stops as he searched for his family in the dark auditorium.

In her dream, Ruth willed him to step forward, whispering under her breath, "Come on, let's go."

Again, the scene shifted, as shepherds and props vanished in a swirling mist leaving only the rough wooden manger in the background and Tim standing at center stage. His face glowed in the blue spotlight. His head stopped moving and his eyes, their panicky darting from side to side. To Ruth it seemed that every hint of nervousness had left him as he walked confidently to the edge of the platform then stood and smiled into the darkness for what seemed an eternity.

Childish jitters gone, Tim turned his gaze toward the ceiling, and then cocked his head slightly as if listening for something. The shadowy congregation, taking his cue, moved to the edges of their seats in anticipation. Not even a cough disturbed the hush that settled over the church.

Ruth had no idea what it was her brother expected to hear until the soft mewling cry of a baby invaded the silence. Tim turned to look over his shoulder, and then slowly nodded his acknowledgement of an unspoken command just as the cries died away.

Squaring his shoulders, he addressed the mystified congregation in a firm, confident voice that belied his age and size.

"The shepherds came to the manger looking for Jesus," he said, flashing a wide smile. "They found Him. I've found Him." Tim paused and squinted into the darkness, as if looking for a particular person. "You," he fairly shouted, "you can find Him too!"

The dreaming Ruth felt her brother's gaze seeking her in the darkness.

"Christ wants all of you to find Him and to trust Him," Tim said, with the persuasive voice of an evangelist rather than that of a little boy.

Ruth squirmed in her imaginary seat thinking, *Tim talks like Jesus is his personal friend.*

A question shouted in her heart for an answer: *Do I know Him like that? I believed everything the Bible says about Him. I believed Jesus was God's son and that He was born of a virgin. I believed He performed miracles and died on a cross for our sins, and that He rose from the dead. But is that enough?* Her heart told her it wasn't.

Shadows of light and dark swirled around her, and Ruth felt herself buffeted from side to side, as if two opposing forces were trying to pull her apart. Was she sure about her relationship with God? Tim's message reverberated inside her head, and again she heard Miss Flowers' words about the little brown man in the picture: "Maybe he's looking for God."

Me, too! Me, too! Ruth wanted to shout, but as in the way of dreams, no sounds would come.

I don't know Jesus, at least not in the way Tim does. But I want to. She felt tears running down her cheeks. At that moment, she said "yes" to the voice softly speaking to her heart; a voice she just obeyed inviting her to move beyond mere belief in the truth *about* Jesus to believe *on* Him as her master and best friend.

Tim walked to the manger, looked down and smiled. "The shepherds were the first to come to Jesus," he said as he turned back toward the shadowy audience and then in a stage whisper so as not to awaken the baby, said, "Now it's your turn."

He stepped back to the edge of the platform, opened his small arms wide and shouted, "Come on everybody, come to the manger ... come to Jesus! If you've not trusted Him, you can trust Him now. If you know Him, come to the manger and get to know him better. Come on everybody; come with me to the manger!"

Her pastor, Reverend Duncan, gave an invitation every Sunday at the end of his sermon inviting people to give their lives to

Christ, but he had never given one like this. Ruth felt herself float-
ing forward, buoyed by a newfound understanding of what it truly
meant to believe *on* and not just *about* Jesus.

For a few moments, she hovered over the platform looking
down into the manger, secure in knowing, like Tim, she had just
trusted God's Son as her personal Savior.

Once more, Ruth's perspective changed. Again, she was an
audience of one, watching as a new scene unfolded on the platform. Tim still stood in the spotlight, but he had traded his shepherd's robe for a pair of blue jeans. Pulled low on his forehead was
a slightly soiled western hat. Around his waist, a silver belt buckle
sparkled in the light.

Miss Flowers materialized out of nowhere and joined Tim
onstage. Ruth was shocked to see her wearing a shabby bathrobe, her hair rumpled as if she had just risen from her bed.
But more astounding was her physical presence. Once, time had
stamped her frail body with osteoporosis so severe it had twisted
her spine until her chin almost touched her chest. Next to Tim,
Miss Minnie stood erect, the weight of her eighty-odd years suddenly lifted from her shoulders, the wrinkles erased from her
cheeks.

"It's a miracle," Ruth whispered.

Smiling, the old woman took her brother's hand.

"Timmy, we must be going," she said and led him toward the
tall pillars looming in the shadows at the left of the stage. "There's
so much for us to see and do."

Hardly had she spoken when another spotlight flashed on, bathing the towering props she glimpsed earlier with a golden glow. Ruth gasped! They weren't Styrofoam stage props at all, but real stone pillars so tall they dwarfed the platform, the auditorium—everything!

Her eyes shot up. The ceiling of the auditorium, its roof, and the whole church dissolved. For a moment, she could see only a star-filled sky into which the tops of the soaring pillars had disappeared. Her sense of place returned and looking about she realized she was standing on a trail winding out of a forbidding forest. Ahead she could see Tim and Miss Flowers had almost reached the stone columns.

Tim stopped, looked back at her, and then pointed to a meadow ablaze with flowers just beyond the pillars.

"Ruthie, you can come with us," he said, this time in his familiar little boy's voice.

Oh, how she wanted to. A longing too deep for words swept over her.

"That's right, Ruth, follow your brother," an inviting voice purred. "There's no reason to be left here alone."

Startled, she looked back toward the edge of the forest. Something moved in the shadows where the branches of three large trees overlapped.

She froze in panic. The image of a snake, slithering in the shadows, filled her vision: two blazing eyes, a gaping mouth, filled with jagged yellow teeth.

Terrified she watched as the image congealed, a body joined the snakehead, legs and feet appearing. From what had only moments before been a co-mingling of reptile, gloom, and shade, a sleek black cougar moved sinuously out into the hazy light. Fixing yellowish eyes on Ruth, it crept forward.

Ruth tried to scream but couldn't.

She forced herself to look away from the cat's mesmerizing eyes. Tim and Miss Flowers had reached the pillars and looked back for her. Ruth willed her legs to move. If she could reach them, she'd be safe.

"Oh, look at the lovely flowers, dear," Miss Flowers called, like a child who had just made a wonderful discovery.

Beyond the pillars, yellow crocuses in full bloom filled the meadow.

Ruth knew she would be too late. Tears streamed down her face as Tim and Miss Flowers passed between the pillars and into the meadow. Heartbroken, Ruth steadied herself against one of the columns and felt her fingers slide into a series of depressions in the stone. Without even looking, she recognized they were same markings she had traced on the Shaman's bench in the picture in the library.

"Go ahead and follow your brother, you little toad." The soft purr of the cougar suddenly became a vicious snarl.

Ruth looked back. A few feet away, the beast sat on its haunches, eying her like a piece of meat in a butcher's shop.

"No one can help you. If you stay here, I'll tear out your liver and eat it before your eyes!"

"There's still time, Ruthie!" Tim and Miss Flowers reached the far side of the meadow, and he waved frantically. "Come on! You don't have to stay behind."

She desperately wanted to run into the meadow and join them. They were so near. Just a few more steps and she could be there. Yet something stronger than her overwhelming desire to join her brother, stronger even than her fear of the cougar, held her back.

Suddenly, a man stepped out of the jungle and started down the trail toward her. Except for a loincloth, he was naked. His skin was the color of tanned leather. Crowned with a halo of feathers, a shimmering black stone hung around his neck.

He stopped and fixed his gaze on Ruth standing between the stone pillars and, as if in recognition, ran toward her with outstretched hands. Ruth could now see his face clearly. *The man in the picture!* Hours of studying those sad eyes had branded his face on her memory.

He cried out with the desperation of a drowning man, "No, don't go without us! Please. Not without us!"

Ruth's hand still rested on the strange engravings and, without thought or intention, she nervously retraced the design's indentions with her finger. The response was instantaneous. A sudden stirring of the wind and a fluttering sound drew her eyes back toward the meadow. The field was awash in butterflies! From among the yellow crocuses, they rose in clouds of swirling color, sweeping upward, encircling and lifting her on their wings. Up... up...

Ruth could no longer see the man's face through the wall of shimmering wings, but she heard his voice clearly.

"Come back," he cried. "Come back! Come ..."

"Come back. Please come back to us, Ruth."

Another voice, a familiar one was calling.

Ruth struggled to open her eyes, while another part of her confused mind tried to hold onto the beauty of the butterflies. The bright light made her blink, and her eyelids jerked closed in pain. Finally, she eased them open again. Her mother's face hovered over her, and in the background, her father's worried frown materialized out of the fog that had held her in its grasp.

"Oh, thank God," she heard him murmur. "You've come back to us." Then he forced a wan smile. "You've been asleep a long time, honey."

"I can't go without them." Ruth found her voice and began to cry. "Not without them!"

"Without who, sweetheart?" her mother asked, rubbing her thumb against Ruth's hand as if she could will her daughter back to full consciousness.

The swirling mists that had held Ruth in their sway cleared even more, and she saw the tears in her mother's eyes.

"Not without whom, dearest?" Diana asked again.

Something was terribly wrong. Ruth could feel it. Her mother's tears…the grief in her father's eyes. Fragments of a terrible memory scratched at her consciousness. Riding Gypsy with Tim behind her. Gypsy rearing. Then falling…falling…into darkness.

"Where's Tim?" Ruth jerked upright in the bed, her brain whirling. She dreaded the answer, her eyes shut tight against the pain she knew was coming.

The silence seemed to stretch out forever before her father finally whispered, "Tim's gone home to be with Jesus."

Somewhere nearby she heard her mother crying softly.

Ruth felt tears well in her own eyes, but her voice, when she spoke, was steady. "He'll be all right. Miss Flowers will take good care of him."

Frank and Diana exchanged a look. There was no way Ruth could have known about the old woman's passing. Their daughter had been in a coma that lasted for nearly a week.

"Miss Minnie and Timmy will take care of each other until we're all together again."

CHAPTER 12

STARLING FARM. TWO WEEKS LATER

"MRS. STARLING, CAN RUTH have company?" Diana was not surprised to find Frank Spencer's son Jerry at the kitchen door when she answered the timid knock. He held a bouquet of flowers in one hand and a book in the other. "I picked these early bloomers this morning," he said holding out the flowers for Diana's inspection. "I thought they might cheer her up." He extended the bouquet for Diana to take as she opened the door wide and invited him in. "Thank you Jerry, I'm sure they will. She is in her room and doing much better. I know she'd love to see you. Why don't you have a seat in the living room while I put these flowers in a vase and then I'll call her.

Frank and Diana had hardly gotten Ruth home from the hospital day before yesterday when Jerry called to see how she was doing. Frank took the call and Diana could tell, listening to his end of the conversation, that Jerry needed assurance Ruth would be O.K.

"She had a small fracture ..."

"Yes, that's right ...

"A very small one ..."

"No, the doctor said there was no permanent damage ...

"Wants her to stay in for a week and not exert herself for at least a month.

"Then ... yes, that's right, then he thinks she should be as good as new.

"No ... with the bouncing and all it probably won't do for her to try to ride Gypsy in the parade."

"Gypsy? Oh, the vet gave her a shot of anti-venom and she's doing fine."

"Yes Jerry ... I'll tell her you called. Give her a day or two to rest up and I know she'll be glad to see you."

"Jerry Spencer's a nice kid," Frank said as he hung up the phone.

A mental picture of the gangly neighbor boy formed in Diana's mind. Jerry was the eldest of the Spencers' four children and turned fifteen about two months before Ruth's twelfth birthday.

Like Frank, Fred Spencer was a deacon in Lone Oak Church. Jerry had known Ruth since she was a baby, but Frank and Diana agreed it was her first day in school when they really bonded and when Jerry seemed to have made Ruth his special responsibility.

Diana remembered Ruth was anxious about going to school for the first time. Hoping to lift her spirits, she took her daughter shopping in Lubbock for some new clothes the Saturday before school started.

That Sunday, on the church parking lot Frank and Fred were in a conversation when Frank mentioned Ruth being a little anxious about starting to school. "I guess the first day can be kinda scary, what with new faces, new surroundings and all," Fred volunteered.

Only when Ruth grabbed his pant leg did Frank realize she had been standing behind him and heard Fred's remark. "Is school really a scary place daddy?" Her eyes brimmed with tears, her chin quivered, and there was near panic in her voice as she looked up at her father. "If it is, I don't wanna go!"

Jerry, who was also nearby, heard his dad's remark, came up beside Ruth, put his hand on her shoulder, and mustering all the confidence a ten year old could manage said, "school's not scary Ruthie, if you're not by yourself ... And you won't be, because I'll be with you."

Jerry's promise must have been all the assurance she needed because she let go of Frank's pant leg and skipped away with the Spencer children to do whatever kids do.

That Sunday evening after church Frank watched as Diana helped Ruth try on her new outfit. After tucking in her blouse, Diana stood back admiring Ruth's reflection in the mirror. "You look great honey," she said, giving her a reassuring smile! "You'll be one of the prettiest girls in kindergarten." Frank knew his wife hoped her upbeat manner would ease the worry both of them saw on Ruth's face.

"Jerry will be there won't he? At school I mean." Ruth sought out Diana's reflections in the mirror for assurance.

"Sure he will, honey. Don't you remember Jerry's promise this morning?" Frank interjected.

The next morning Frank stood in the front yard with Ruth, watching as a distant trail of dust announced the coming of the yellow school bus. He felt Diana's eyes watching them through the living room windows. Seeing her baby leave for school for the first time was especially sad for her so after helping her dress they hugged and said their "goodbyes" in the house.

He would never forget the look of relief on Ruth's face when the bus came, the door opened, and there stood Jerry, as good as his word, on the top step.

"Come on Ruthie." He was smiling from ear to ear. "I've saved a seat for you by me," he said as he reached down and took her hand.

Jerry stood as Ruth entered the living room holding the vase containing his flowers. After putting them on an end table, they exchanged hugs and sat down together on the couch. "Thanks for the flowers." She gave him that familiar flick of a smile Jerry felt hinted at more unspoken.

"I brought this too." He picked up the book beside him and gave it to her.

"My favorite," she said glancing at its familiar title.

"I know. I had to look a long time before I found it in the library. With Miss Flowers gone and all I ..."

"I know." A radiantly youthful Miss Flowers and Timmy, surrounded by yellow crocuses flashed in Ruth's mind.

"But we'll be with both of them again."

"Both?"

Jerry's questioning look told her he did not understand what she meant by *both*. "Tim and Miss Flowers I mean ... I saw them both in my dream," she said.

"But they're ..."

"Dead? Jerry, my dream told me dying is just the way God sometimes moves us from one place to another. They're both in a beautiful place and someday we'll join them."

"Maybe you Ruthie ... I'm not so sure about me."

Jerry felt the conversation taking him somewhere he'd rather not allow his mind to go. Like those stormy Sunday nights the pastor always seemed to pick to preach on the return of Christ. Those sermons, filled with descriptions of war and earthquakes, he delivered to the accompaniment of booming thunder and lighting, were double wallops to his conscience, reminding him he wasn't ready for the great event.

But Jerry's uncertain response was the opening Ruth needed to tell him about her dreamed decision to trust Christ, and its real follow-up in the hospital after she came out of her coma.

"Jerry, you can be sure just like me," she said, and added, "next Sunday when Pastor Duncan gives his invitation for folks to come forward and declare their faith in Jesus I'm going. He came to see me yesterday and I told him about my decision. When I told him in my dream, God showed me the difference between believing *about* Jesus and *on* Him, he said he wanted me to give my testimony in church."

Ruth looked at Jerry inquiringly. "Do you know the difference Jerry," she asked, never letting her eyes drop from his.

Jerry's look of befuddlement dissolved into one of conviction. Dropping his eyes, he said wistfully, "I'm happy for you Ruthie. I guess I'd like to have what you have, but I'm just not ready to make the kind of decision I think you're talking about. There are things you don't know about me, things I can't ..." Jerry's voice trailed away leaving his thought unfinished.

"I hope you understand the risk you're taking Jerry," Chief Detective Walters of the Lubbock police department said the next day as he fixed Jerry with an appraising stare.

"Look," Jerry said, returning it. "I took on this job because I'm tired of seeing school buddies being sucked down a black hole of drugs and I'm not quitting until you guys know the supplier and put him away. Just last week I visited one of my friends in the hospital who tripped on something that fried his brain. They had him tied to a bed and he was screaming to the top of his lungs. The doctor told his folks not to expect him to ever be normal again."

"I'm sorry about that Jerry. I just wanted you to understand the downside of this operation," Walters replied, "and the possible consequences if the drug dealers at your school finger you as a snitch." Having given his warning, he yelled "pull" and Jerry launched another clay pigeon that shattered in mid-flight at the blast of Walters' shotgun.

It was here on this gun range Jerry first met Walters several months ago. His keen eye and steady hands with his 22 along with a mature manner for one so young had impressed the officer and quickly won the crusty officer's confidence and respect. It was also here, a few weeks before Ruth's recent accident, Jerry told Walters he thought he knew who was selling drugs in the high school. "If we knew for sure, we could trace them to their distributor, work up the gang's operational chain and break this case wide open," Walters observed.

That was when Jerry put himself on the front line of the probe by volunteering to try confirming the sellers' identities, then win their confidence and learn the name of their source. "I have a plan that might do the trick," he said without discussing what it was.

Jerry immediately started dropping inquiries about where he might pick up some "meth" with kids at school he knew used drugs and after several dead ends, one finally volunteered he might want to talk to the Brady brothers.

His inquiries must have circulated quickly because a few days later one of the brothers approached him in the lunchroom wanting to know about his interest in "meth." "I've never taken you to be a user kind of guy," Brady said eyeing Jerry suspiciously. When he told him his interest was financial rather than personal, it seemed to perk Brady's interest because he suggested they meet at his car on the parking lot after school to discuss some possibilities.

Both Bradys were in the car, one behind the wheel the other in the back seat, when Jerry joined them. He floated his drug networking idea, involving the recruitment of kids in the city's middle schools as sellers and both brothers immediately warmed to it. "If we work together, you guys can make added profits now as well as making new customers for later in high school," he said, adding that if they liked the plan his cut would be a percentage of sales in the middle schools. A deal was struck when he added his network of sellers would only be an extension of theirs rather than a separate operation.

"You're quite the businessman Spencer, for a country boy," the brother at the wheel said as he reached across and opened Jerry's door. "Not a bit like most of the other hicks from the sticks the schools bus in."

"Just tired of being poor I guess," Jerry replied then grinned and faked a laugh.

"We'll give you a heads up after we talk to our supplier," the brother in the back seat said as Jerry shut the car door, "I'm sure he'll want to meet you."

As Jerry walked away from their car, he was glad they brought up the subject of the supplier, sure that had he done so it would have raised suspicion.

Yesterday when Jerry told Walters his suspicions were right, it came as no surprise the sellers were the popular Brady brothers. "Too fancy a car for kids and too much cash being flashed," he observed stoically, adding, "it will sure blow the minds of the local football fans to know their star quarterback and defensive right end are dealers."

"I think the Bradys have bought my idea," Jerry loaded another clay pigeon into the launcher as he was speaking. "Yesterday they told me they would give me a 'heads up' when their distributor was ready to meet me and discuss my plan."

"To discuss your plan? Well maybe." Walters cocked his head and squinted down the barrel of his shotgun. "But to check you out ... most definitely," he said dryly just before shouting, "pull" and blasting the last clay pigeon from the sky.

CHAPTER 13

THE BIG DAY HAD arrived. Lubbock's annual parade announcing the beginning of the biggest rodeo in West Texas would start in only a few hours. A wag sounding off in the gossip column of the local news paper described it as "amnesia day." One where the spectacle of horses, floats, marching bands and old men riding midget cars made folks forget the harsh winter just past and focus instead on the prospects for new life that come at planting season.

Frank couldn't suppress a smile as he reflected on what his neighbors might think if they saw him now, ensconced with Diana in the back seat of the Spencers' car with Jerry at the wheel and their little Ruth sitting beside him.

Frank and Diana tried hard during Ruth's recuperation to help her move beyond what they saw as her shock response to losing her brother. "She seems so calm and at peace ... almost as if nothing has happened," Frank observed. "That dream she had while in the coma seems to have insulated her against grief and a sense of loss."

But could it be more than that? Frank remembered his own frightful dream before Ruth was born, one that had followed him ever since and at times seemed real enough to touch. *Is it possible,* he wondered, *that, though in a coma, Ruth's vision of her brother and Miss*

Flowers as still alive and happy is real and that that reality is what gives her such peace?

However, Frank and Diana both felt the need to bring closure to their lives as a family of four, adjust to one of three, and felt that giving Ruth something to look forward to would help all of them.

It was the very day he and Diana last discussed this concern that Jerry appeared at the kitchen door with a question. "Mr. Starling," he asked nervously, "would you and Mrs. Starling and Ruth let me drive you into Lubbock for the parade?"

Jerry explained he had recently gotten his driver's permit and had been gaining experience driving his mother and dad back and forth to Lubbock. "They think I'm a good driver, good enough for them to let me take the car and drive you to the parade ..." Jerry paused and looked at Diana, who had just walked into the kitchen, as if seeking her approval. "... at least if me driving is alright with you."

Frank took Diana's smile as a "yes," and said, "Jerry, we would be happy to let you drive us in. Knowing we're going with you will be a big boost to Ruth's morale. She had really looked forward to riding in the parade, you know."

"Yeah, I hoped us going together might make her happy and able to forget ..." What Jerry hoped she would forget he left unsaid as if its mere mention was too painful even for him.

"Yes Jerry, we do too or at least help a little," Diana answered, as Frank dropped his head and brushed a tear.

Frank was glad the city had been thoughtful enough to erect some bleachers along the parade route so those needing to sit would have a place to do so ... a place that is if one got there early enough. He appreciated a thoughtful friend who, knowing the parade would be one of Ruth's first outings since her accident, had come early and saved four seats for them.

After Frank helped Diana and Ruth to their seats, he and Jerry went to the concession stand where Frank bought pop, peanuts and popcorn. They had just started walking back to the bleachers when they bumped into the Brady brothers. Frank recognized them not only because he had watched them play football or even because the smaller of the duo, the first string quarterback, had more pass completions to his credit than any in Lubbock High's history, but because of their swaggers, swaggers that shouted "look at me, I'm important!"

As they passed, one turned and quickly said something to Jerry. Frank could not make out what he said but Jerry's nod made it clear he did. *Strange*, Frank thought. *What could two seniors like the Bradys, so-called big men on campus, have to discuss with a sophomore farm boy like Jerry?*

Back in their seats, Frank couldn't help noticing the Bradys standing at street level just to the right of the bleachers. The street vibrated with the blare of bands and marching feet, the hum of trucks displaying girls on flattering floats, and the steady clop, clop, clop of prize horses bearing proud riders. However, Frank realized the Bradys weren't noticing, but looking toward where they were sitting. He also noticed Jerry's eyes kept shifting back and forth between the parade, the Brady boys, and someone he was texting on his cell phone.

Frank thought he saw a quick nod from one of the Bradys just as Jerry stood, and without explanation, said he had to leave but would be back in a little while.

Jerry's abruptness and sudden lack of interest in the parade mystified Frank. He covered his bewilderment however with an understanding nod to the boy just as he saw the Bradys disappear around the corner of the bleachers.

"You took your own good time dude," The older Brady scowled at Jerry, obviously irritated.

I couldn't just rush off like that ... might have raised questions," Jerry replied, trying to cover his jitters with a tone of casual indifference as they started walking across the parking lot.

"Where to now?"

"To your car," the other Brady boy replied. "It's over there." He pointed several car lanes over. "We saw you drive in."

"Oh, so I'm driving?" Jerry felt a flash of sudden nausea.

"You can, can't you," the younger Brady snapped.

"Sure, I got my license two weeks ago," Jerry replied, but felt very small when both Bradys began to snicker.

"A licensed driver!" the older one hooted, slapping his thigh. Well Mr. Businessman, we wouldn't want you breaking the law and driving without one. That would be bad for our reputations."

"And for business if you couldn't even drive to pick up and deliver the product," the younger Brady added as they reached the car, opened the doors and got inside.

For several minutes, they traveled in silence, broken finally by the older Brady who had positioned himself in the back seat behind Jerry. "You're driving good for a dude who just got his license. Maybe just a little nervous..." Both brothers snickered again at their inside joke. "But in your situation who wouldn't be?" the older brother added, patting Jerry on the shoulder.

"You haven't told me where we're going," Jerry said, glancing into the rearview mirror.

"Haven't needed to so far. You're going in the right direction. Just turn right at the next four-way stop sign then left on the gravel road at the top of the hill."

"To where?"

"Where do you think? We're going where you've wanted to go ever since our first conversation. We're going to see the man. He wants to check you out, have a little visit with you, and see if you're up to the job."

Jerry saw the gravel road on the left and turned, surprised to see a sign above it that announced, "City Cemetery."

"Just go straight in and all the way to the back side... Our supplier will be parked in his black Caddy near a small grove of trees," the older brother explained.

Jerry could see the Cadillac now just where the brother said. He felt his heart racing and his palms sweating. *If I have to shake his hand, he'll know I'm scared,* he thought, just as he stopped his car beside the suppliers.

He glanced at his watch. *We've been gone twenty-five minutes. How will I explain to the Starlings if I don't get back before the parade is over and they are stranded?* Just then, a window in the Cadillac lowered and a diamond-ringed hand reached out and motioned.

"The man wants you to come over," the younger Brady said. "Don't keep him waiting."

After Jerry joined the supplier in his car, the man said nothing for some time but only looked at him with heavily hooded eyes. "I can smell a snitch a mile away," the supplier finally said. "Are you a snitch?" He paused, then not waiting for an answer asked, "Your name is Jerry, Jerry Spencer, is that right?"

"Yes," Jerry answered, hoping his voice did not betray the fright.

"Are you a snitch, Jerry?"

"No"

"No? Then tell me Jerry Spencer what are you?"

He tried to answer. "My name is ..." but was not permitted to finish before the supplier grabbed his head and jerked it toward him so that Jerry had to stare directly into his hate-filled hooded eyes.

"Not *who* are you, stupid! If you're not a snitch, *what* are you?"

Jerry knew he had to think quickly, and did. "Mister, I'm someone who doesn't want to always be poor but will be unless I can get off the farm," he blurted, never taking his eyes from those of the supplier. "Setting up and managing a network selling drugs to middle-school kids will be my ticket off the farm and away from this podunk place."

"Do you know the danger kid?" The supplier smiled.

"You mean the law?"

"Oh, that's a danger alright, but there's a lot bigger one."

"What's that?"

"ME!" the supplier suddenly snarled. "If you so much as mention my name, even in your dreams, or ever try to short me or welsh on a deal, I'll be your greatest danger, your worst nightmare and your last."

"My last?"

"Yeah, your last because you'll be dead." The supplier gave Jerry another appraising look. "Now, are we clear?"

"Yes sir," Jerry replied sheepishly, relieved to look away from the murderous face of the supplier.

"Good, then we almost have a deal."

"Almost?"

"Yeah, almost. Just need to nail our understanding down so you never forget."

"How do we do that?" Jerry couldn't hold back the quiver in his voice.

The supplier displayed a yellow-tooth grin as he reached under the car's seat and felt until he found a small bottle filled with a red liquid.

"Are you a Christian kid?"

"Well, I go to church if that's what you mean."

"That's good enough," the supplier said. "Then you know about Communion, right?"

"I know it's what our church calls "the Lord's Supper." The preacher says it's a way of remembering Jesus' death on the cross."

"Right on," the supplier said, flashing his yellow-toothed grin again. "Well Jerry, just we two are going to have a little Communion service right here so you will always remember your promise never to snitch on me, OK?"

"I guess," Jerry whispered as the supplier reached into the glove compartment and retrieved a small cup into which he poured a little of the red liquid.

"Here," the supplier said almost gently as he placed the cup in Jerry's outstretched hand, "drink this in memory of me."

"That wasn't so bad was it dude?" the older Brady jibed as he settled again into the back seat of Jerry's car.

"Not bad at all," Jerry replied feeling a sense of unexpected confidence.

Glad to be going, he started the car and was about to pull away when the older Brady told him to wait while he had a few words with the supplier. Jerry watched anxiously as the two conversed, but now Brady's jovial tone implied all was well.

But all wasn't well. Jerry sensed it just as they exited the cemetery and entered the main road leading back into town. His hands began trembling on the wheel, and the road suddenly appeared wavy. Passing cars, weirdly distorted like reflections in a fun house mirror, left contrails of blues, reds and yellows as they streaked by.

That drink, Jerry thought as he felt himself exit the body at the wheel and become a mere onlooker to what was unfolding.

"Yeah, the man gave you thumbs up," the older Brady said, "and threw a big word at me. Said you should be *ecstatic* about your new business."

"Ecstatic as in *ecstasy,*" the younger Brady said, as he laughingly mimicked his brother.

For Jerry, the observer, their little private joke that sent them into fits of laughter was no longer private.

They know the supplier put something in the wine I drank and are enjoying watching my reaction, he realized just as his foot, no longer obeying his brain, floor boarded the accelerator pedal sending the car weaving crazily down the road faster and faster.

The car's rocking and careening from side to side shook the jollies out of the Brady boys. "For God's sake Spencer, slow down!" a Brady shouted.

Jerry heard the cry of alarm but could not respond. All he could do was look on, feeling the same terror as they, as the car raced toward the four way stop just ahead. He saw the huge grain truck as it slowly entered the cross street, but knew the mindless body at the wheel of this car wouldn't stop. *Besides,* he thought, as if watching a film in slow motion, *it's already too late and we're about to crash. I might as well take a nap,* which he did. His body tilted into the lap of the younger Brady just as the car, to the shriek of sheering metal, slid under the bed of the truck.

"Well, I see the patient is doing better." Detective Walters managed a slight smile as he looked down at Jerry on his hospital bed. "The doctor said he probably would check you out later today if the test came back positive."

"Yeah, he told me the same thing when he came by a little while ago," Jerry replied wishing the detective would get on with the business that had brought him to the hospital. "How's the school taking all that's happened?" he asked trying to move the conversation along.

"About like you would imagine, considering two star football players were decapitated in a car driven by another kid high on acid. A kid, by the way, who, in a lot of students' minds, escaped what was coming to him by passing out before the truck's undercarriage sliced off the top of the car."

"Sounds like my reputation is shot."

"To say the least ... for now at least, thanks to someone in the hospital shooting off their mouth. We wanted to keep the fact drugs were found in your blood under wraps. But someone blabbed to a reporter the Brady brothers' blood was clear, but yours showed traces of LSD."

"Thanks to your text message from the parade we were able to follow you to the cemetery, and then follow the supplier back to his place. We found enough drugs there to put him away for a long time.

The prospect of spending fifteen to twenty years in jail has him singing like a bird. We're keeping his arrest out of the papers and have put him on a leash and back on the streets to try drawing higher-ups into the net. Which means ..." Walters paused.

"Means what Detective Walters?" Jerry asked, dreading what his answer might be.

"Means we can't clear you publicly for now or tell the good folks of Lubbock their two heroes were drug pushers and that you're the one that deserves the applause."

Walters threw up his hands in resignation... "They say justice is blind Jerry. Sad truth is it's sometimes deaf and dumb as well."

Walters reached and put a hand on Jerry's shoulder. "But now isn't forever. Right now, all we can do is privately clear your record of the drug and reckless driving charges and get you somewhere safe where you can finish high school out of the spotlight. After that ..."

Walters paused as if trying to visualize what would come "after that" then said, "Jerry, after that I promise to do all in my power to help you fulfill your dreams whatever they may be."

CHAPTER 14

TWO YEARS LATER

Subject: Graduation Plans

From: jspencer@netscape.com

To: rstarling@horizon.com

Hi "Ruthie,"

Mother just called and gave me the good news you would be
coming with them to my graduation from Waco High next
Sunday afternoon. It's been hard being away from you and
the family these last two years but I am grateful my aunt and
uncle were willing to let me live with them. They have done
their best to make me feel a part of their family and I will
always be grateful for their help.

Detective Walters has also been a great encouragement. He has
nominated me for a scholarship through the National Police-
men Association. After he told the association my story, he
said he was almost sure I would get it. If I do, it will pay a
large part of my tuition and expenses and make it possible to
go to college right here in Waco at Evangel University.

I guess you've heard Detective Walters has a promotion and is now with the Dallas Police Department. Ever since that drug supplier and his accomplices were put away, he's tried to get the Lubbock police to issue a report clearing me of the drug and reckless driving charges. The family of the boys killed in the accident is well connected. Walters says the police have been under pressure to keep the real story of what happened under wraps to protect the family's reputation, which I guess, means mine doesn't matter. One thing for sure, as things stand now, I will never be able to live in the Lubbock area again.

Mother said she passed on my e-mail address to your pastor in hopes he would encourage me. For whatever reason, I've never heard from him. I suppose that since I had never joined the church he didn't want to become involved in my situation. I guess if I had been a member of the church, things might have been different but oh well...

The most important thing Ruthie is that you have stood by me and believed the best even before you knew the truth. You proved I was right that day I "adopted" you as a special friend your first day in school.

Since the folks will be coming down Friday evening, maybe I can take you for a picnic at Cameron Park on Saturday. Thanks again for coming to my graduation but most of all for being the special friend you are.

Jerry

Unlike most of the girls her age, dating had still not made it to the top of Ruth's "to do" list. She had many friends of both sexes and enjoyed going out in groups. One of the boys showed a special interest in her, always arranging to sit beside her when the group went out to a movie or a ball game. He was nice looking, had a great personality and was active in his church's youth group, so when he asked if she would go on a "real date" with him she had to admit she felt a little special.

"You're going aren't you?" one of her girlfriends gushed.

When she said "no" her friend couldn't believe it and asked why not. That was when, for the first time, she found herself hinting at feelings about Jerry she had never expressed, even to herself. "The boy is nice and I like him a lot as a friend," she confided. "I know I would be comparing him to Jerry every time we went on a date and that wouldn't be fair."

Sitting in the back seat of the Spencers' car on the drive to Waco, the word *special* kept echoing in her mind. *In his e-mail, he said our friendship was special. How special?* She agreed with his sentiments. Their relationship was special; had been since that morning ten years ago when he met her on the steps of the bus to escort her to first grade.

She thought of the morning two years ago and her near fatal fall from Gypsy. Her dad had been busy, but set his work aside, took her hand, and let her lead him to the corral to watch her ride. "Dad, I want to marry a man just like you someday," she said laughingly as he cupped her heel and helped her into the saddle. "I'm sure God already has someone special picked out for you Ruth," he said as he slapped Gypsy on the flank, sending her trotting around the corral.

As she rode along in the car she dozed somewhere between awake and asleep, but was jolted alert when Mr. Spencer announced they were only five miles from Waco. The echo of her father's words lingered and she wondered, *Is Jerry that special someone? If he isn't then why are we special to each other now? What's the purpose? One thing's for sure,* she resolved as they passed a sign announcing Waco's city limit, *until I know the answer to that question there will be no dating for me.*

"My, you've changed Ruthie." Jerry gave Ruth a broad smile as he entered his uncle's living room. He thoughtfully appraised the blue-eyed beauty with hair the color of spun gold before sitting down beside her on the couch. "Wow, two years can sure make a difference," he said, reaching out and taking her hand.

"I'm glad you noticed," Ruth said teasingly, but blushed when she realized his parents and aunt and uncle were watching them with smiles of approval.

"I'm sorry I wasn't able to be here when you came," Jerry explained. "Today my shift at Starbucks didn't end till 6:00; but tomorrow…" He flashed a grin at Ruth. "I've made arrangements to be off and of course on Sunday for graduation."

Jerry's dad looked at his watch. "Well son, it's almost 7:00," he said, rising from an easy chair. "We better get to the motel and check in. I hear Evangel University is playing a big game tomorrow and I'll bet the hotels and motels are probably booked solid. We sure don't want to loose our reservations."

Jerry saw them to their car, opened the back door for Ruth and as she got in, kissed her lightly on the cheek. "That will have to do till tomorrow Ruthie," he said with a laugh as he closed the door.

They traveled in silence to the motel and Ruth was glad. It gave her mind free reign to imagine she could still feel the imprint of Jerry's kiss on her cheek.

"Dad, I appreciate you letting us use the car today," Jerry said the next morning when his parents and Ruth returned to his aunt's and uncle's.

"Glad to do it son. Your mother and aunt haven't had a good visit for a long time. This will give them some time to catch up."

Jerry turned his attention to Ruth. "Ruthie, I want to take you out to Cameron Zoo and after that we can have a picnic in the park if that's ok?"

"Sounds like fun," she said, thinking as she did, *I wish Jerry would call me Ruth.*

"Just don't be out too late son," his dad reminded, "with graduation and all tomorrow ..."

"I won't dad. I'll have Ruth back here no later than 9:00"

Just then, Jerry's aunt came to the door. "You mentioned wanting to have a picnic," she said, handing Jerry a basket, "this should take care of you kids."

"Thanks," Jerry said as he and Ruth turned and walked to the car.

As they drove away Jerry looked at his watch. "It's only 9:30, plenty of time to go to the zoo and see something special before lunch."

"Special? What in the world are you up to Jerry Spencer?" she asked, mimicking seriousness.

"You'll see. For now let's just say you're going to meet El Rey de la Montana."

"I don't understand Spanish.

"Me neither, not much at least, only that those words mean king of the mountain."

"Oh, I see. That explains everything," she said sarcastically as they entered the zoo's parking lot.

Inside the zoo proper, Jerry led Ruth to a bench where they sat while he explained his mention of El Rey de la Montana. "That's what people in the Amazon call a certain species of bird called a king vulture. The zoo has an Amazon jungle exhibit that includes all sorts of wild animals; vultures, monkeys, two-toed sloths and jaguars just to name a few."

"Jaguars!" A jolt of fear shot through Ruth at the mention of the dreaded beast of her dreams.

"Yeah, but don't worry Ruthie, they'll either be in cages or behind thick glass so they can't get at us."

"Speaking of jaguars and jungles, after I came here I started looking for a copy of that book you've always been so interested in."

"Beyond the Far Horizon?"

"Yeah, that's the one all about the girl who married a wildlife photographer and traveled with him around the world to jungles and all."

"Did you find it, and if you did have you read it?" She hoped his answer was yes. *If it's yes, he's probably had the same weird experiences reading it as I.*

"Yes and yes," he replied. "I finally found one in a used bookstore and have already read it through. In fact, I've re-read several times the chapter about the Amazon jungle and its people."

He paused before dredging up an observation he'd made while reading the book. "What about that full page picture of the Shaman?" As he reflected on the sad faced man, his voice trailed away as if he did not expect a response from Ruth, but was only verbalizing a private thought. "Kinda gives you the willies how he stares off the page at you as if reading your mind or waiting for you to answer a question. "Well anyway," he said, moving on, "that character gives me the creeps."

"I know," was all Ruth could manage in response since she had never discussed the more horrific details of her vision while in the coma. She knew her folks thought she would feel better if she did, but rather than being pushy, they patiently waited for her to speak to them in her own good time. Once she tried to talk about it with her dad, but like just now, at the mention of the jaguar, all he could say was "I know," as he turned away to hide his discomfort before changing the subject.

Just as advertised in the zoo's brochure, the Amazon exhibit was a realistic reproduction of jungle habitat complete with a trail overshadowed and bordered by all manner of ferns and trees. Along the trail, cages and fenced in enclosures were positioned so that patrons could watch the animals in a natural setting. To Ruth, the habitat made her feel uncomfortable and steadily more so as they rounded a corner to find the trail ahead blocked by a wall of thick glass.

I don't want to be a wet blanket. Jerry has gone to such trouble to make this a fun experience. She struggled to put on a happy face, fearing at the same time her walk down this trail would end just as her vision walk, confronting a beast intent on killing her.

Beyond the barrier, Ruth saw birds flying from tree to tree and monkeys scampering limb to limb. A brass sign below the glass read: "There is a jaguar here. They frequent the shadows during hot afternoons and their camouflaged coats make them hard to see. One is probably looking at you now. Can you spot it?"

The jaguar ... hiding in the shadows ... about to spring. Her mind froze when she remembered its snarling threat: "I'll eat your liver before your eyes."

"Look Ruthie." Jerry's voice called her away from her dark thoughts as he pointed. "See, up there ... the branch over the clearing. Its leaves are moving. Something ..." Jerry had no time to describe what the something was because just then a jaguar right out of her nightmare sprang from the branch into the clearing, crept up to the glass, settled on its haunches, and fixed its cold, pitiless eyes at her.

"Wow, would you look at that," Jerry said, excited at seeing the dramatic display of the jaguar's instincts. Ruth, however, saw more, much more than animal instinct on display. Its migration out of her dreams into reality confirmed her darkest fears. This beast whose whirlpool eyes were drawing her deeper and deeper into themselves was bent on destroying her, those she loved, and the plans God had for her life.

She wanted to scream but could not. It was as if by a look, the beast had robbed her of her voice. Now she felt the same look was drawing her closer and closer to the glass partition until her head and that of the jaguar were only inches apart. *Those eyes, drawing me down the vision trail to the pillars, to the meadow, and to death beyond.* Her head spun as she felt herself slip into darkness.

" Honey ... Are you alright?" In the darkness she heard a woman's voice and felt arms about her lifting her up ... up.

She opened her eyes, dazzled a moment by the sun, then held out her hand and took a glass of water offered by the woman she sensed had just spoken. "Thank goodness you're ok dear," the woman said obviously relieved.

She felt a hand squeeze hers. *Jerry's,* she realized.

"I don't know what happened to you Ruthie," he said. "One moment you were looking at the jaguar and the next ..."

"I know," she said groggily, "I must have fainted," and added a wish she had never expressed before. "Jerry, please don't call me Ruthie."

"What?"

"Never mind, I'll explain later," she said as she took Jerry's hand and let him help her to her feet.

"Jerry did you see or feel anything strange just before I fainted?" Ruth asked as her dark blue eyes probed his. They had found a large tree in the park near the cliff called lovers leap, spread a blanket and just finished off the last of the pimento cheese sandwiches Jerry's aunt had prepared when Ruth broke the lingering silence with her question.

"The only thing I noticed, except for the jaguar acting like a jaguar, was what looked like his special interest in you. Others stood around us at the glass partition, but for some reason he seemed to take no notice of anyone but you. As he moved closer and closer to the glass you did too until you were almost eye-to-eye. That was when you started to fall and this lady caught you and several of the men helped me carry you outside."

"Are you sure that's all you remember Jerry?"

"Ruthie!" There was exasperation in his voice. "Tell me what's going on? What am I supposed to have heard or seen? Are you still grieving over Miss Minnie, Timmy, everything...? "

"Everything? What do you mean by everything?"

"Everything you've never told me, probably have never told anyone, about your interest in that book, your coma, the jaguar, everything."

He reached and took Ruth's hand and drew her closer. "Open up Ruthie. You're the most special girl in the world to me but I can't help you unless you level with me."

"Am I really Jerry?"

"Are you really what, Ruthie?"

"Am I really the most special girl in the world to you?"

Jerry pulled Ruth closer and looked into her eyes as his lips found hers in a long lingering kiss. "If you don't know by now you never will Ruthie. You're a lot more than just special. You're the ..."

Her kiss blotted his words before he could finish.

"I've always hoped I was, she said, I know you've always been more than special to me." Ruth felt a load of uncertainty lift and for the first time since she discovered the book, *Beyond the Far Horizon*, felt she could share her strange experiences with someone without them thinking she was crazy.

For the next several hours, she told Jerry everything about her out of body experience when she first traced the sign on the Shaman's bench, and the pity she felt for the Shaman when she looked into his eyes. "Eyes that seemed to say he was searching for something and sad because he hadn't found it," she said.

She described her dream visions in the church, the children's Christmas program and Tim's altar call and a young Miss Minnie on the platform calling for Tim to follow her.

She told of finding herself on a jungle trail, much like the one today at the zoo, and Tim and Miss Minnie in a field of yellow flowers calling her to follow them beyond the stone pillars, " to death I thought," she said and shivered.

She described the jaguar threatening to kill her. "His eyes were so full of hate; just like the one today that seemed to have stepped out of my dreams and was following me."

"Well, that explains at least your reaction today," Jerry interjected.

"Yes, but I think there is more to it than just being reminded of my dream. " She pulled Jerry close again. "Since I became a Christian I've had a feeling my visions in the coma were God's way of preparing me for something." She felt Jerry's body stiffen.

"And the devil, the jaguar, whatever, is trying to stop you?"

"Maybe," she said putting her head on his shoulder.

"Preparing you for what Ruthie?"

"I'm not sure, but I keep remembering the natives in my vision and their begging me not to leave without them."

"Are you telling me you think God may want you to be a missionary? I always hoped that whatever we did we could do together."

"Me too Jerry," she said squeezing him tightly. "Only ..." Her voice trailed away.

"Only I'm not a Christian so that leaves me out, right?"

Ruth felt tears welling as their eyes met. "It wouldn't have to Jerry if only ..."

"If only I'd accept Jesus? Ruthie, I wish I could as easily as those people the missionaries describe.

"I remember them coming to our church and telling of all the people who become Christians through their preaching. Well, I've heard preaching all my life. Why does it seem so natural for them to believe in Jesus and so hard for me?"

Ruth had no ready answer, but wished she could ease the pain she heard in his voice.

Jerry had not waited for Ruth to respond anyway, but had gotten up and walked over to the high bluff overlooking the Brazos river. It was getting late and the setting sun cast a golden highway across the water.

Ruth got up, joined him, and for some time neither spoke.

Finally Jerry said, "They call this bluff 'lovers leap' because of the legend that here, an Indian princess of the Waco tribe and her sweetheart, a brave from the enemy Apache tribe, leaped to their deaths rather than letting their tribes separate them."

Jerry turned and kissed Ruth again. "You seem so sure that God has a purpose for your life," he said.

"Not just for me, but for both of us," she said as she laid her head again on his shoulder.

"I want to believe, I really do," he finally said wistfully. "But not just to please you but because I really mean it."

"I'll never stop praying you will, that Christ will become as real to you as He is to me," she whispered.

"And that we'll always be together ... that nothing will ever separate us?"

"I'll pray nothing will ever separate us from our love for each other," she said, "and that it will be God's will we always be together."

"Don't ever stop Ruthie," he said as they walked to the car.

When they got in the car Jerry took Ruth in his arms and kissed her one last time, "No matter what God's plans may be, I'll always love you Ruthie, and always be there for you."

CHAPTER 15

LOST IN A SEA OF MEMORIES, Akhu studied his reflection in the still water of the pool. Much time had passed since Twanke had appointed him Shaman, yet his mind constantly drew him back to earlier days, remembering the wise teacher's words. It seemed just yesterday, he was standing in this exact place, questioning all that was to come...

What is it Twanke sees in me that makes me worthy to be the old man's successor as Shaman of theYanoako? A young Akhu looked up and saw a friend, a little older than himself, standing ankle-deep in the water a short distance away. He stood perfectly still, studying the water, his spear at the ready. A slight ripple of tensing muscles in his right shoulder the only hint of movement before he plunged his spear into the water.

Akhu recalled it had been only a few seasons since his friend endured his Marake test and entered manhood. Already he was gaining fame among the other men for his hunting and fishing skills.

Realizing Akhu was watching him, the man grinned and proudly held up a wiggling fish.

Akhu noted the man's success with a nod, smiling when he remembered the shy glances his friend received from the young women whenever he passed one in the village.

Why choose me as Shaman rather than a man like my friend?

Still pondering the question, he turned and started walking toward the village, sure of only one thing. Whatever Twanke saw in him that made him worthy to be his successor, the pool did not reflect it.

Rustling leaves announced a sudden breeze that brought with it the memory of Twanke's last words to him yesterday. "Akhu, only you beside me have journeyed into the Stone of Memory and seen the pale-skinned woman and only you has she called by name."

Akhu was certain Twanke's words supplied the answer to his nagging question. It wasn't some physical trait such as his appearance or even a finely honed talent like hunting or fishing that qualified him to succeed Twanke. What the old man saw in him was an inner experience even the clearest, calmest pool could not reflect. Only he and the Shaman had made the terrifying journey and seen the woman and only him had she called by name.

"*You must prepare yourself.*" Those words spoken by Twanke as they returned from searching out healing plants still haunted Akhu.

As he reached the edge of the village, he could see ahead in the courtyard the yucca press used to make cassava bread. Beside it was a brightly painted canoe to hold the kasil.

Only a few sunrises now until the Garden Festival begins, Akhu realized. With the planting season over and prayers entreating Wanadi's blessings on their labors offered, the joyous festival of singing, dancing, and feasting could begin.

Akhu felt a sudden chill when he thought of the dreaded and mysterious rite proving manhood that would follow, one he knew must bring pain, and one for which Twanke had said he must prepare himself.

In a nearby tree, monkeys chattered angrily. He smiled at their cries of challenge to some intruder. Until now, he had been like one of them, ready to fight even a jaguar, foolishly believing he was ready for anything. Now as the dreaded Marake ritual loomed before him he was not so sure.

As he neared the longhouse, he saw a little girl trying to feed her pet parrot. Tethered by one leg to its perch, the creature pecked disagreeably each time she withdrew her hand to get another piece of banana. Suddenly, the child let out a howl of pain as the ill-tempered bird finally managed to sink its beak into her finger. The child's mother came running as the parrot, amid a flurry of ruffled feathers and noisy squawks, retreated to the far side of its perch.

Learning can be painful, Akhu thought, remembering Twanke's words concerning the Marake test.

Even the oldest in the tribe could not remember when the *Marake* ceremony had begun. They knew only it was the stack pole around which the men built their lives.

He glanced again across the courtyard. Except for the parrot, now asleep on its perch, it was empty. Only days before, women filled it, some busily weaving kunana baskets while others fashioned feather ornaments and prepared the paints the men used to decorate their bodies for the Garden Festival.

Akhu, like the other boys, approached his Marake with mixed feelings. There was joy in knowing that when the rite was over he would earn the right to hunt with the men, adorn his body with the sacred signs, and take part in village ceremonials instead of doing women's work in the garden. However, fear of what awaited him in the Place of Meeting or that he would disappoint Twanke by proving himself weak, haunted him.

Several sun risings later dawn brought the mournful sound of wamehiye bark horns announcing the beginning of the Garden Festival. The men of the village marched solemnly down the path from the communal garden singing an invocation to the spirits of the forest.

"Come, oh spirits of river, rocks, and trees, guard the labor of our hands," they chanted.

Then he and the other boys chosen to experience their rite of passage into manhood watched as, Elders first, then the other men, began the festival by dipping their gourd cups repeatedly into the canoe filled with kasil. Akhu marveled at its power to put songs on their lips and free their bodies to dance.

Twanke explained to him kasil's true purpose. Drinking the brew not only inspired dancing and singing, but brought forgetfulness. This magic liquid helped the Yanoako forget the outsiders' broken promises, the devouring of their hunting lands, and the deaths of loved ones at their hands. When they drank it, they forgot for a little while that the outsiders and their greed were destroying their beloved forest and driving them closer and closer to the border of the taboo land.

A sudden breeze stirred the dust in the courtyard into whirling plumes in which Akhu imagined he saw the dancing figures of long-dead Elders.

"I see them too my son," Twanke joined him and laid a quivering hand on Akhu's shoulder.

"Soon I will join them," Twanke reminded him again.

In campfire talks with the boys, Twanke had reflected several times how quickly the seasons of his life were passing. However, today he spoke of his death as being at hand. Though his teacher's announcement saddened him, there was comfort in the feel of Twanke's hand on his – confirmation they had just shared a common vision and now were joined at the heart by a bond even death could not break.

The Garden Festival with its dancing and singing soon ended and the villagers became strangely quiet. Women gathered up their little ones and retreated to the long house. Then, as if answering a silent summons, Akhu watched as the men filed into the Place of Meeting.

The Place of Meeting stood apart from the rest of the village, its mysteries unknown to all but the men. All Akhu knew was that it was there the Shaman led the men in the sacred ceremonies. When sickness came to the village, the soil of their garden died, or game became scarce, it was there Wanadi spoke to the Shaman, giving him wisdom and guidance. It was there that Wanadi revealed to him the time had come for the people to collect their families, burn their village, and begin another "time walk," taking the tribe back to a time the forest was untouched by the outsiders and all was as it was in the beginning.

Though numbed by fear and dread of what awaited inside, Akhu allowed an Elder to lead him into the Place of Meeting for his passage into manhood.

Entering, he saw a small fire in the middle of the hut waging a losing battle against the darkness pressing in about it. From somewhere in the shadows, Twanke started speaking.

"You are here to prove yourself a man," he said solemnly. "Suffer the pain in silence, my son. Cry out, and you will be fit only for women's work."

Akhu could almost taste his fear as an Elder stepped from the darkness and stirred the coals into flame just as another joined him and placed a clay pot at Akhu's feet.

Twanke stepped into the firelight and approached Akhu carrying a kunana. He had seen a woman weaving one before each Garden Festival, but she was silent about its purpose.

Twanke took the kunana and laid it beside the clay pot as another Elder came with a gourd cup,and after kneeling scooped what looked like dirt from the pot into the bowl-shaped kunana. Twanke then took it and quickly pressed its mouth against Akhu's chest.

"Remember, do not cry out," Twanke commanded as he tied it there with narrow strips of hide.

Akhu felt ashamed because he trembled, but in only moments, his shame dissolved under a wave of pure terror.

Ants! Not dirt, but ants had been poured into the kunana. Panic gripped him. Experience in the forest told him they would attack with fury anyone unfortunate enough to stumble into one of their hills. He felt hundreds of the stinging creatures scurry across his naked chest. *In a moment, they will impale my flesh with their stingers. The pain will be unbearable.*

"Remain silent," Twanke said, his eyes searching for any hint of fear on Akhu's face. "Pain will brand the story I tell you on your memory."

As suddenly as they started, the ants stopped moving. Akhu imagined them poised, their quivering stingers raised to strike.

As if released by his thought, they did. A single-minded army of the venomous little messengers of pain barbed his flesh on their wicked stingers. His chest exploded. Gasping, he gulped a breath of stagnant air and held it until he felt his lungs would burst.

The pain spread, winding its fiery threads around his body, wrapping him in a cocoon of absolute misery.

Just when he thought the dam holding back his scream would burst, he heard Twanke's voice again. He felt lifted by his words out of his body of agony when, for the first time, he heard the sacred story of the man and woman and the forbidden land.

In a time long ago, a time when Wanadi still spoke to all his children, a man and woman journeyed into the forest. They walked for many days until they came to a place where the trail turned back toward the great river.

Ahead lay the taboo land, the place Shi, the god above all gods, said no Yanoako could go. But the man was deaf to Shi's words and said to the woman, "Let us go on. Perhaps in the forbidden country, we will discover the secret of our beginning."

Soon, the man and woman came to a tree whose branches seemed to reach to heaven. They were tired from their journey, so the man said, "Listen. The tree frogs say night is coming. Let us lie down and sleep beneath this great tree until morning."

The woman agreed, so they lay down on the soft moss and were soon asleep. When they awoke, it was still dark. Because they had broken the taboo, they feared the sun might never shine again, so they called for Mado to come and lead them back to their village.

When he came, the man said, "Mado, we have entered the forbidden country, and the sun will not shine. In the darkness, we cannot find the trail leading back to our village. We fear the demon Yoluk hides among the trees and waits to steal our souls. Along the trail, the fer-de-lance or bushmaster may lie coiled to strike us as we pass. Please lead us back safely."

"Why should I?" Mado replied. "It is true you have broken the taboo, but see? Nothing has happened. Now that you are rested, let me lead you on to the place of your beginning."

The Shaman paused and Akhu shut his eyes for fear they might reveal his pain, but quickly opened them in relief as Twanke untied the kunana. He knelt and scooped more ants into the basket, then retied it, but this time to Akhu's back.

Again, he felt the tickling of scurrying feet, a pause, then burning pain that forced his attention back to Twanke's story.

Mado finally agreed to lead them back to their village, but on the way, he reminded them of all they had missed. "Too bad," he purred as he turned to leave them at the jungle's edge. "You were so close to finding the answers to your questions. So close ...so close..." His voice lingered on a gentle breeze as he melted into the jungle.

The Elders met the man and woman as they came out of the forest.

"Where have you been?"

"Why were you gone so long?"

"Were you lost?"

"Have you been hurt?"

"Look at me," the Shaman finally ordered. At this command, the Elders grew silent.

The man and woman raised their eyes, but quickly dropped them under his piercing stare.

"Children, have you broken the taboo?" he asked.

The fear the Shaman saw written on their faces answered his question.

"Father, we only wanted to visit the land of our beginning," the man stuttered. "Like you, when you journey into the stone—"

"Mado said he would lead us there," the woman interrupted.

At the mention Mado offered to lead them, the Elders tried to speak at once. "She blasphemes Wanadi!" they screamed, as they jerked the couple to their feet and pushed them toward the village. "These taboo breakers must die!"

The movement under the kunana tied to Akhu's back had stopped, the ants quivers of stinging arrows emptied. Only a constant throbbing remained to remind him of their attack on his flesh.

Even though his eyes were closed against the pain, Akhu sensed Twanke had drawn close when he felt his warm breath on his face.

"You have done well, my son," he whispered. "Your test is almost over. Now listen to the rest of the story."

Under Yanoako law, the Elders could give only one sentence for breaking this taboo... death. However, there was another law that decreed no Yanoako could shed another's blood except for revenge or in battle. Therefore, the Elders decreed Wanadi's Damodedes would receive them for judgment.

The Damodedes or spirit beings live within the fiery coils of the eels in pools of stagnant backwater and are Wanadi's agents of judgment on those who break his laws.

On the night the man and woman were judged by Wanadi's Damodedes, the Shaman, driven by a burning need to understand, questioned them one last time. "I ask you and you must answer," he said. "If you speak the truth, perhaps Wanadi will forgive you and protect you on your journey to the world of spirits. What did you see at the border of the forbidden land?"

The firelight washed over the Shaman's face as he leaned closer to hear the condemned man's words.

"We saw a great tree reaching to heaven," the man said, looking directly at the Shaman. "We were tired, so we lay down and slept under its branches."

"And?" The Shaman leaned still closer.

"I...we...dreamed," the man stammered.

"What did you dream, my children?" He turned from the man and for a moment looked at the woman, who was staring with dead eyes into the fire.

"We both dreamed the same dream," the condemned man finally said. "Night had fallen, and we stood on a trail beside what I thought was another great tree. Only it wasn't a tree at all, but a finger of stone, taller than the tallest tree, and across the trail from it, we saw its twin.

"Beyond the stones, a treeless land stretched to the horizon that glowed with hidden fire. I looked at the stone and in the dim light saw strange markings cut into its side."

The man paused in the telling of his story, as one might before leaping into a dark river.

"Mado was in our dream," he said, his voice quivering. "He told us we should follow him beyond the horizon."

"It is time to enter the taboo land," Mado said. "Wanadi wills it."

"And did you follow?" The Shaman leaned closer to the man and again looked into his eyes as if searching for the truth behind his words.

"No, Father," the man replied, "the woman would not let us."

"Woman? What woman?" The Shaman could not hide his surprise. He reached out and touched the head of the man's companion lightly. "Do you mean this woman?"

"No, Father, it was another—a beautiful woman with skin white like the clouds of the dry season. It was she who spoke to us."

"And what did she say?" The Shaman's voice shook with excitement.

"She said we must go no farther until she comes, that the god above all gods would someday send her to us with his message."

"And?"

"And after we heard his message, she promised to go with us into the land of our beginning."

After his Marake test, Akhu went to the longhouse and waited, as the other boys who had endured it entered. The angry red welts on their bodies testified to their ordeal. Like him, Akhu knew they would never forget the story of the woman and the forbidden country.

Now proven a man, Akhu searched out Twanke the next morning to ask a question about a part of the story he did not understand. "What caused the Elders' outburst of anger when the woman said Mado told them they could enter the taboo land?" he asked.

"The woman blasphemed by daring to say Wanadi's servant Mado tempted them to break Shi's taboo. Shi has spoken only once to the Yanoako people and that was long ago before the first flood time. He decreed none must ever go into the taboo country until he speaks again and tells them it is time. After he gave this command, he created a lesser god, Wanadi, and his servant, Mado, to help us until He sent someone to lead us to the forbidden land. I believe that someone is the woman of our vision."

That night, for just a moment, Akhu dreamed he looked into Mado's fiery eyes. The next day he told Twanke of his dream and the old man smiled knowingly.

"Mado has confirmed my words," he said. "You will be the voice of Wanadi to our people. Mado, his messenger, will come at your bidding often as you sleep to guide you to healing plants and to show you where the enemy hides. Most of all, he will protect you from Odosha, master of the underworld, and the evil souls who serve him.

Akhu had thought often since his Marake test about the woman's claim that it was Mado who tempted them to go into the taboo land. After Twanke's explanation, however, he understood the Elders' anger at the pair. If Wanadi was Shi's messenger and always did his will, it would be sacrilege to say Wanadi's servant Mado tempted them to disobey the supreme god's command.

But, what if the woman spoke the truth? What if Wanadi's servant Mado did tempt them to break Shi's law? Until now, such an idea was unthinkable so he tried desperately to resist it, but, like a dreaded fever, it continued to plague him.

CHAPTER 16

IT FOLLOWED THE PATH of moonlight marking the boundary between the jungle and the clearing around the village. In his dream, Akhu heard no wind, but saw leaves parting, as though brushed by the hands of an unseen presence. He sensed its command for silence, an order quickly relayed by nature through every root and tendril of the forest to the canopy overhead.

Glowing coals, suspended in darkness, appeared before him. They grew larger, nearer, until Akhu recognized them for what they were: eyes encased in a great head atop a sleek black body. Just as predicted by Twanke, Mado, the jaguar, had come. *But not in response to my summons,* Akhu realized, feeling a sudden unease. *He's come uninvited.* Twanke's whispered warning, just before departing to the world of the spirits, that Wanadi might not be what he seemed only added to the fear creeping over him.

The jaguar stopped within a few steps of Akhu's hammock. He could feel its burning eyes sweeping over his sleeping body. *So close,* he thought, dreamily. *He would be an easy target for my arrows. But my quiver is empty.*

Fear gripped him when he realized how powerless he was against the creature whose blazing eyes were branding on his mind a single command: *Follow me!*

Desperately he tried to awaken, but couldn't.

In nighttime talks around the campfire, Twanke had explained to him the mysteries of his Akito or spirit double; how in dreams, by imagining he expelled the breath from his body, he could release his spirit to follow Mado on nocturnal journeys through the forest. But now he feared that if he did, it might never return. In spite of this, he felt his resistance crumbling before the fiery-eyed stare of the beast, powerless to obey the voice of his own instinct shouting, *Escape!*

He could not. Through closed eyes he watched terrified as his Akito, now captive to the great cat's will, spilled like water from his body and reformed into a cloud-like copy of his sleeping self.

For a moment, its grip on his mind relaxed, and his Akito turned to look at his body in the hammock. He had never seen himself through these eyes before. *So helpless.*

Mado's tail swished lazily from side to side, its black eyes exploring Akhu's, as if searching for his most secret thoughts.

I should trust him, Akhu thought, trying to quiet his fears. Still, he remembered Twanke's warning: *Wanadi may not be what he seems.* Now, staring into the cat's eyes, he suddenly realized a twin possibility—*Mado likewise might not be, either.* Then an even more terrifying thought, until now unthinkable. *What if Wanadi and Mado did not serve Shi at all? What if their master was the dreaded stealer of souls, Odosha, lord of the underworld?* Akhu felt all he believed about the spirit world slipping away. *What if Wanadi, Mado, and Odosha were the same being in a different form?*

The names swirled in his mind, gripping him in a whirlpool of terrifying uncertainty as Mado turned and commanded his Akito to follow him into the jungle.

In a moment, he was skimming silently along in Mado's shimmering wake, trees and bushes dissolving into mist as they brushed past. Soon they came to the place where the trail ran close to the great river. Still Mado did not turn back, but continued toward the forbidden land.

None but the man and woman in Twanke's story had ever violated its border. Only the Shaman, gazing into his Stone of Memory, had ever approached so close.

"You must follow me, Akhu." The jaguar stopped, turned, and again grasped his mind in a claw-like grip. "The man and woman were too timid. They saw little," Mado purred, reading his thoughts. "Soon you will see all the wonders they missed. Now, follow me!"

Akhu's Akito flew forward, and gradually the jungle began to thin as the vines and creepers tying trees together disappeared. Ahead, in the dim light, he saw shadowy outlines of great trees standing solitary watch. He thought he must be close to the border of the forbidden land when suddenly a familiar voice confirmed his fear.

"Come no farther till I come," it warned.

The cat also heard the voice. "Follow me," it ordered.

The soft voice spoke again, "Akhu, come no farther."

It was the voice of the pale-skinned woman, he realized, just as the great beast snarled, "Follow me now!"

"Not yet," the woman pleaded.

"Follow…no farther…follow…no farther…" A battle of wills raged as Akhu's Akito drew closer and closer to the border.

The battle seemed to slacken as Akhu and the jaguar reached the top of a low hill. There, the beast stopped and faced him again. "Look, Akhu, do you see the glow in the distance? Beautiful isn't it?"

With a paw, he pointed toward a pulsating light spilling over the horizon. At that moment, his forelegs began rising from the ground.

The beast is changing! With horrified fascination, Akhu watched as its legs became arms, its paws became hands. In a flash, the beast stood erect before him on human legs and feet, its flickering yellow eyes, black head, and canine teeth the only reminder of what he had been just moments ago.

Yes, I see it, Akhu thought, trying desperately to suppress any hint of fear. *The shimmering light is beautiful.*

"And more wonderful than you can imagine," the man-cat replied as he opened his new arms wide toward the glowing horizon.

Akhu felt torn apart. One part of him desperately wanted to close his mind to Mado's seductive voice and flee the place; the other longed to enter the forbidden land and learn its secrets.

"There," the man-cat said, pointing toward the distant glow, "at the heart of the light are the answers you seek. You want to know the secret of your beginning? It is there."

Akhu remembered what Twanke said when he described his journeys into the Stone of Memory. *"Beyond the pillars and within the light is knowledge enough to make you the wisest of men."*

The man-cat drew so close Akhu could feel his hot breath and sense his blazing eyes probing his thoughts.

"Yes, Twanke is right. All knowledge will be yours for the taking. But something else awaits you there. Can you guess what it is?" the man-cat purred seductively. Before Akhu's mind could even form a reply, the jaguar answered his own question.

"There, you will never die!" He pointed again toward the horizon. "Think of it, Akhu. You will know everything and have forever to use and enjoy your knowledge!"

The man-cat's words caressed his mind, like a cool breeze over his body. *"To know all things and never die."*

He felt his will's resistance collapsing before the assault of the creature's temptation.

"You have waited long enough for permission to enter that wonderful land." The man-cat's words were like gentle waves washing over him. *So understanding. So reasonable.* "Wanadi has sent me to tell you it is time for you to enter."

Akhu felt again the brush of fur against his cheek.

"You want to know its secrets, don't you?" Mado whispered. "Now you can." The creature reached out his hand and grasped Akhu's. "Let us be going."

"Come no farther until I come."

Again, Akhu heard the warning of the pale-skinned woman.

But what Mado says is true, he told himself. *I do want to finish the journey and discover the secrets that lie beyond the great stones. The woman says Shi forbids it, but Wanadi is the only god who speaks to me. If he says I can finish the journey...* He desperately wanted to believe Mado's words of permission. And yet...

Wanadi may not be what he seems.

Come no farther.

His mind echoed with the conflicting voices.

The man-cat sensed Akhu's indecision and pressed its will on him even harder. Akhu felt himself wavering.

The woman cried out her warning again in his mind. *No farther, no farther!*

Mado's grip grew tighter, his tug more insistent. Akhu felt the timbers of his will splintering under the pressure of the beast's demonic insistence.

"*Shi!*" his mind cried out in panic.

He had never invoked that most sacred name before, even in prayer. Wanadi was the god he called upon for help. But Mado, at Wanadi's bidding, had come to him uninvited and drawn his Akito to this place and was speaking of things he somehow knew were not from Shi.

At the mention of the sacred name, a scream of rage and frustration tore from the man-cat's throat.

Akhu prayed more fervently. "Shi, god above all gods, help me! Please! Help me!" But Shi did not answer his pleas. Instead, powerless to resist the will of the beast, he felt himself drawn closer and closer to the border of the forbidden country.

Mado turned and faced Akhu as he continued backing toward the border.

"I grow weary of your delay," he hissed. "We must cross the border ... now!"

Akhu saw the stone columns and waves of cascading radiance breaking toward them, and beyond, the forbidden country.

"A little farther, Akhu, and you will know all." Mado had almost reached the columns. He turned and gestured impatiently. "Come quickly," he snarled.

The waves of liquid light had reached the stones and were lapping at their base.

If I cross the boundary... A vision of the disobedient pair in Twanke's story, coiled about with eels and dragged beneath some stagnant pond, flashed before him. *I will deserve to die just like them.* However, nothing, not even his vision of a horrible death, diminished the power of the man-cat's will as it pulled him closer and closer to the border.

In another moment, my Akito will reach the stones, Akhu realized, but he was unable to resist.

"Just a few more steps," Mado urged as they reached the columns rising in solitary majesty.

Again Akhu prayed, "*Shi, please help me!*" He reached out his hand and braced himself against the column.

Just then, he felt the stone grow warm, and the man-cat's grip upon his will weaken.

In the golden light washing against the column, he saw a familiar design carved into its surface. *The same as that on Twanke's jaguar bench!* He looked closer. *Yes!* He was certain. Just like on the sacred bench, two lines chiseled close together, thrusting upward then turning away from one another in graceful downward curves.

Driven by some inner impulse, he began retracing the sacred sign with his finger.

The beast felt Akhu's renewed resistance and changed form again. Its fur dissolved into something like liquid silver that spread over its body from neck to feet. Its jaguar head reformed itself into that of a man with shimmering silver hair cascading about his shoulders. Only the jaguar's burning eyes remained to remind Akhu of what the man had been only moments ago.

Again, he spoke to Akhu's mind in a tone as soothing as the sound of a rippling stream. "Please, we must be going," he pleaded.

Though an inner voice urged silence, Akhu heard his Akito reply, "*The boundary is for a purpose. Shi has said—*"

"Shi!" The being spat the name before Akhu's spirit double could finish its thought. "Shi has told you nothing but lies!"

For the first time, Akhu heard fear in the creature's voice.

"Who reveals to you the secrets of the forest and speaks to you in dreams and guides your Akito?" the being asked.

Wanadi, Akhu's mind whispered.

"Correct," the creature, snapped. "And who reveals to you the power of healing plants and the words to fight off evil?"

Wanadi.

"Tell me, Akhu," the being again spoke gently. "Who's will is it that you take Twanke's place as Shaman of the Yanoako?"

Akhu hesitated, remembering Twanke had said it was Shi's will he become Shaman.

"Wanadi will have no rivals when you are Shaman. Soon he wills you sit on the jaguar bench, but now he wills you follow me into the land beyond the stones."

The creature's thoughts were like darts, piercing Akhu's mind, but the stone's warmth somehow gave him courage to lift his eyes and confront this strange being.

"Only Shi can give permission to enter the taboo land. Not even Wanadi can grant it."

"Are you sure?" A low growl erupted from the being's throat.

"Yes," Akhu answered, feeling new resolve. *"Just as I am sure it is Shi who wills I become Shaman."*

"You fool," it snarled, "*I* am Wanadi, and I serve no one but myself. Not Shi, not anyone!"

For a moment, Akhu's fingers froze on the stone's design. *I was right to fear Mado,* he thought, feeling the stone grow still warmer. Suddenly, his fear left him.

"What is the purpose of the Stone of Memory?" he demanded.

"It was not of my making, but Shi's," the being replied. "He made it to torture you, to draw you into its depths to revive memories of what you've lost and can never regain. To bring you to these very stones, to lead you this far only to forbid you go farther. Is this not torture? You saw the others in the tunnel. Were they walking *toward* the light?"

The man-cat's words awakened memories of Akhu's childhood journey into the Stone. What he said was true. As he moved forward toward the light, he met lines of men and women walking away from it into the darkness.

The creature read his thoughts. "They all tried and failed to enter the land beyond the stones," he said.

"But Shi has promised one day—"

"Shi! You're a fool, Shaman. You wait for his permission, but he will never give it. You can enter the land right now. With me."

The creature seemed to sense Akhu's growing strength and resolve and paused, searching for the right words to overcome it.

"Something of great power has been lost, Akhu." He spoke softly, seductively, as if confiding a great secret. "But you can be the one to find it, and when you do you will need no one's permission ever again to do anything or have anything you desire."

"But there must be ... there has to be, a purpose for the taboo." Akhu stood his ground and challenged the being who claimed to be Wanadi.

"A purpose!" All trace of beauty suddenly vanished as the being's face froze in a grimace of pure hate. "Oh, there's a purpose all right," it howled. "Shi wants to deny his children what he enjoys himself!"

His children! The hateful creature did not realize it, but his words were like cool water to a thirsty man. Akhu felt the promise revive his heart. *His children!* Shi was not far away as he had been taught, but close ... like a loving father. *My father!* Akhu shouted silently in his mind as joy born of trust in Shi alone flooded over him.

This new assurance infused him with courage to shout defiantly at the being. "*Mado, Wanadi, whatever the name you bear, I am a child of Shi! I will obey only him!*"

Akhu's words sent the waves of light spilling back toward the horizon and in a moment, all that remained was their dim glow in the distance.

"*Akhu, truly you are my beloved child.*" The words tenderly spoken from the shadows enveloped him with love.

The creature screamed its frustration. It, too, heard the voice. Frantically, it clawed the air, changing form in a moment from a being of great beauty into the man-cat, and then into Mado before leaping away into the darkness.

Akhu watched as soft morning gray broke night's grip on the jungle.

The sun will soon be rising.

Free of the beast, he quickly found the trail and started back toward the village. Just ahead, he saw someone approaching. With a start, he recognized who it was. The pale-skinned woman! Her hand held the same black, gold-edged thing she had carried when they met on his first journey into the Stone of Memory. The woman held it out, as if urging him to take it, just a moment before she vanished in the dawn mist.

From the air around him, the tender voice spoke again. "*Soon the woman will come again, Akhu, and show you what you must do.*"

Sunlight streamed through the entrance of Akhu's hut, announcing the arrival of the morning. His dream journey ended. He woke smiling, his Father's promise still echoing in his mind:

"Soon she will come."

It was a promise he knew his Father would keep.

Chapter 17

Palestine, the Fortress of St. Jean Five Years Later

"Hurry, Frederick, the workmen have broken through!"

Father Henri Bodien could hardly contain his excitement as he rushed under the awning where Frederick Neisen sat cataloguing artifacts recovered from the Fortress of St. Jean.

Neither Bodien nor Neisen was satisfied with their progress thus far; nor, they suspected, were their sponsors. As curator of the Vatican archives, Bodien was sure the Holy See expected more from its investment in the project than an elaborately carved sword handle, some cooking pots, and a few coins.

He knew Dr. Francis Abelard, the aged emeritus professor of anthropology at Oxford, had cut through yards of red tape to get permission from the Israelis for Neisen and him to lead the dig. Even after every contractual *i* was dotted and *t* crossed, the final go-ahead came only after the Israelis understood that funding for the project would come from the Catholic Church and from several private foundations.

"Israel's Department of Antiquities has little interest in expending resources to unearth sites of purely Christian interest," Abelard had explained, shortly after learning that the

Brotherhood wanted Neisen and Bodien to lead a dig at St. Jean that summer.

Abelard had recruited both of them into the Brotherhood while they were students at Oxford and had been their mentor ever since. Over the intervening dozen or more years, they had learned a lot about the ways of the old man. They knew, for instance, that he never wasted his considerable influence on trivialities. They had seen what a few well-placed words in the right ears could accomplish.

As early as that night six months before their graduation, both young men felt the power of the man when he invited them to his flat to discuss their futures. Abelard's bland tone had been that of some TV meteorologist giving a weather report as he laid out the courses he had decided their careers would take.

"Neisen." A small cloud of pipe smoke gathered above the professor's head. "You will be placed on the tenure track of a Christian university in the United States where, in time, you will rise to the chairmanship of the department of anthropology."

"As for you, dear boy." He turned to Bodien. "You will take Holy Orders, and in a short time will be made curator of the Vatican archives. From your positions of influence, you will be able to provide invaluable service to the Brotherhood."

Abelard read the amazement written on their faces and with a sly wink added, "Trust me, it has all been arranged."

Now Bodien and Neisen held exactly the positions the professor had predicted. The Brotherhood's execution of its plans for them had indeed been flawless.

Before embarking on the excavation, they asked what exactly they should expect to find.

"It is not necessary I tell you," Abelard said, adding cryptically, "You will recognize it when you find it."

His answer had given them little satisfaction until a member of the Brotherhood, who served as an archivist in the Templar depository in London, reported the discovery of an ancient document concerning the Crusaders' occupation of Palestine. Both men agreed this revelation was behind their sudden assignment to lead the excavation at St. Jean.

Bodien had never heard such excitement in Abelard's voice as when he called to announce the discovery of the document.

"What has been found," he gushed, "may put the Brotherhood on the path to controlling a power capable of changing not only the course of history but of creation itself!"

When Bodien pressed him for details, he refused to share any particulars. So they began their preparation for the dig completely in the dark, only certain of one thing: what they would be trying to find must be immensely important.

When Bodien received Abelard's order to prepare for the dig, he immediately started searching the Vatican archives for any references to St. Jean. He learned that it had been a Templar fortress, abandoned when its commander, a knight named Balian, led his men in a failed attempt to reinforce the besieged city at Acre, which fell shortly after, in 1291. During the nearly eight hundred years since, the fortress had been reduced to a scattering of mud bricks, with only its foundation stones still clearly defining its dimensions.

A special relationship between the fortress and the mountain behind it also became clear as they unearthed around the foundations. As the workers cleared away the rubble from a section of the ruins abutting the steep slope, they discovered a rectangular border of worked stone set into the mountain itself.

This archeological oddity made no sense until they broke through and found the stones formed the border of a cave.

Now, after two days of intense labor in hundred-degree-plus heat, the workers had removed the last of the stones blocking the entrance and for the first time in nearly eight centuries the cave was revealed.

"Neisen, come on!" Bodien could hardly contain his excitement. "Whatever we're looking for may be in there."

"Right," Neisen clipped curtly, as he picked up his flashlight and followed the Reverend Father toward the mouth of the cave.

The tunnel twisted several yards into the mountain before finally opening up into a small, low-ceilinged room carved from solid rock. Neisen and Bodien played their flashlight beams about the room. Their first discoveries were disappointing: a wooden cot with a cross above it and a chair and table made of rough planks. It might have been a monk's cell for its austerity. Then the feeble light picked out a shelf holding what appeared to be a leather binding of some sort and, hanging in a far corner, a broken armor harness and a threadbare tabard emblazoned with a faded crimson cross. Though Frederick speculated the room served as quarters for the commander of the fortress, the finds were hardly of a value that justified the labor involved in sealing the cave.

The only item of interest taken from the cave was the length of leather, which, when unwound, was found to contain a parchment scroll. The task of translating it from medieval French into English had hardly begun when the name Balian of Ibelin, the fortress's last commander, appeared.

With their working knowledge of modern French, both men found the task of translating the ancient language, though tedious, not at all intimidating. By early evening, they had finished. Bone tired, Neisen excused himself after dinner and retired to his tent. In a little while, the last of the workers bedded down as well and silence descended on the camp.

Bodien remained at the table where they had eaten. By the light of a single lamp, he began to study their translation of what was clearly Balian's personal journal. *What had this Balian of Ibelin looked like?* In his mind's eye, he saw a raw-boned man, bronzed from years of fighting the infidel in the desert sun. Bodien could picture him, wearing the coarse wool kirtle of a soldier, seated and writing at the crude table in his cell-like quarters. He visualized him pausing, only to dip his quill in ink, his words flying across the parchment as if fearful of being overtaken by a lapse of memory. Eerily, the Vatican curator felt as if he were looking over Balian's shoulder as he read the translation.

Today I, Balian of Ibelin, Templar Knight to the Vicar of Christ and Master of the Fortress of St. Jean write in my own hand of the events that have unfolded this day. I write in haste, lest death should come to me and any record of these marvelous happenings be forever lost. My faithful scribe will copy all I write herein for the eyes of Master De Molay and the Holy Father. When a member of The Brotherhood makes his way to Cypress, he will deliver the document and stone to you.

I call on the Angels of heaven, Cherubim and Seraphim, together with the holy Apostles and the Virgin, ever blessed, to judge me according to my words. If I speak falsely, or should Satan or his demons have seduced my mind so that I believe a lie, may my lot be banishment to outer darkness for all eternity.

As evening was coming on today, Cornelius, a trusted member of our Order, brought a Bedouin shepherd boy, of slight acquaintance, to me. Cornelius and his men were on patrol near the ruin called by the ancients Qum Ran when they found the lad. He was walking about, babbling in a manner that greatly distressed the men and caused them to fear for the boy's life if left to wander through the night in such a state.

When the boy was brought to the fortress, Cornelius gave to me a scroll and leather pouch that he declared the lad was carrying when found. Cornelius said the boy raved as he took the pouch from him and screamed none should touch the stone it held lest the sun be lost forever. So fearsome were his screams of whirling colors, long dead armies, and ancient cities rising from the earth that the men drew back in terror lest they be striving with a demon. At long last, the boy's screams dissolved into weeping of the most piteous kind, causing the compassion of even the most hardened soldier to flow toward the poor creature.

After hearing Cornelius's report, I sought to allay the boy's fears by commanding food and drink be set before him. Only after he had eaten did I ask the source of his soul's distress. Still overcome by fear, he pointed a trembling hand toward the leather pouch and scroll on the table declaring he had found them in a cave above the Sea of Salt.

As I reached for the pouch, he screamed so frightfully that I called for a guard, entrusted the lad's soul to God, and commanded he be given shelter for the night and victuals for his journey on the morrow. Only after he left my presence did I view the objects that had occasioned his distress and after viewing it called a guard, ordering the boy be given a merciful death.

The scroll was written in the language of the Jews, and had I known this tongue, I warrant its revelation of the other object's purpose would have much comforted my mind.

On opening the pouch, I found therein an oblong stone of pendant size, encased within a thin gold band, inscribed about with letters in the Hebrew tongue. The stone was black as pitch, and when I touched it and the light fell full upon it, a rainbow of colors appeared and washed in waves across its face. As I watched, the colors rose above the stone then wove themselves into a veil of shimmering radiance that, for two breaths, hung in space before my eyes, then vanished.

Unease assails me as I write this portion of the tale, lest I omit some part needful for His Holiness or Master De Molay's understanding of the events that shortly came to pass.

No sooner had the colors vanished than I discerned a raised design, of simple form, graven upon the stone: two lines ascended side by side, then bend away from one another at their highest point, then downward, thus.

What this strange stone and its sign may mean, I leave to wiser men than I. One thing of certainty I know. When I gave my fingers leave to trace the marks, this action linked the times and set in motion all that followed.

That was all—a story with a strange beginning and stranger ending. Bodien wondered what had followed as his hand lightly brushed Balian's drawing. What had happened to cause the man to hide his journal away in a cave behind tons of rock? Again, he let the tip of his finger softly trace the lines on the delicate design on the scroll.

Bodien's head swam. His rational mind told him it must be a dream, yet he had no recollection of leaving the dining tent and going to bed. A moment ago, he was looking at the drawing in the Templar's journal and now suddenly his familiar world had disappeared! Tent, table, the entire camp—everything vanished into a fog. He no longer sat under the canopy at the ruin of St. Jean but stood in the cool shadows of a cave's entrance, staring down on a narrow sea. It snaked away to the lip of the horizon where it became one with the sky. The sea's oily waves lapped wearily against the stony shore, its battle to break free of the deep rift holding it captive long since lost.

A dull sound caused him to turn and look back into the cave. As his eyes adjusted to the gloom, he made out a figure. A boy, dressed in the loose-fitting robe of a Bedouin, had just removed the lid of a large stone jar. The thud as it fell to earth caught his attention.

He watched the boy reach into the mouth of the jar and feel around for something hidden there. Somehow, he knew the boy would withdraw his hand clutching the scroll and the leather pouch containing the stone described in Balian's journal.

What drew the boy to the cave? Was he simply seeking shelter from the cold wind blowing down from the mountains? In some mysterious way, he knew he had transcended time and space and been linked with the Bedouin boy of Balian's journal and was now seeing through his eyes, experiencing his excitement and the fear that gripped him before Balian's knights found him wandering about at Qum Ran.

He isn't seeking shelter. Bodien knew this with the certainty of an eyewitness. *A raging curiosity, whetted by the hermits' tales he's heard around their campfires draws him here.*

The hermits tell of golden treasures and holy things hidden in ancient times among the bleached cliffs around the Sea of Salt. Some among the boy's people say such tales are the ravings of men driven mad by loneliness, but the lad's father is not so sure. He has told the boy the men in the fort on Mt. Quarantana worshiped the same god as the hermits and have come to their land in search of his holy things.

From the cave's mouth Bodien surveyed a gray, dusty valley winding into the distance. Bricks, like shedding scales of a monstrous snake, lay scattered about, marking the ruins of an ancient town. He knew, beside those shattered walls, the father and son once walked together and in his mind, he heard the father speaking.

"*Men of great knowledge built this village,*" he said. "*They spent their lives writing down the words of their god and waiting for his coming. But evil men came first. They destroyed the village and killed the people. Some say that hidden nearby are the sacred things belonging to their god. The hermits say when the time rolls round again, he will come and claim what is his.*"

Bodien looked back into the cave again. The boy had opened the leather pouch and was walking to the entrance. He looked disappointed as he withdrew a small black object and began examining it in the light.

Bodien drew closer so he could see more clearly. It was the stone of Balian's journal: one side polished to such brilliance it shimmered with bands of color, the other graven with the design the boy just now began to trace.

Bodien remembered Balian's words: *I touched the marks. This action linked the times and set in motion all that followed.*

Bodien felt a sudden rush of panic and he opened his mouth to warn the boy but no words came.

Against his will, the Priest found his eyes drawn to the valley below. It was as if he were watching a video on fast forward. Moments before, the sky was cloudless with no hint of a breeze. Now clouds raced by, as though driven by a storm. On the valley floor, what moments ago had been a ruined village, suddenly changed into a stretched, distorted image, then changed again into an obscene assemblage of grotesque angles, shapes, and colors, like the meanderings of an insane artist's brush on canvas.

He felt he was looking into a fun-house mirror. A wild collage of colors and ill-defined forms were bending and weaving, thickening and flowing, out, then back again. The world outside the cave seemed captive to the whims of a potter who had not yet decided what shape his work should take.

As quickly as it started, the shape shifting stopped. What had been a town in ruins was now a community of neat stone buildings. Men dressed in white gathered in what appeared to be the town square and looked westward where black smoke spilled over the low mountains.

Bodien knew his history. It was 70 AD and the Roman general Titus was doing his grisly work just over those hills. The people of Jerusalem were being put to the sword and the Holy City torched. Soon Titus and his legions would make their move on Massada. There he knew a thousand of Israel's bravest soldiers and their families would battle the Romans to the death.

Again, Bodien heard movement within the cave. He turned, expecting to see the Bedouin boy again. Instead, he saw a soldier, his uniform caked with blood and dirt. A large leather bag hung from his shoulder, and a weary sadness lay heavily on his dark, swarthy face. He removed the lid from the stone jar and reached into the bag.

Bodien was not surprised when he retrieved the familiar scroll and leather pouch and placed them in the jar. But nothing could prepare him for what followed as the soldier drew his sword, drove its handle into the earth, and then pitched forward onto its point, crying out as he did: "I have done my duty, oh God."

The soldier's final words followed Bodien through the fog that suddenly filled the cave and into the light of the dining tent at St. Jean. With a start, he realized he was still sitting at the table with Balian's journal spread out before him. He looked at his watch, his mouth dropping open in amazement.

It had been just before nine when Neisen retired. It couldn't have taken more than fifteen minutes for him to read the translation of the scroll, to ponder the crude drawing and trace its outlines with his finger, however, in his vision he had spanned the centuries in that brief time. But how long had it really taken? He held his watch closer to the light and gasped as he watched the second hand sweep forward. In exactly fifteen seconds, it would be 9:16!

I have done my duty, oh God.

The soldier's words still echoed in his mind as he retrieved his camera from a chair. For a brief moment, he felt a tinge of anxiety and looked about. Satisfied he was still alone, he positioned the light so that it fully illuminated the scroll and snapped several pictures.

Finished, he rolled the parchment, put it safely away, and walked toward his tent feeling all the while unseen eyes were watching from the darkness.

CHAPTER 18

WASHINGTON, DC

SHUT AWAY IN HIS small study just off the Oval Office, John Howard Stewart, President of the United States, struggled to come to terms with the seemingly impossible. Dark shadows, announcing the coming of night, draped themselves over the White House where he mourned the death of his vision: a world free at last from the threat of war.

The report, presented a few hours ago by Dr. Conner Mills, Director of the Central Intelligence Agency, had buried it. The operative, code named Melchisedec, had been brutally straightforward. Earlier, during the intelligence briefing, Stewart had willed himself to remain as emotionally detached as possible. Alone now with the complete report spread before him, he felt helpless, a witch's brew of disbelief and fear simmering in his mind as he scanned Mills' introductory remarks.

The Director summarized the background of the operative, an anonymous informant who had contacted the CIA regarding the existence of an international network of prominent people holding unpublicized meetings in various parts of the world. He claimed to be privy to information leading him to believe this network posed a threat to the United States as well as the whoile international community. The Agency had sought to learn the informant's identity and his possible motives, but all inquiries had hit a dead end.

After several more contacts, the informant had finally agreed to reveal his name, but only to Mills, with the assurance he alone would conduct any vetting. He expressed fear the network might extend to the highest levels of government and, if so, the risk of compromise was too great if others in the Agency knew his name.

Ultimately, Mills became convinced that because of the informant's unique relationship with the group, he should be authorized to conduct surveillance on the government's behalf.

Because Mills gave his personal pledge, the operative's name would never be revealed. The code name "Melchisedec" was assigned both to the agent and to the operation.

In the President's briefing, the Director emphasized the religious, esoteric, and historical content of the report. Because of Melchisedec's position, and the uniqueness of his background, Mills assured the President he was qualified to offer informed judgments on these issues.

The President rubbed his eyes and flipped open what Mills had titled:

"The Melchisedec Memorandum"

The focus of this report is on a security threat posed against the United States as well as the rest of the world by a secret organization calling itself The Brotherhood of the Sign, a society formed following the near extinction of the Knights Templar in the fourteenth century.

The Templars were a Holy Order of warrior monks committed to freeing Palestine from Moslem control and protecting pilgrims journeying to the Holy Land.

After discovering that Pope Clement was plotting with King Philip of France to steal their wealth and destroy The Brotherhood, this splinter group of Templars rejected organized religion in general and the Christian view of God in particular. However, they never allowed bitterness to blur their vision of a future utopian world.

Having shed themselves of religion, they equated this perfect world with one led by enlightened men such as themselves. Among other things, their belief system rejected outright faith in a God who loves and cares for man. The Brotherhood does believe, however, a Supreme Being created a perfect world (Paradise) then moved on, leaving man to care for it. In their view, it was failure to manage Paradise properly that led to its loss.

Since rejecting Christianity five hundred years ago, this society has been bound together by a single conviction: a door back to Paradise exists and they are destined to find the key to unlock it.

The key, they believe, is an amulet given to Adam when God banished him from Eden; one meant to be both a reminder of what he had lost and also of what, one day, would be regained. After the fratricide of Abel, the society believes Adam gave the stone to his other son, thus engendering the references to the mark of Cain.

In time, their tradition says it was given to Abraham by Melchisedec, the ancient king of Salem, or Jerusalem, where for generations it remained with his family until passed on to Moses.

Following the construction of the Tabernacle, they believe Moses placed it, along with other sacred objects, in the Ark of the Covenant and when Jerusalem fell in 70 AD, all traces of the Ark were lost and with it the fabled stone.

If used correctly, The Brotherhood of the Sign believes this stone can literally reverse time, and return the world to its original state of perfection. As I said, they believe their destiny is not only to find the stone, but also to use its powers to recover Paradise, and more important, to rule it.

One may question how such curious beliefs pose a threat to national and world security. Dr. Mills, I am sure you have investigated by background and know I am a rational man and not given to exaggeration. Credible evidence exists supporting my belief that such a stone as I describe actually exists and represents unimaginable power, both for good and for evil. The Brotherhood has sought its whereabouts for centuries, devoting their lives and fortunes to its recovery, and for only one purpose—to control its power to regain Paradise and to remake it in their own image. Soon I hope to have proof they are well on their way to finding this stone.

The President closed the folder and dropped his head into his hands. To sway his Cabinet, the Congress, and the American people securing proof of such a plot was essential. Claims of an international conspiracy conducted by a shadowy group with its foundation dating back to the Middle Ages would be hard, if not impossible, to sell without something concrete to go on. However, the President needed no such proof. In his heart, he knew he had just read the truth.

And it scared him to death.

Chapter 19

Washington, DC
Several Months Later

A MASTER HAD RECRUITED the man whose first report lay before the President.

"The boy is intelligent, highly motivated, and well positioned to be useful," Mills told the President when he first announced the recruitment of a backup to Melchisedec.

"And what will be his *nom de guerre*?" The President smiled as he remembered Mills's reply.

"I'm calling him "What If," he said, and then described how the man had come to the agency's attention.

At the height of the cold war, President Eisenhower inaugurated an annual intelligence briefing for senior or master's level college students showing an interest in public service. Because attendance was by invitation only, academics and various law enforcement agencies were encouraged to nominate students they believed to be promising candidates for government service.

Each student nominated submitted a paper dealing with some real or imagined threat to national security. Mills told the President of the several thousand nominated, fewer than twenty percent made the cut and received invitations to attend a special security briefing at the Capital.

Of course, the meeting was merely a cover for identifying and recruiting bright young men and women for the Agency. Other than a vigorous security check, insightfulness reflected in the student's paper was the deciding factor in their selection.

It's like this kid's been reading our mail, Mills said to himself, recalling the astounding insight the young man had displayed. The similarities between the imaginary situations described in his paper and the facts contained in Melchisedec's reports were remarkable.

"What if," the student had asked, "there exists a secret organization composed of powerful men from the highest strata of the world's economic, political, academic, and religious life? What if their loyalty is only to the group and their purpose is world domination? What if their motivation is not power for power's sake but driven by a conviction they alone possess the wisdom to save the world from a coming catastrophe?"

"Insightful," the President responded after Mills had shown him the paper. "Where did the kid get such an idea?"

"You can bet that will be the first question I ask when I meet him," he replied.

The student turned out to be the graduate assistant for a Dr. Frederick Neisen, professor of cultural anthropology at Evangel University in Texas. The young man told Mills the idea for his paper had come following a conversation he had with his professor, Dr. Neisen.

That revelation, and the fact Melchisedec mentioned this professor in a number of his reports, was enough to spark Mills' interest in the boy and ultimately win him an appointment. At this morning's intelligence briefing, Mills had given the President What If's first report.

The President opened the file and began perusing its contents.

Not bad for a first effort, he thought as he read the captions beneath the pictures on the first page. Mills said the agent had retrieved the pictures from a CD he found in Neisen's office. To the uninformed, they might have appeared to be nothing but paparazzi shots, taken in informal settings and obviously from a distance.

"Our photographic specialists tell us the grainiest of the pictures suggest whoever took them was using a telephoto lens in the two hundred millimeter range," Mills said.

"Which means the photographer didn't want to be seen," the President speculated.

"That's our best guess, but that opens a whole new can of worms," Mills replied.

"How's that?"

"Well, for one thing Melchisedec has a unique relationship with the organization. He'd never have to be secretive about taking pictures."

"Then who's taking them, and why?" The President tried unsuccessfully to mask his frustration.

"It's obvious someone else is as interested in getting a fix on this group as we are. Interpol, remnants of the KGB, Mosssad. Take your pick."

"What's your best guess?"

The President knew his CIA director did not like to deal in guesses and sensed Mills' discomfort at being put on the spot. Mills had a well-earned reputation for controlling the agenda, for anticipating questions and having his answers prepared ahead of time.

"The more important question is how the pictures got into Neisen's hands in the first place," he replied, betraying a hint of defensiveness in his voice.

"Why?"

"It may indicate that Melchisedec's cover has been compromised."

"What do you mean?"

The President's voice must have registered his impatience because Mills dropped his head and scanned the carpet, as if searching for an answer.

"I mean, Mr. President, that these pictures are the same as those Melchisedec furnished us nearly two years ago as proof of The Brotherhood's existence."

President Stewart let his gaze drop again to the young man's report. The photos, arranged in a series of four montages and labeled as to place and date, also included the names of those pictured. Taken nearly a decade earlier, the oldest bore the caption *Thailand*. Others were labeled *Hilton Head Island, Canary Islands,* and the most recent, *Luxor, Egypt*. They included photos of men dining on hotel verandas, walking down ships' gangways, and deplaning from private jets.

"When we got the pictures from Melchisedec," Mills said, "we spent the better part of a month putting names to faces. This attachment to What If's report contains the background information we collected on these men."

The President's attention fastened on one particular picture of four men snapped in conversation beside a hotel swimming pool. Three were identified as a Father Henri Bodien, Dr. Francis Abelard of Oxford, and Dr. Frederick Neisen, whose name kept cropping up with such interesting frequency. For a moment, the President studied Neisen's finely chiseled features.

There was no need for a caption identifying the fourth man. The President recognized him instantly as his dinner host while attending an economic summit in Germany less than a year ago: His name was Erik Stiediger, Board Chairman of CGA, a German conglomerate invested heavily in steel, banking, and petrochemicals. A recent issue of Fortune Magazine had described him as one of the five richest men in the world.

The Stiediger family had played a prominent role both politically and economically in Europe since the turn of the twentieth century. Curiously, though they were free marketers to the core, it was widely believed the Stiediger wealth had supplied Lenin with much of the capital he needed to finance Russia's Bolshevik revolution.

After the Second World War, Stiediger's great-uncle Hans was tried at Nuremberg on charges CGA used slave labor in several of its plants that supplied needed materials for the Nazi war machine. Although sentenced to five years in prison, powerful friends in America and Great Britain arranged for the commuting of his sentence after he had served only six months. Numerous magazine articles speculated on the source of the funding that fueled CGA's meteoric rise from the ashes of Germany's defeat, but that source remained a mystery.

The President's eyes swept the photomontage and list again. *What was Stiediger doing with a Priest and two college professors? Moreover, what about the others?* He marveled at the intellectual, political and economic power they represented: a retired chair of the International Monetary Fund, Russia's leading theoretician in the field of hydrogen fusion, an American televangelist. There was a Saudi prince, CEOs of a dozen Fortune 500 companies and chairs of some of the world's largest philanthropic organizations. Rounding out the list was a British cosmologist, an authority on dead Middle Eastern languages he had never heard of, a rabbinic scholar specializing in the Kabala, a Buddhist mystic, and a defeated third-party candidate the President knew only too well.

What common thread bound such a disparate group together?

A cloud passed over the sun and dulled the light spilling through the Oval Office windows. From somewhere beyond the White House grounds, an ambulance siren wailed. He turned his attention again to the CIA addendum to the young agent's report.

"*A trans-national organization of gifted and influential men,*" it read.

Gifted? Without a doubt, the President reflected. And obviously organized. Meeting in out-of-the-way places all over the world demanded both good communications and the ability to travel under the radar. But for what purpose?

Did the photos provide sufficient evidence these gatherings were not only unusual but also conspiratorial? Did they bolster the new agent's hypothesis, the one he had first suggested in his application paper? No matter, the bottom line was clear. He needed incontrovertible proof, solid enough to satisfy his critics before he even contemplated labeling this group a threat to national security.

The President retrieved his Bible from his desk drawer. A personal treasure, it had been his father's and the one on which he had taken his oath of office. He opened it to his dad's inscription on the flyleaf: "Son, read this book every day. Let it be a lamp for your feet and a light for your path."

And I have opened it so seldom, Stewart thought, remembering how his father would read it aloud to the family each evening after dinner when he was a boy. He felt his eyes well with tears. *Oh God, I need your wisdom now,* he prayed silently as his fingers felt along the Bible's edge until they randomly selected a page deep in the book. His gaze was immediately drawn to Revelation 20:1.

"And I saw the beast and the kings of the earth and their armies assemble to make war against Him who sat upon the horse and against His army."

Memories of chilling intelligence briefings came back to him, each more alarming that the last. He thought of his many meetings in the Situation Room buried beneath this very floor. He could see Mills, the Joint Chiefs, members of his National Security Council—each reciting a litany of threats to the nation.

"Mr. President," one said, "our sources have confirmed at least two dozen suitcase-sized atomic devices are missing from the Russian arsenal, and may be in the hands of terrorist organizations. Already we've heard rumors of plots being formulated against major cities and industries in the West."

And another, "Hackers have been intercepted on the verge of accessing both ours and Russia's ballistic missile codes. The hackers' intent is unclear, but we must assume they are trying to deactivate the missiles. Or, even worse, trying to trigger a launch."

Another threat concerned the seas. Not only were they being polluted and depleted of fish, but also rising at an alarming rate. Changing weather patterns were producing spring-like conditions at the North and South Poles for several months each year. As a result, the ice packs were melting. He had read one ominous report from the Academy of Science so many times he had practically memorized it. *"If the current rate of meltdown continues,"* it said, *"we can expect a number of cities along the eastern seaboard and Gulf of Mexico to become uninhabitable within less than a hundred years."*

The Horsemen of the Apocalypse are riding over the world, he thought, closing the Bible and dragging his attention back to the young agent's report. *And now this!* He glanced at the pictures again and shook his head sadly.

"Oh, dear God, I need you now. Please show me what to do," he prayed aloud, resting his face in his hands before turning to stare through the office windows. Since he began studying the reports the sky had completely overcast. Branches, neatly stacked earlier by the grounds crew for pickup, were blowing about as a line of rainsqualls moved through the city.

Again, in the distance he heard the wail of a siren. *Like the scream of an enraged beast,* he thought and chided himself for giving way to his overworked imagination as he let his head drop once more into his hands.

Chapter 20

Jerry had not known what to expect as he and Neisen crossed the two bridges connecting the mainland with Hilton Head Island. He checked his watch. Mechanical difficulties in Dallas stretched a normally two-hour flight to Savannah into five, leaving him exhausted at nearly ten o'clock at night.

Lights winked timidly through gathering fog as they drove down Highway 278 toward the heart of the island. What little he knew about the place, he had learned in the library the day before they left. One article said archeologists found evidence Indians had lived there for thousands of years before the white man arrived. Before the Civil War, it was a hideout for Negroes escaping from slavery. Called "Gullah," their descendents still inhabit the island, now known more as a sanctuary for the well-to-do.

He told Ruth about his invitation to accompany Dr. Neisen to an important meeting on Hilton Head Island during the Christmas break, but he gave her no details except that relationships established there might help to further his career.

"Who are these men Dr. Neisen wants you to meet, Jerry?" Ruth asked.

"All I know is that he says most of them are very rich and very powerful ... world changers he calls them." He could tell by her tone, his explanation provoked more questions than answers.

"And these very rich and powerful men want to meet you? What for Jerry? What can they possibly...?"

"See in a lowly student from a college that's not exactly Ivy League?"

What Ruth's question implied hurt and he wished he could tell her he had moved beyond struggling to find himself but that was impossible. For now, he could only hope that unfolding events would show her there was more to him than she imagined.

"Well, I know your mom and dad will be disappointed, but I guess they'll understand the importance of you getting to know the right people." Jerry heard only disappointment and sarcasm in Ruth's voice, so he changed the subject.

Neisen had been vague about what he should expect at the conference. Even during the flight he responded mostly in generalities to his questions, saying only he would be meeting an international fraternity of friends with common interests who looked forward to his joining them.

Jerry pulled an in-flight magazine from the seat pocket and began flipping through it. "What kind of common interests?" he asked Neisen, keeping his voice casual.

"To make a better world," Neisen replied without hesitation, as if that explained everything, and then closed his eyes.

Jerry waved away a flight attendant offering drinks and stared out the window of the first class cabin. *Nothing but the best,* he mused, remembering the photos he had found on Neisen's computer. *My sponsors, some of the wealthiest and most prominent men in the world, all gathered in one place.* "An inner circle of power," Neisen called them. *And I will be a part of that circle.* Neisen had also said he would be expected to make a decision of some sort at the end of the meeting, but gave no hint what it might involve.

Jerry jerked himself back to the present as Neisen turned off 278 onto a side road that ended abruptly at a dark parking lot, bordered on three sides by palmetto palms and on the fourth by Calibogue Sound. Once parked, he collected his bag and followed Neisen down a path to a lighted pier where a large cruiser awaited them. An ancient Negro man dressed immaculately in white, his white hair haloed in the light from a single dock lamp swinging overhead, raised his hand as they approached.

"We're not staying on Hilton Head Island?" Jerry asked through his exhaustion.

"Just a short ride," Neisen explained patiently, "to a smaller island, one with no bridge to the mainland. Too many tourists here. Not enough privacy."

As they walked out on the dock, the old man finished untying the bowline.

"Evenin' Dr. Neisen," he said courteously as he stored their luggage onboard. "T' other folk is already suppered and bedded down."

"Enough, Henry," Neisen replied with a wave of his hand, "just get us to the island. It has been a long day and we are worn out."

The man absorbed Neisen's rudeness as though calloused to it, started the engines, and pulled away from the pier into the darkness.

"Mr. Spencer, welcome to Daufuskie Island! I'm so pleased we can finally meet."

Francis Abelard extended a clammy, claw-like hand, which Jerry felt obliged to shake as he entered the foyer of the mansion.

"Our host, Dr. Stiediger, sends his regrets for being unable to greet you tonight, but he will join us tomorrow."

Jerry shivered at the old man's touch but tried to project warmth. "Thanks so much, Dr. Abelard, for inviting me."

"Frederick has told me so much about you." Abelard stepped back and gave Jerry an appraising look. The tick of a clock from somewhere was all that disturbed the silence as his buzzard-like eyes took his measure.

"Henry!" The uncomfortable hush ended as Abelard switched his attention to Henry who was carrying their luggage into the entrance. "You know better than to come through the foyer. Use the back stairs. "

Neisen shot a glance of contempt at the old man whose head hung down, his eyes avoiding either of the two arrogant white men as if anticipating another insult. Jerry squirmed in embarrassment for him and took the opportunity of the diversion to study Abelard, the man Neisen had described as the world's leading anthropologist.

His sheer bulk was striking. Probably once of a stately build, age had reduced him to a great heap of rubble, a ruin of at least three hundred pounds of disorganized flesh, draped in a black cassock.

"Henry is Gullah, a fascinating group," Abelard went on, as if the servant were a piece of furniture. "They even have their own language. As you might expect, I have a great interest in their culture, but it is always good to make sure they remember their place, don't you agree?" Again, he flicked a contemptuous gaze, masquerading as goodwill, at Henry. "Run along now, there's a good lad."

Abelard beamed at Jerry and swept an arm to his left.

"Shall we?" he said, as Jerry feeling his face burning with embarrassment, preceded him reluctantly into the dining room.

"As I said, the Gullah interest me greatly. Not just because of who they are, but because of what they represent."

They had taken their seats at the table, and Jerry was in the process of devouring a medium-rare cut of a prime rib. Thankfully, he thought, it prevented him from having to respond to Abelard's comment.

"And what is that, Francis?" Neisen looked up from his dinner and peered down the massive dining table at his mentor seated at its head.

"Humanity's helplessness in the face of inevitability."

Jerry cringed when he realized Abelard had directed his response not to Neisen, but to him. His mouth still full, he nodded and hoped that would satisfy his host. Apparently it did, because Abelard continued as if he were delivering a lecture to one of his classes, although Jerry's research told him Abelard had not taught in over ten years.

"History, like water, flows downhill from its source and the Gullah, like the rest of humanity, is swept along by its current. Their rescue here on Daufuskie from this current's downward pull is only temporary. All humanity feels caught in it and looks for escape in one way or another. Some seek it through a hoped-for medical breakthrough that will delay their dying, others, by overcoming humanity's obsession with war and the establishment of a lasting peace. And some quaint souls, even in this enlightened age, still insist on reversing history's downward pull through faith in a compassionate God."

Abelard turned his head as he spoke and looked into the darkness outside the dining room windows. "Every man seeks an island of safety," he said, as if to himself, "but sooner or later all are swept away by the current of history."

Jerry had not said anything since shaking hands with Abelard in the foyer. The professor's manner, like everything else in Stiediger's house, seemed designed to impress and intimidate: the twin staircases curving majestically up from the foyer, this dining room with a chandelier worthy of the Palace of Versailles, the massive table dominated by a throne-like chair at its head, obviously placed there for Abelard. All this opulence declared proudly in the language of polished woods, finely worked stone, and sparkling crystal, *I have the power. I am in charge.*

"You speak of a river...and history's source. What might that be, sir?" Jerry was surprised how weak his voice sounded, how his words seemed to lose themselves somewhere between his lips and the vaulted ceiling looming overhead.

However, his words obviously reached Abelard because he nodded knowingly, folded his hands together in a prayer-like pose and for several seconds said nothing. When he did speak, it was to Neisen.

"Frederick, you were right in inviting Mr. Spencer into our circle. But I am afraid he has asked the wrong question."

Abelard glanced at Jerry. "You ask me *what* is history's source. That is not how I would frame it, young man. More precisely, your query should be not *what* but *where*, that is, where in time did the river of history begin its downward plunge?"

He did not wait for a response but heaved his huge bulk out of his chair and shuffled to the door.

"Tomorrow we will discuss your question further. I think you will find the answer interesting." Abelard gave Neisen a broken smile as they exchanged knowing glances. "It is past midnight, and I am sure you are both weary from your journey."

"Henry." Abelard hardly raised his voice to call the Gullah before he appeared, as if on cue. "Henry will show you to your room," he said, gesturing at Jerry. "Sleep well."

Half his meal uneaten, Jerry reluctantly arose and followed the servant up the stairs, aware that Neisen had stayed behind. A quick backward glance confirmed he had followed Abelard into a room across the foyer from the dining room.

"We have much to do tomorrow, Frederick," Jerry heard the old man say just before he closed the door.

The next morning, Jerry tried not to stare at the two muscular, flint-featured guards who stood with cold detachment at the door to the dining room.

Over a huge breakfast, he and the four other young men exchanged names, but avoided revealing anything else too personal. He did learn that, like him, they had not been told what to expect at the meeting. One said he understood that they would learn the history and purpose of the society and would be asked to make a decision that would change their lives for the better. All of them speculated, privately, about what that might be, but none of them was willing to give voice to his thoughts, except for one brash member of the group who insisted that it was merely a formality.

"After all," the tall, blond one said, "if they didn't want us to be part of their group, we wouldn't be here in the first place, right?"

Maybe, and maybe not, Jerry thought. Still, he was sure, all shared one common feeling—a burning curiosity about the men one called "*their destiny determiners.*" More specifically all of them were anxious to know how these titans would benefit their careers. He looked up, startled, when one of the guards entered the room.

"You will follow us," he said in heavily accented English. "Dr. Abelard is ready to receive you in the great hall."

And so it begins, Jerry thought as he and the others pushed back their chairs and followed the guards into the hall.

With the exception of Abelard, all the men in the room stood when they entered.

For the first time, Jerry had the opportunity to meet their host, Erik Stiediger. He greeted each recruit stiffly; then, like a mongoose avoiding a cobra's bite, moved in jerky starts and stops around the room, introducing them to the other members of the group. Delicate hands, unaccustomed to work, voices deeply accented and courtly manners made their graciousness seem more theatrical than real.

When the social pleasantries were over, Stiediger called the meeting to order.

"Gentlemen," he said crisply, "welcome to Daufuskie Island. Though I have had the honor of hosting you and our esteemed leader many times," he gave Abelard a nod of acknowledgement, "only once before have we met on my lovely island."

As he watched Neisen take the chair next to Abelard, Jerry wondered if Henry and his fellow Gullahs would appreciate Stiediger's assumption he owned the whole island.

"Since we are all very busy, we will move as quickly as possible to deal with the business at hand." He gestured toward Abelard, whose multiple chins wobbled as he smiled. "Dr. Abelard, we await with interest your remarks."

Abelard remained seated after Stiediger's introduction. "Thank you, Erik," he began. "Please forgive my not standing. These ancient legs you know." He patted a knee as the men nodded their understanding.

"I have called you together with mixed emotions," he continued. "First, joy, as I anticipate the decisions these five young men will soon be making." Abelard's eyes swept the room, and his lips drew back in a smile more canine than human. "As they say in certain Christian traditions, their professions of faith." There were chuckles as members of The Brotherhood exchanged glances as if privy to a well-kept secret.

"Like you, I have also come to this meeting anticipating our good Father Bodien's report that the search for the talisman, the so-called mark of Cain, is almost over."

Heads turned toward a slight, balding man in clerical garb in the corner of the room. Spencer recognized Bodien as one of the men in the pictures he had taken from Neisen's office. He also noticed Neisen's glare at the mention of the Priest's name, one a quick glance from Abelard erased.

"Yes, I feel joy at the prospect of what we will hear." Abelard fingered his signet ring, his face grave. "At the same time, I feel sorrow because of a painful duty I must carry out."

His eyes sought Neisen's, almost as if looking for permission—or perhaps absolution. The others cast questioning glances, obviously unprepared for Abelard's grim announcement.

Jerry wondered how many had noticed Neisen's hand go to his mouth a beat too late to hide a satisfied smirk.

Abelard's tone became more upbeat. "But let us first deal with more pleasant tasks." He gestured a bony hand toward the newcomers. "For these fine young men, this is a day of revelation, and for the rest of us a day of information, so let us move on."

Jerry could feel the grip of Abelard's cold eyes as they swept the room before fastening on him. *Those eyes...* They seemed to take on lives of their own, to become creatures with claws that grabbed his gaze, dug into his mind and rummaged about, groping for his most secret thoughts.

Much retelling had polished the story Abelard related. In conversations with Neisen, Jerry had heard it in bits and pieces but never from start to finish or with the level of intensity Abelard displayed.

"As you probably know," he began, "primitive tribes pass on their history orally."

Primitive tribes. Jerry remembered the old Shaman in Ruth's favorite book, and the disdain with which Abelard had treated Henry and his Gullah ancestors.

"However, they aren't the only ones with an oral history. Our Brotherhood has had its own for centuries. For the benefit of our young friends here, I want to retell it now. Afterwards," Abelard paused and scanned the faces of each recruit, "you will make your decision."

"Hugh De Payne founded our order in the thirteenth century. He did so with the purest of motives. Though born into wealth, it was never his master but rather the means by which he showed his love for God, Holy Mother Church, and the land of Christ's birth. Through The Brotherhood, he tried to inspire that same love in other young men of privilege. He saw himself and his followers as the church's military arm with a calling to protect those on pilgrimage to the Holy Land from the Muslim infidels."

Abelard related how thousands of Europe's brightest and best young men joined The Brotherhood. Called Templars or Poor Knights of Christ, they pledged fidelity, chastity, and obedience to The Brotherhood and dedicated their lives and their wealth to the service of the church. Over the next two centuries, their pooled wealth grew to such an extent that they became not only the church's military arm but also Europe's chief banker.

"That was a good thing," Abelard continued, "because the cost of financing the Crusades was draining the treasuries of Europe, and its kings needed a generous banker. This was especially true of Philip IV of France. As the Crusades were ending, he found his treasury empty and his debt to the Templars enormous.

"The final blow to the Crusaders' dream of wresting the land of Christ from Moslem domination came when the port city of Acre fell, and with it Europe's last foothold in Palestine.

"With this final defeat, both King Philip and Pope Clement were faced with personal dilemmas. Philip needed money to replenish his bankrupt treasury and Clement needed a scapegoat to explain the defeat of a movement the church had said enjoyed the special favor of God. What better choice for achieving both goals than the Templars? They still had great wealth to be tapped, and as for blame...weren't they at the forefront of Acre's defenders? Could it be their cowardice had led to its fall?"

The sun had been shining brightly through the tall windows behind Abelard when they first entered the room. However, as the old man spoke, the sky became overcast; raindrops peppered the windows, and a soggy gloom, common to coastal winters, settled over the island. Outside, long pointed fronds of palmetto palms swayed in the wind, as if trying to shoo away the mist settling over them.

"The storm arrives, just as the plot thickens," Abelard stage whispered from the gloom invading the great room. For several moments, he seemed to listen to the wind, as if waiting for it to remind him of something he had forgotten.

From his seat at the far side of the room, the evaporating light made it impossible for Jerry to see more than the barest outline of Abelard's great bulk. Though normally calm, Jerry found himself shifting uncomfortably in his chair as the raspy voiced Abelard continued speaking from the shadows.

"Fixing blame on the Templars was easy. The church leadership's widespread envy of The Brotherhood guaranteed no shortage of persons ready to testify to their cowardice. Gaining control of their wealth was another matter. Sanctioned by the church, the Templar enjoyed its protection. Unless…"

Spencer sensed a stirring in the shadows and in spite of his distaste for the bloated Abelard, he, too, found himself leaning forward in anticipation of the rest of the tale.

"Its wealth could not be touched unless heresy could be proved, and proving it would be harder than spreading rumors questioning the Templar's courage. Bribed witnesses were not enough to convict them. They must be made to confess their crimes which meant—"

Without warning, the silhouette leaned forward for a moment from the shadows, and Jerry Spencer gagged as a cry caught in his throat. He prayed it was some trick of the light…the way the shadows fell across Abelard's face, or a nightmare born of his own imagination, but he knew it was not. Nothing, not even Ruth's love, could ever erase from his mind the vision of the spawn from hell that had been Abelard; its vulture-like head moving slowly from side to side as if searching for some dead thing to devour, its serpentine neck wrapped in folds of leprous skin, the soulless stare of its pitiless eyes seeking his. Jerry knew he was looking into the face of pure evil and this vision would haunt his dreams forever.

"They had to be made to confess," the being that had been Abelard hissed as it drew back into the shadows, "and torture was required if a confession was to be believed."

Again, there was a rustling sound. *That thing's reforming into Abelard,* Jerry thought, feeling his mind seized by a sickening horror. Frantically, he searched the face of the recruit beside him for some hint he too saw the nightmare but his engrossed expression told him he had not. Reason abandoned him as he imagined the demonic transformation taking place within the shadows.

"You understand, for reasons that will become clear, how important it was to the church that Templar leadership be tortured." Abelard was speaking again in classic Oxford style. "The religious carry a burden we do not share. They must hide their lust for power beneath a veneer of piety."

Without explaining what he meant, he went on to describe in lurid detail the kind of tortures the church used to gain confessions.

Just as Jerry was wondering why Abelard had drifted from the story to focus on the grisly details of torture, he dropped the subject entirely, proceeding to describe how King Philip and Pope Clement had hatched a plot to get what they wanted.

"Witnesses were bribed to make false statements accusing the Templar of all manner of crimes. Europe's ears tingled with tales of their consorting with the devil, offering human sacrifice, and committing homosexual acts.

"Jacques De Molay was Grand Master of the Templar at the time," Abelard explained, "and had made Cypress his headquarters shortly before the fall of Acre. When rumors began circulating in Europe about The Brotherhood, he chose at first to ignore them, confident his God would defend their cause.

"God!" The way Abelard mouthed the holy name was blasphemous. "De Molay believed The Brotherhood's years of faithfulness to the church would quickly silence the lies being spread, but the storm continued to grow, and the heavens were silent.

"Finally, feeling only he could defend The Brotherhood, De Molay returned to France to face their accusers. It was too late. On Friday night, October 13, thirteen o seven, Philip's troops fanned out across France and in a matter of hours, all but small remnants of the once mighty Templar were in chains.

"What was their mistake, Mr. Spencer?"

Jerry felt as if he had been pinned in his chair by the whiplash of Abelard's voice. He swallowed hard and forced himself to reply calmly.

"Sir, I'm not sure I understand your question."

"I mean exactly what I said. What was the Templar's mistake Mr. Spencer ... their mistake?

CHAPTER 21

LUNCH HAD ENDED; THE morning squall had washed the sky clean of clouds, and the sun shown brightly through the windows as the men re-gathered in the great room to hear the much-anticipated report from Father Bodien.

Abelard was just concluding his introductory remarks. "Thank you for coming," he said. "Please accept my apologies for calling the meeting on such short notice, but certain circumstances, which will become clear as we move along, have warranted it." Questioning glances between the men followed as to what these "circumstances" might be.

He announced that following Bodien's report and a final bit of business, the meeting would stand adjourned and all but Bodien, Neisen and the recruits would be free to take a water taxi back to Hilton Head.

"And now, good Father Bodien." Abelard gestured in a dismissive manner reeking of bored indulgence rather than interest, for the Priest to come forward.

Not just indifferent, Jerry thought. *I think Abelard hates the man.*

Bodien appeared to ignore the slight as he began his report. "For centuries," he said "our order has believed the mark of Cain existed, that it was a stone designed by God's own hand with power to restore lost perfection to the world."

Engaging and oozing confidence, Bodien continued his much-awaited report.

"Our Brotherhood believes the stone was given by God to Adam; and he, after leaving Paradise, gave it to his son Cain following his murder of his brother Abel. This stone gave birth to the mark of Cain tradition referred to in Genesis. History, with the exception of several vague references in books considered unreliable by the early church fathers, tells us little about it.

"Being curator of the Vatican archives has given me access to the church's most ancient documents including those of a Jewish mystical order called the Kabala. Like us, they too believed in the stone's existence. According to their tradition, it later came into the possession of Melchisedec, an ancient king of Jerusalem, who presented it as a gift to Abraham at their meeting referred to in Genesis, chapter fourteen.

"The Kabala tradition relates that just before Abraham died he gave it to Isaac who then passed it on to Jacob as part of his inheritance. After Jacobs's arrival in Egypt, tradition says the stone was entrusted to Joseph's family. Then, shortly after the beginning of the exodus, it was given to Aaron, Israel's High Priest, for safekeeping. "Centuries of silence followed during which nothing was known about its location. But seven hundred years ago, the silence was finally broken in a letter from the Templar to His Holiness the Pope."

It was obvious to Jerry that Bodien relished the anticipation he saw reflected on their faces and paused, letting it build before continuing.

"I have found that letter," he announced triumphantly. "It states that just before the destruction of Jerusalem in 70 A.D., the stone, along with other sacred objects, was taken from the Temple and hidden in the hills above the Dead Sea."

A gasp erupted from the men as the significance of what he said dawned on them.

For a moment, Bodien hesitated, casting a quizzical glance at Abelard, who had been whispering to Neisen and jumped when their host's voice boomed out.

"Get to the meat of your report!" Stiediger growled impatiently.

Bodien blushed and continued.

"Until now the bits and pieces of information we had about the stone provided no clues to its location." He paused again and nodded in deference to the German. "But since our host requests haste, the meat of my report is this: Dr. Neisen and I have recently made a discovery in Israel that leads me to believe the stone will soon be in our possession."

Everyone, with the exception of Abelard, Stiediger, and Neisen, greeted the news with another burst of excited chatter. Jerry had been sure Abelard's lack of excitement over the news was because he already knew about the contents of Bodien's report, but Stiediger and Neisen's lack of enthusiasm was puzzling.

"But how can you be so sure?" Stiediger asked impatiently.

"Herr Stiediger," Neisen said, "please allow Bodien to get on with it and tell you what we found."

"Dr. Abelard knows that several months ago Dr. Neisen and I made an exciting discovery while excavating a Crusader fortress in Palestine. In a sealed room, we found the personal diary of its commander, Balian of Ibelin.

"The last entry in his diary is dated twelve hundred and eighty-four and relates how a Bedouin shepherd appeared at the fortress one day and gave him a leather pouch containing a stone and an ancient Hebrew scroll. The man said he had found the objects in a cave above the Dead Sea near Qum Ran and added cryptically that strange things happened when he held the stone up to the light. Balian's descriptions of the strange happenings that took place when the stone came into his possession, along with other facts that will shortly become clear, lead me to believe that it is in fact the storied mark of Cain.

"Brothers, you may remember that in twelve hundred and eighty-four Palestine was on the verge of being lost to Christendom. Balian wrote how he expected Jerusalem to fall to the Moslems at any moment. Fearing the precious stone and scroll might fall into their hands, he describes his plan to deliver them to William of Beaujeu, the Templar commander in the port city of Acre, for safekeeping."

He paused and looked at Neisen as if for confirmation.

"I'm sure Dr. Neisen would agree that the most exciting thing about our discovery is that for the first time we have the name of a credible and relatively late witness to the stone's existence."

Jerry sensed Bodien growing uncomfortable because of the obvious disinterest of Abelard, Neisen and Stiediger in what he was saying. He also noticed the Priest had begun to perspire and seemed to be forcing himself to look away from the trio and concentrate on the others in the room.

"Church history has been kind," he said. "For several years I have mined the Vatican archives and have finally struck gold!"

When Stiediger and Neisen heard this, they sat up in their chairs.

Here is something they have not already heard, Jerry realized.

"I've found a letter in the archive dated 1284 to Pope Clement from William of Beaujeu and along with it a transcript of the heresy trial of Jacques de Molay, Grand Master of the Templar. Both are exciting finds because of what they tell us, doubly so because of what one also shows us.

"In his letter Beaujeu declares that after he received the stone and scroll he gave them to a Father Ricoldo Monte Crèche for delivery to De Molay on Cypress. Shortly after, De Molay went to France to defend The Brotherhood and there was arrested, questioned under torture, and finally, as you all know, burned at the stake. The transcript of his trial reveals he confessed to heresy but neither rack nor fire could loosen his lips to tell the stone's location. Even at the end, when told his life would be spared if he would tell where it was, he insisted he did not know."

"Then you've reached another dead end," Stiediger blurted out impatiently.

"I think not," Bodien replied, betraying growing irritation. "I said the letter is exciting not only because of what it tells, but also because of what it shows us. You see . . ." Bodien paused again and looked around the room. "Beaujeu included a small drawing of the stone in his letter to the Pope. Now, for the first time, we know its shape and most importantly, we have a drawing of the design on its face.

"I immediately gave Dr. Abelard a copy of the letter." Again, he nervously looked at the old Oxford Don for confirmation. Abelard was not listening, but whispering to one of his bodyguards.

"I . . . uh." Bodien stammered as his eyes followed the man who was circling those seated and walking toward him. "Dr. Abelard felt that with the clues furnished by the letter he was ready to use other sources for information as to the stone's present location. This brings us to the primary reason for our meeting. Dr. Abelard has made exciting progress in his investigation and is ready to share the results with us."

For the first time since Bodien had begun speaking, Jerry could tell he had Abelard's full attention.

"I do indeed have good news about my findings, but unfortunately news of another sort as well," Abelard began. "But before we move on, I would like to ask the good Father several questions."

Bodien glanced nervously to the side, apparently aware Abelard's bodyguard had taken up a position behind his chair.

"What do you believe to be the function of the stone," Abelard asked.

"We can only guess." Though obviously troubled, Bodien held himself perfectly still as he spoke. "Some recent discoveries about the universe may give us a clue. According to Einstein's general theory of relativity, space and time curve. Because of this, some speculate that at some point the past might curve back along a path parallel with the present and—"

"And what do you think, Priest?" Abelard interrupted, his voice sharp and cutting. Neisen and Stiediger's looks were even grimmer as they glared at Bodien.

However, Bodien faced them, only a slight quaver in his voice betraying his nervousness. "The discovery of black holes," he said, his eyes fixed on Abelard, "has also given us a possible theory. Some scientists speculate these may be conduits connecting parallel lines of time. The stone might be the key to accessing and navigating these conduits between our time and the past. "

Bodien was obviously feeling the pressure of trying to answer the unanswerable and tried to shift attention back to Abelard. "Dr. Abelard," he said weakly, "you remember the discovery made years ago by one of our order. You said it might hint at this very possibility."

"Do you refer to the Gilgamesh Epic?"

"Yes," Bodien answered, "specifically the piece of the tablet that was broken off."

"Ah yes, the piece our brother broke off after discovering part of it referred to 'time rolling round again.' He agreed with your hypothesis that the mysterious phrase might mean at some point the distant past might actually parallel the present and that black holes might connect the present with—"

"Paradise," Bodien interrupted, whispering the word almost reverently. "'Time rolling round again' might have been the ancients' way of expressing just that possibility." The nervous quaver in his voice was getting more noticeable to everyone in the room. "Perhaps some believed that possessing the stone would give them power to cross the gulf of time and space to Paradise."

"Some? Exactly who are these 'some'?" Abelard snarled.

The image of a black robed inquisitor, glowing poker in hand, materialized in Jerry's mind.

"Well, we . . . that is, I believe . . ."

"Exactly." Abelard cut him off before he could finish. "You alone, Priest, believe its purpose is merely to regain the Biblical Paradise!"

"Well, I thought you . . . that is, all of us . . ." Bodien, gestured helplessly to the others as if pleading for support. "I thought we all wanted to get back to Paradise."

"That is where you betray yourself, Bodien. We do not! We do not want merely to regain Paradise. We intend to remake it! Your naive religious outlook has perverted your mind, and you have forgotten what else the Gilgamesh fragment said."

"I'm not sure I—" Bodien began.

Abelard would have none of it. "You don't remember its promise, do you? Let me refresh your memory.

"'By it the vaults of knowledge are opened, vaults hidden by Him who cast you forth . . .'

"Or this prediction— 'By YOUR POWER . . .'" He pounded his fist on the arm of his chair. "'BY YOUR POWER, you will return and claim what is yours by right. '"

"Another theory concerning the purpose of the stone might be . . ." Bodien was gasping like a drowning man struggling for air, "one based on a multidimensional view of the universe."

"Spare us any more of your theories, Bodien," Abelard hissed. "We don't want to return to Paradise, to simply relive history . . . never!" Abelard's eyes flashed pure hate. "No! It will be as the fragment promised—by our power we will return, claim, and remake what is ours!"

Abelard's voice suddenly softened. "My poor, poor Bodien," he cooed as one would to a baby.

Sensing danger, Bodien rose but was quickly pushed back into his seat by Abelard's bodyguard.

"Haven't you guessed by now? You are the last unpleasant and unfinished bit of business. You poor deluded man. Hearing your report was not the primary reason you were brought here. I could just as easily have given it myself since I had read most of it already."

"I don't know what you mean." Obviously afraid and confused, Bodien tried to stand again.

"I mean I baited you," Abelard snarled, "with the promise of the last bit of information you and your 'godly' friends needed to find the stone for yourselves."

Something passing for sorrow replaced Abelard's snarl. "How I pity you," he said. "To have betrayed your brothers for a fantasy." Mockingly, he made the sign of the cross and pointed a bony finger upward.

"Dr. Abelard, Neisen can tell you I". . . Bodien reacted like a convict searching for a stream to hide his scent from tracking bloodhounds.

Another bodyguard joined the first behind the Priest and with a nod from Abelard, they gripped the Priest's shoulders and lifted him from his chair.

"Neisen already has," Abelard replied. "Neisen saw you take the pictures of Balian's diary at St. Jean. When you failed to tell him, he became suspicious and told me. We have eyes everywhere. You are not the only one who serves us in the Vatican. When our man searched your office, we learned of the Pope's little group and its intrigues with various intelligence agencies. He also found these."

Abelard reached inside his coat pocket and took out a packet of pictures. "Your little gang has been quite busy, Bodien." He flung the pictures into the air and watched as they fluttered down around the startled men. "Brothers, all of you will find yourself in at least one of the pictures," he said.

"Take Father Bodien to the room our host has prepared," he ordered his bodyguards, as casually as asking a waiter for the check. "We will finish our business and then tonight deal with him in a fitting manner." He watched as they led the Priest away and shook his head in mock sadness. "What a waste," he said.

"Mr. Spencer."

Jerry was startled when Abelard suddenly turned his attention to him. "You and the other recruits take a long look at the Priest. Locked away and left alone he will wonder how his treachery will be repaid, I am sure he will pray fanatically to his God for deliverance. And thereby make the same mistake that the Templar made. Have you decided what that was Mr. Spencer?"

Jerry sat frozen in fear that he, like Bodien, had been discovered.

Abelard shook his head in a show of mock disappointment. "No answer yet, Mr. Spencer? Perhaps it will come to you tonight."

His face erupted in a display of yellowed teeth, his closest imitation of a smile.

After Bodien was led away, Abelard addressed the group again.

"We could have eliminated Bodien without going to the trouble of bringing him here. Some poison in the warm milk the Sister brings him each evening would have done quite nicely." His lips curled back again in just the flicker of a smile.

"I had two reasons for not choosing the simpler solution: First, to make him an example to any others who might entertain the idea of betraying us, and second, to answer the question I have asked several times already today."

For a moment, his eyes sought out Jerry again.

"Let me share with you the information Father Bodien and his friends in the Vatican were so anxious to have." Abelard's triumphant gaze swept around the room, leaving Jerry limp with relief.

"After he discovered the letter to Pope Clement, I personally started searching Templar records in London. In a notation by the keeper of the Priory House dated January 1306, I found a report that one Ricoldo Monte Crèche had arrived from Cypress and lodged there for several weeks before going on to Paris.

"I sent one of our men to Paris with instructions to search their National Archives for any records concerning this Priest. There, a member of our order directed him to a high public official who found the complete list of those Templar remanded to the secular arm by the church for execution. Ricoldo Monte Crèche's name was among them. It recorded he was burned a month to the day after the Grand Master's execution.

"Our operative believed he had reached a dead end until on impulse he asked if a record existed of the prison where Ricoldo was held. To his surprise, one did and more, Ricoldo's exact cell number.

"The ancient building has been preserved and converted to a museum containing a large collection of medieval artifacts. Our agent went immediately to the building and inspected Ricoldo's cell, and this is what he found."

At Abelard's nod, his bodyguards unrolled a large banner and held it up before the group.

"Behold the sign of the stone!" he said, pointing to the banner.

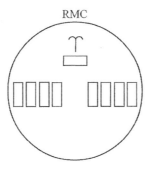

On it was drawn a large circle. Within the circle were eight oblong boxes arranged in groups of four lying to either side of twelve o'clock on the circle. At that position, a single box separated the quartets of boxes. Above the box was a drawing of the engraving on the stone depicted in Beaujeu's letter to Clement. And just outside the circle, at twelve o'clock, were the letters *RMC*.

"This," Abelard said, "is an exact reproduction of the drawing our man found amongst the graffiti scratched on the wall of Ricoldo's cell.

"As we leave..." Everyone rose as Abelard's bodyguards rolled up the banner and helped the ancient man to his feet. "Be encouraged by this, yet another confirmation of the stone's existence. I feel certain Ricoldo's drawing is a crude map and, in time,

will lead us to the stone's location. In the meantime, be patient."
He nodded to Neisen, who managed a slight smile. "And one last
thing."

Jerry felt the power of Abelard's presence as he, with a slight
gesture, drew him and the other recruits forward, his great bulk
looming over them, as they formed a semicircle around him.

"Will you join us in our service to The Brotherhood without
any reservations?" he asked as he searched each man's face.

"I will," each answered in turn.

"And you?" Jerry realized Abelard was looking at him and waiting for him to make the pledge.

"I will," he said softly.

God help me, he thought.

CHAPTER 22

THAT EVENING AFTER AN early dinner, Abelard dismissed Jerry and the other recruits to their rooms. "It's been a long day," he said, "and a stressful night is coming." He flashed an approximation of a smile. "While we make preparations get some rest gentlemen. Reflect on your pledge and await our summons."

While we make preparations ... preparations for what? Jerry closed his eyes, his mind a whirl of ill-defined and overlapping images and thoughts -the Gullah Henry, the vulture-like thing sliding from the shadows, Bodien, the pledge.

Jerry was startled awake by a knock on the door. One of Stiediger's men was there. "I've been sent to collect you and the others," he said in a heavily accented voice. "Drs. Abelard, Neisen and Stiediger will meet you on the boat."

They pulled away from Haig Point into Calibogue Sound with Henry at the helm of Stiediger's sports fisherman. As it picked up speed, its wake flashed silver in the moonlight. Through the cabin windows, Jerry could see the lights of Sea Pines Plantation twinkling dimly all the way out to the point where the sound kissed the Atlantic.

"We should be at Bloody Point in a few minutes," Abelard said. "Henry assures me it's an excellent place for night fishing. He says we will go a mile or so into the Atlantic then turn back and begin laying a chum line. With the tide coming in, it should draw some big ones to our bait."

Jerry looked across the cabin where Stiediger and Neisen sat and saw them exchange knowing glances. What seemed an after-thought remark by Abelard this afternoon now came back to Jerry as a witch's cauldron filled with ominous possibilities. *If you agree to join us, you will seal your vows tonight.*

All seemed anxious to join and quickly expressed willingness to make whatever vow was required. Like the others, he had seen vow taking as a mere formality, a quaint rite of passage, borrowed from a time long ago. But now?

Now he saw fear written on their faces. *They probably see it on mine as well,* he thought. They know now there is no turning back, that the vows are serious with a deadly price to pay if they are broken. Proof lay sprawled at their feet where Father Henrì Bodien lay bound and gagged.

The opulent stateroom of polished woods, chrome and leather in Jerry's fevered imagination had become a medieval torture chamber. As in a dream, he heard Henry announce they were passing Bloody Point and would soon be ready to turn about and begin laying down the chum line.

"De guts be ready in de stern," he said looking over his shoulder at Stiediger.

"Right." He motioned toward the rear of the boat. "Get to the stern. Abelard's bodyguards moved away from the hatch and took up their positions. "Begin dipping out the chum when Henry gives the word," he ordered.

Across the cabin, Jerry saw Stiediger move to a locker and remove a large rod and reel. He stripped line from the reel and fed it through the rod's eyelets. From a nearby cabinet, he retrieved a huge stainless steel hook, swivel, and several feet of steel leader.

Panic pounded on the door of his mind as he glanced at the other recruits. All were watching in morbid fascination as the German tied the hook and leader together, attached the rig to the line, and took a seat near where Bodien lay.

One of the recruits gasped as Stiediger began to dangle the hook's needle-sharp point before the Priest's terrified eyes.

His look of terror and the wild gyrations of his head as he tried to avoid the hook caused an immediate change in the German's manner. He was no longer the stiff and formal man Spencer had met that morning. Now he was like a wild animal toying with its prey, as he swung the hook closer and closer to the Priest's face.

Back and forth, back and forth, the hook's movement was hypnotic. Bodien's muffled scream suddenly broke the spell. The poor man had jerked his head away just as the hook brushed his nose, misjudged its position, and succeeded in driving it past its barb, deep into his cheek.

Jerry's head spun. As if on a merry-go-round, he whirled past Neisen who pointed and laughed at the Priest's shocked expression. Another turn and Abelard appeared, sitting toad-like on a chair, his eyes empty of feeling, watching as Bodien struggled helplessly.

The room turned full circle and Stiediger reappeared tightening, then releasing, the tension on the fishing line. Bodien tried to scream through his gag as the hook dug deeper and deeper into his cheek with each click of the reel.

"Careful, Eric," Abelard said, with an easy casualness usually reserved for dinner conversation, "Henri will need all his strength for the battle." He held out his hand to Stiediger. "Pass me some pliers from your tackle box, and then be kind enough to get me a damp cloth."

Stiediger laid down the rod, pulled a pair of pliers from a drawer, handed them to Abelard, and then went to the head for a towel.

"Mr. Spencer." Abelard motioned toward a newspaper beside him on the seat. "Please pass that paper to me. We wouldn't want Bodien bleeding all over the carpet of our host's lovely boat."

His hand trembled as he passed the paper to Abelard who acknowledged his nervousness by saying, "the path of progress, dear boy, is sprinkled with blood," as he adjusted the paper under the Priest's head. "I believe the Bible says 'without the shedding of blood, there is no remission of sin' or some such drivel."

He managed a little chuckle as he took the pliers, bent and grasped the hook's curve and with one quick jerk tore it free, along with a small patch of Bodien's skin.

The Priest was choking as he tried to scream through the gag.

"There, there Bodien." Abelard patted the Priest gently on the head. "There's no need for this," he said, pulling the gag from his mouth. "At this hour we're quite alone out here on the water. No one but God can hear you."

Bodien gasped as he turned his bloodied face away from his tormentor.

His grimace of pain reminded Jerry of Abelard's lurid description this afternoon of the torture the Templar endured.

Abelard had become the black-robed inquisitor he had described torturing a man strapped to a wooden frame.

For a moment, he broke the nightmare's grip and looked at the other recruits. Their expressions told him the horrible vision was his alone just as Abelard turned and flashed him a yellow-toothed grin. Now, instead of pliers, he held a glowing poker in his hands!

The body of the poor man on the frame was a patchwork of seared and mutilated flesh, his stomach a seeping, red, raw mass, with his peeled back skin hanging apron-like across his groin. His terrified eyes bulged from their sockets as they watched his tormentor bring the poker nearer and nearer.

Abelard leaned over the helpless man. "Tell me," he said gently, "I cannot ease your pain unless you tell me."

"I have confessed everything!" the man whimpered. "I've worshiped the devil, eaten the flesh of children. I have done everything you say. Please, have mercy. Free me from the pain. Let me die. No more . . . no more," he begged as his words dissolved into gasping sobs.

"You have made a full confession and asked for absolution, my son. In the name of the blessed Virgin, I give it," Abelard said as he laughed and brought the poker closer to his eyes. "I will release you and dispatch you to Paradise, but first you must tell me. Where is the stone?"

"The religious carry a heavy burden." Jerry remembered Abelard's cryptic remark that morning. *"They must hide their greed under a veneer of piety."*

After Bodien gave his report that afternoon, Abelard explained what he had meant. "The religious labor under the burden of pretense," he explained. "Pope Clement was far more interested in discovering the stone's whereabouts than rooting out heresy.

"Proving the Templar guilty of heresy would lead to the confiscation of their wealth, but the Pope knew it would flow directly into Philip's treasury and be of no profit to the church. Enrichment of the French treasury was hardly a reason for him to sanction torture unless . . . "Abelard smiled knowingly as he paused for effect. "Unless he could use the search for heretics as religious cover for his effort to find something of far greater importance."

"The stone," the recruits replied almost in unison.

"The stone," Abelard echoed.

Henry switched off the motors. "Mr. Shark be a'comin," he called.

Jerry felt bile rise in his throat at the sight of Bodien lying bloody and whimpering on the cabin floor as Stiediger and Neisen, like pit bulls, looked at Abelard for the command to attack.

"What are you going to do?" Though tied on the cabin floor, Bodien managed to turn his head and look at Abelard.

"You'll know soon enough." Abelard motioned to a bodyguard who jerked Bodien to his feet. "In the meantime, there's no need for you to be uncomfortable. Take him to the stern," he ordered.

Through the cabin's glass hatch, Jerry watched them push Bodien into the fighting chair.

"As I said," Abelard turned and faced the recruits, "one of the main reasons I chose not to dispatch Bodien in Rome was that I thought he would make a good object lesson for you young men."

He paused and looked at Jerry again before he continued.

"Several times today I have asked Mr. Spencer a question that he has yet to answer. Let me repeat it for the final time. What mistake did our brothers, the Templar, make that led to their downfall? It is important that each of you knows so that none make it again.

"I have arranged a unique departure for Bodien to demonstrate their mistake if you will be good enough to follow me to the stern."

"Henry, turn on the aft spotlight, and then join us," Stiediger said as he picked up the rod and reel and exited the cabin behind Abelard and the others.

Jerry saw Bodien handcuffed to the fighting chair. Abelard's bodyguards had just finished removing all the Priest's clothes except for his underwear.

"We must leave the the good Father a little dignity." Abelard patted Bodien's bony shoulder, then took several steps back and looked down at the helpless man and asked, "Are you really a man of prayer Bodien?"

Except for his cry of pain when the hook was jabbed into his cheek, the Priest had said almost nothing since his confrontation with Abelard earlier in the day. It had been eerie watching him walk zombie-like onto the boat between the guards, seemingly resigned to whatever fate was coming.

He looked up at Abelard, the pain from the wound on his cheek still reflected in his eyes. "Yes, I pray," he said softly.

"I know you say your Hail Marys, but do you make your prayers personal? Do you ever ask your God to do something and fully expect him to comply?"

Jerry was sure prayer had something to do with the question Abelard had asked him and the object lesson he planned to make of Bodien.

"Yes, I pray to God in a personal way." Bodien's face had already swollen terribly, and his speech was slurred. "I've even prayed for all of you." For a moment his pain-filled eyes looked directly into Jerry's as if seeing something none of the others could see.

He can't know who I am! I would be suffering the same fate if they found out. Fear mingled with shame as Jerry turned his eyes away, regretting he could not have answered Abelard's question as had Bodien. *I've never had the faith to believe as Bodien does ... or Ruth.*

Jerry remembered the evening on Lovers Leap when he kissed Ruth for the first time and told her of his struggle to believe. Then, it was some jungle native he sensed could come to faith in Christ so naturally; now it was Bodien, who held so tightly to his faith he could even pray for his tormentors in the face of death. How he envied them. How he wanted that something that made their faith possible.

"Well, knowing you're praying for me is a comfort," Abelard replied sarcastically to the helpless Priest, "but are you praying for yourself right now?"

"I've prayed for courage to bear my cross."

"But have you prayed for deliverance from it?"

"Yes," Bodien answered weakly.

Jerry realized the last few hours had taken an awful toll on Bodien's strength. His words slurred more and more as Abelard continued to goad.

"Like my Savior in the garden," he whispered, more to himself than to Abelard and the others.

"As when He said, 'let this cup pass from me'?" Abelard leaned forward and turned an ear to Bodien's swollen lips. "Tell me Priest, has the cup been taken away? Have you been delivered by your God?" Abelard turned from Bodien and faced Jerry and the other recruits. "Tell me gentleman, has God delivered him?"

With one voice all answered, "No."

Turning again to Bodien, Abelard asked, "Wouldn't you like to ask him to deliver you right now?" Abelard laid a hand on

Bodien's shoulder again and pointed toward the stern of the boat where the spotlight painted a narrow ribbon of light across the calm water. "You really should, you know. Do you see the slick on the water?"

Bodien did not answer.

Jerry could see the oily sheen made by the chum reflecting in the light as it trailed out behind the boat before disappearing into the darkness.

"The chum line," Abelard said. "Five gallons of beef blood trailing from the Atlantic to this spot."

Everyone's eyes were on the ribbon of light. Watching. Waiting.

"Mister Shark!"

The Gullah's cry hit Jerry like a clenched fist. The nausea he felt at seeing Bodien's cheek impaled returned as he braced against the gunnels of the boat praying the shadows would hide the horror he knew was on his face.

He thought he was prepared to see Bodien murdered. Since this afternoon when he saw him led away, everything pointed to it. Now, with sickening certainty, he knew he and the other recruits would play a part. He knew something stronger than a simple oath must bind them to The Brotherhood and accomplices to murder would be a tie none of them could break. But to murder a Priest! Jerry ground his teeth together and willed himself not to vomit.

"Why don't we bow our heads right now, Bodien, and let you offer a last prayer before Stiediger baits his hook?" Abelard's voice was heavy with mockery as Stiediger again dangled the large hook before Bodien, who closed his eyes as it brushed his forehead.

"Look! He is praying." Abelard lowered his voice to a stage whisper. "Just like the Templar all those centuries ago. They prayed for deliverance from the rack and the flames; now Bodien prays for deliverance from the terrors of the deep.

"What was the Templar's mistake? What led to their downfall?" He looked directly at Jerry and obviously expected an immediate answer.

"They believed God would save them," he heard himself finally mumble.

"Exactly!" Point made, Abelard almost shouted. "Like all the religious, they nursed on the teat of an illusion. They believed God was near and cared for them, when in fact he had long since deserted this planet for other worlds."

He swatted a moth drawn to the light, then crushed it in his hand. "He cares no more for us than I do this moth," he said, tossing it into Bodien's lap.

Jerry saw the Priest's lips were moving.

"He's praying, but no one is listening." Abelard's voice was acidic with sarcasm.

He turned again and faced the recruits. "We of The Brotherhood have learned from the Templar's mistakes. We are realists. God has left us here to make this world a heaven or hell. He will not help us to remake it. The work is ours to do, and we shall accomplish it with the aid of the stone. Then we will get what is due us—both the power and the glory."

"Mr. Shark be here," Henry hollered, as he pointed down the pathway of light.

Jerry saw a wake break the calm surface of the sound and move straight toward them.

"Throw over a big piece of bait," Stiediger barked at Henry who immediately reached into a box at the stern and pulled out a whole dressed chicken. He tossed it into the water as more wakes appeared behind the boat.

The wakes paused for a moment just before reaching the chicken. Then there was an explosion of snapping jaws and thrashing tails as six or more monster sharks fought for the choice tidbit.

"I see our guests have arrived." Abelard motioned to his bodyguards who reached down, unlocked Bodien's handcuff, and pulled him to his feet.

"Get your rod, Stiediger," Abelard ordered as the guards led the Priest to the railing at the stern.

"Now, gentlemen, it's your turn to help." Abelard motioned to Jerry and the others to gather around him. "Give them the hook."

Stiediger quickly stripped off some line and handed the hook to one of the men as the bodyguards forced Bodien's body forward against the rail.

"The rest of you, take hold of the hook," Abelard ordered. "It is time to seal your vows."

The recruits threw frantic glances at each other.

"Now!" he commanded.

Shaking hands reached and took hold of the hook in any way they could. One grasped the first one's hand, another a wrist, and still another a forearm.

"You too, Mr. Spencer," Abelard commanded.

Jerry glanced at Neisen who, with a nod, confirmed The Brotherhood.

Abelard reached and grasped the arm of the recruit holding the hook. "Put the point of the hook on the skin between his shoulder blades just here."

To Jerry it seemed Abelard's voice was coming from far away and that he had become an observer rather than a participant in the horrible act. However, he knew he was no mere spectator.

In his newly entered world of subterfuge and conflicting values, Jerry tried to persuade himself the greater good sometimes outweighed the means of its accomplishment, yet he knew, like the other recruits, he could never wipe Bodien's innocent blood from his hands.

"On my command push the hook completely through his skin," Abelard ordered, then, rubbing his hands together, laughed manically and shouted, "Are you still praying, Priest?"

Pushed as Bodien was against the rail, Jerry could not see his face or his lips moving in prayer, but he could feel himself and the others trembling. *God forgive me*, he prayed, just as Abelard gave The Brotherhood.

"Now," he shouted, "push!"

Spencer tried to will himself out of his body, to insulate himself from the crime being committed, but he could not. They all jerked, driving the hook deep into Bodien's flesh.

He screamed, then screamed again as the point was pulled completely through the fold of skin, and blood began to flow.

"Any last words, Priest? A final blessing for us poor sinners perhaps?"

Again, he didn't reply to Abelard's goading.

"Very well," Abelard said, "push him overboard. Let's see if the sacrament of his flesh will be accepted."

The two bodyguards grabbed the helpless man by the ankles, lifted his feet off the deck, and then dropped him head first into the water behind the boat.

"Start the motors, Henry. Go ahead slow," Stiediger ordered.

Stiediger let out line on the helpless priest as the boat began to slowly inch forward and he futilely grasped for its gunnel.

When the boat had moved ahead twenty or thirty more yards, Stiediger put the reel in gear and tightened the line. Bodien screamed again as the hook pulled open the wound and a ribbon of red formed on the surface behind him.

Suddenly, wakes came out of the darkness from three directions and glided toward the Priest.

"Pray, Bodien, pray," Abelard shouted as Neisen laughed and Stiediger braced for a strike.

It was not long in coming. There was a churning of the water around the helpless man, a momentary calm then...

"The sharks are coming up under him," Abelard shouted over Neisen's laughter. "Get ready Stiediger."

"Oh, dear God...no...no," Bodien cried out helplessly.

Jerry would never forget Bodien's piercing scream or his own nausea as he turned away from the gory sight. Then silently, though of little faith, Jerry prayed for this man of great faith who, only hours before, believed he was above suspicion.

A last shrill cry, so loud it seemed to be tearing the Priest's vocal chords from his throat, interrupted his prayer. Then silence... then, a clicking sound.

Jerry opened his eyes and looked. Stiediger had put his reel in free spool and set the clicker. One of the sharks had locked the hapless man in its jaws, dived, and was taking out line. A spreading red film marked the place where Bodien had struggled with the beast.

Click...click...click...clickclickclickclick. Line peeled from the reel in a blur as the shark continued to sound. Faster, faster.

Suddenly the clicking stopped.

"The shark's mouthing the bait," Stiediger said with a chuckle just as the clicker sprang to life again, and the fish took off.

"Now he's feasting," Abelard squealed in sadistic delight.

For what seemed an eternity to Jerry, all eyes were on the taut line descending down into the depths of the sound.

Then again, there was a pause.

"Now," Abelard shouted. "Set the hook!"

At Abelard's order, Stiediger flipped the reel in gear and came back hard on the rod. It almost doubled as the star drag sang.

"He's on," Stiediger yelled, as the line peeled off the reel. "He's going to take all of it," he said, just before the line snapped.

"Let him enjoy his prize," Abelard said as he turned to go back into the cabin.

Jerry and the other recruits watched as Bodien's bloody signature on the surface yielded to the pull of the outgoing tide and drifted toward the Atlantic.

CHAPTER 23

CONNER MILLS WAS WORRIED. It had been two days since the conference at Hilton Head had ended, and still there was no word from either Melchisedec or Spencer. He was almost sure there had been no breach in Spencer's cover. *Almost.*

Melchisedec was another matter. He had not seemed alarmed when Mills told him Neisen had a duplicate set of the pictures. Since several besides himself were assigned by the Vatican to investigate The Brotherhood, he felt confident the pictures could have reached Neisen in any number of ways.

Yet the gnawing in Mills' gut wouldn't go away.

Dr. Henrì Bodien, *nom de guerre* Melchisedec, as curator of the Vatican Archives, was one of several Priests selected by the Pope to assess the dangers, if any, posed by The Brotherhood. Since only the Pontiff knew the identity of those charged with this surveillance, any one of them could have taken the pictures and passed them on. All Bodien said he knew was that he had received his copies in an envelope secured by the Pope's own seal. Since he did not know the photographer, he saw no way the pictures were traceable back to him.

It was not long after Mills' first contact with Bodien that he learned the Vatican had known of The Brotherhood's existence for many years. But even they had little concrete information about the group, just vague rumors suggesting it might represent a challenge to the true faith.

Until Bodien came to the attention of the Pope, there had been no opportunity to infiltrate the organization. Other than names of some of its members, there had been no useful information garnered except for one name: Dr. Francis Abelard, an Oxford professor of anthropology.

Bodien, a recent graduate of the Sorbonne in that specialty, had descended from a long line of French clerics, his uncle having been an intimate of the Holy Father. From Bishop of Cherbourg, the uncle had been elevated to cardinal and eventually appointed Papal Nuncio to England.

Shortly after his graduation, Bodien received an invitation for a private audience with the Pope. Mills assumed the Vatican's influence brought the young man to Oxford to study under Abelard. However, his own brilliance, tenacity, and guile gained him access to The Brotherhood's inner circle. Mills thought it ironic that Bodien's taking of Holy Orders had been exactly what both the Pope and Abelard had wished for him.

Mills also suspected that only after the gravity of the threat posed by The Brotherhood became clear did the Pope order Bodien to pass the pictures and other information on to the Agency. He was sure the Vatican hoped the CIA would join them in confronting a threat far greater than first imagined.

So far, Bodien's information, while intriguing, had been sketchy at best. His case file contained a patchwork of references to ancient texts and speculation about the existence of a mysterious stone, although there was no hard evidence such an object existed, much less posed a threat. However, the fact that powerful men such as Erik Stiediger believed it did and were devoting their fortunes to finding it, were sobering.

There was another consideration. Mills knew the Vatican usually played its hand close to its vest and never overacted, so its desire to team up with the agency to investigate the organization was enough to make him take the threat even more seriously.

Mills opened the Melchisedec file and flipped through its contents. The introductory letter from the cleric and the pictures had arrived at CIA headquarters by registered mail about two years before with all correspondence since then routed through Mills' secure email site.

There had been no contact with Bodien since last summer's dig at St. Jean until duplicates of the pictures he sent the agency were found by Spencer in Neisen's office. Hard on the heels of Mills' warning Bodein's cover might be blown, came another startling piece of information from the Priest.

"Enclosed," he wrote, "is a copy of a letter sent by Francis Abelard to all in The Brotherhood's leadership.

"I assume Abelard is sending us a translation of an ancient text called the Lamech Fragment as a means of whetting our appetites for even more revelations when we meet in Hilton Head, South Carolina, during Christmas."

It certainly had done that, Mills thought as he continued browsing Bodien's report. It said Abelard's letter to his leadership also referenced an ancient cuneiform tablet called the Gilgamesh Epic. A rumor had circulated in archaeological circles for years that its discoverer had deliberately broken off a corner of the tablet for reasons unknown. What made this information intriguing to Mills was that Abelard disclosed its discoverer was a member of their order and that the corner was broken off because it contained information regarding the fabled mark of Cain referenced in Genesis – information its discoverer considered vital to The Brotherhood's continuing search for the key to reclaiming Paradise.

Mills read again the translation of the Lamech fragment Bodien included in his report. Like other intelligence he had received about the stone, it simply added another layer to a mystery that seemed beyond solving.

"Hear oh sons of Lamech," it began:

Give heed to the words of your father. The stone of Cain our father is your gift…(Undecipherable)…birthright. By it [through it?] the vaults of knowledge…(Undecipherable)… hidden by him who cast you forth…are opened…(Undecipherable)…by your power and the stone you will return and claim what is yours by right, when time rolls round again.

Pointless to speculate about its meaning, Mills thought. Of more immediate concern was the last paragraph of an email he received from Melchisedec just days before he left for the conference of The Brotherhood's leaders in South Carolina. As he read it again, his feeling of foreboding grew.

"I have made an exciting discovery in the archives," it said. "Abelard is also on the trail of something. Everything may come together when we meet at Hilton Head. I will inform you of the outcome of the meeting as soon as I return to Rome. Melchisedec."

So far, Mills had not heard a word from his agents—either one of them.

Chapter 24

Ruth Starling should have been happy, in spite of the cold teeth of a Blue Norther that had come screaming out of the panhandle into central Texas several hours ago. As she walked across campus toward the Student Union Building, the gale bit into her face and ears. The cold, however, was nothing compared to the chill in Jerry's voice when, after several days of trying, she finally reached him at his dorm.

"Jerry, I have something important I must talk to you about. I've been calling you ever since I got back. I've checked by your carrel in the library, looked for you in the cafeteria ... everywhere. I've been so worried."

She hoped her tone conveyed both sincerity and her feeling of urgency.

"I know," He replied.

There was a long pause, and Ruth knew immediately that someone else, probably his own parents, had given him the news ahead of her. She wanted to be the one to share with him one of the most important decisions of her life, but his tone of voice told her she was too late.

She remembered her promise on the night he first kissed her five years ago in Cameron Park, a promise she knew he must feel she had broken.

"I'm sorry," she said, knowing he would understand her meaning, "But I still need to see you."

"Where and when," he snapped, betraying deep hurt..

"In the student lounge, right after your last class?" She waited. "Is that okay?"

For a moment, she thought he'd hung up.

"Fine," he finally said curtly.

"Jerry…" She had no idea what she would have said had she not heard the click on the other end of the line.

Ruth made her decision while home for the holidays, and had wanted to call and tell Jerry about it immediately. However, knowing she could not reach him at Hilton Head, she decided to wait until she returned to school. Today was her first opportunity to give him the news.

Last Sunday she had been hard-pressed to explain her actions, even to her parents. As they had sat around the old wooden table in their kitchen she tried to express her feeling of *rightness* about the decision she had made that evening in response to the visiting missionary's message.

Based on a text taken from Matthew 24:14, where Jesus said, "This gospel of the kingdom will be preached in the whole world as a testimony to all nations, and then the end will come," the missionary's message was entitled The Last Tribe.

His sermon, meant to challenge young people to consider missionary service as a calling for their lives, had certainly challenged Ruth, especially at the conclusion when he said, "some young person here might be God's choice to share His message with the last people on earth never to have heard about Christ before He returns."

"I can't explain it exactly," Ruth said, as she searched her parents' faces for understanding, "but do you remember the book in the church library that captivated me when I was a little girl?"

"You mean the one you were always bringing home, the one with all those pictures?" her mother asked.

"Yes, that's the one. But it wasn't all the pictures, just a particular one, of an Amazonian Shaman that fascinated me. He seemed to be looking right at me with his sad eyes. I could almost hear him saying, 'Please, help us,' every time I opened the book."

"Don't you think that might have been just your childish imagination working overtime?" her father asked.

"It might have been. All I know is that picture planted a thought in my mind that grew into a conviction I had to make a commitment to mission service. Mom and Dad I just had to," Her eyes teared as they sought her parents' assurance and understanding. "I have to have a part in sharing God's word with people like the Shaman who have never heard about Jesus." She wiped her eyes, adding, "my decision has made me both sad and happy. Sad because it may change forever the plans Jerry and I were making, but happy knowing I'm doing what God wants me to do."

"Well, honey, I…" Her father's voice trailed away as if he suddenly had no words to express his emotions.

However, Diana filled in for Frank's loss of words saying, "Ruth, your decision sounds to me a lot like having a baby—pain just before it arrives, but a lot of joy after."

They all laughed, but Ruth saw, beneath her father's smile, tears rolling down his cheeks.

Ruth reached the main entrance to the Student Union Center, opened the door, and paused as she entered the foyer, letting the warm air from inside sweep over her. She drew a deep breath and stuffed her hands deep into the pockets of her jacket then slowly climbed the stairs to the second floor.

Each of the quiet, cozy rooms along the hallway contained an overstuffed sofa, a desk, and a chair. Since coming to Evangel University nearly four years ago these comfortable surroundings had been her and Jerry's favorite place for conversation. Jerry had laughingly called it their "cheap date place." It was here, one rainy night of her Freshman year, that Jerry had formally stated the obvious - that he loved and wanted to marry her as soon as she graduated.

The most constant refrain of Jerry's relationship with Ruth over the years was his promise to be there always for her ... and he had been.

My rock of Gibraltar on whose strength and love I know I can depend, she thought, peeking into several rooms as she passed.

Humanly speaking, Jerry seemed perfect for her, possessing some of the same qualities she most admired in her dad— patience, ambition, dependability, and most of all, love . Though undeclared for years, he had shown his love for her in countless ways, ever since her first day in kindergarten.

Jerry's so much like my dad, she had often thought, *except for one thing.* That one thing, like a passing cloud that for a moment blocks the sun, cast a shadow on their conversation each time the subject of Jerry's relationship with Christ was mentioned. Though his lack of a clear-cut commitment to Christ was troubling, Ruth could see his doubts gradually dissolving and knew in her heart that it was only a matter of time before he accepted Christ as his Lord and Savior.

Yes, humanly speaking Jerry was enough, and more. In her heart she knew she could never love anyone more than him. *Except God.* It was that realization that led her to respond to the preacher's invitation last Sunday. Until then God's will for her life was a mystery, but one that was solved as she made her decision and for the first time saw clearly the path her life would take.

As she searched each room and alcove for Jerry, she prayed silently that God would guide the conversation, that Jerry would understand and that her commitment made last Sunday would not dull his love for her.

She finally spotted Jerry in one of the rooms and slipped in quietly. He sat, seemingly lost in thought, staring out a window at the cold, gray day outside.

"I saw you walking over from the dorm." He did not turn his head when he spoke. "All we had…our plans…the places we were going to see together. I thought…" He seemed to be talking to himself rather than to her. Then his voice fell silent, as if retreating to some secret place for shelter from the hurt he knew her words would bring.

This is not the right time for explanations, she thought as she walked over to the couch, laid her hand gently on his shoulder and joined him in gazing silently through the window.

"Ruthie," he finally said softly, never taking his eyes away from the scene outside the window.

"Yes?" She choked back tears at his mention of her pet name and the sadness in his voice.

"Do you remember how afraid you were your first day at school?" He did not give her time to answer. "Do you remember my promise?"

"Yes." Ruth waited, unable to bring herself to speak as the curtain of silence descended again.

Finally, Jerry broke the quiet. "It was that book wasn't it? God used it and the dream when you were in the hospital to prepare your heart."

Her grip on his shoulder tightened and she felt buoyed by Jerry's spiritual insight that was both surprising and encouraging. *Of course, he was right,* she realized. Her decision was not made in a vacuum. The book, her fall, her strange dreams while in the coma, had all played a part.

"And yes, I'm hurt and disappointed—all the negative feelings you'd expect a man to feel when his dreams fall apart," Jerry spoke in a voice that seemed drained of emotion. He turned away from the window and looked into her eyes. "Do you remember the day I brought up the subject of us getting married as soon as I finished graduate school?"

"And you started apologizing for not having the money to buy me an engagement ring," Ruth answered, a small smile cracking the layer of sadness on her face.

"I'll never forget what you said. Do you remember?"

"That it didn't matter, that I loved you as much without a ring as with one."

"What else?"

"Jerry, let's not go…"

"When I tried to go on, you put a finger on my lips and said we could talk about it later. It was as if thinking about marriage made you uncomfortable."

Did I somehow know even then? Aloud, she said, "I'm sorry. I didn't realize—"

"I know you didn't, Ruthie." He reached out, broke down his wall of reserve, and put his arm around her. "But from that moment, things between us were somehow different. I couldn't put my finger on what it was, but when Mother phoned and told me of your plans—"

"I wanted to be the one to tell you." For a moment, she wished Jerry would simply take her in his arms, kiss away her sadness, and tell her nothing had changed between them. But he didn't. And it had.

"Since we had never even discussed being missionaries, I knew your plans didn't include me."

"They can't, Jerry. Not unless God calls you like He called me."

His eyes took on a far-away look as he removed his arm and cupped her face in his hands. In her eyes, he saw the frightened little girl mounting the school bus steps for the first time and her joy at seeing him there waiting to take her hand. He saw her on Gypsy, her ponytail bobbing, as she rode her little mare across a field on a summer day. He glimpsed her, deadly pale and locked in a coma from which the doctors feared she might not awaken. *But, I prayed,* he thought, *oh, how I prayed!* And God had healed her.

Even now, he wondered why that prayer and God's answer to it by healing Ruth had not been enough to lead him to trust Him with his own life. Nevertheless, for some reason yet unknown to him, it had not, and he still tottered on the knife-edge of complete surrender to Christ.

He was not ashamed of the tears he knew Ruth saw in his eyes.

"Darling, that's the misery of it all," he said. "God's plan for your life doesn't include me."

As he dropped his hands dejectedly, she took one and squeezed.

"Since Mother called, he said, I've prayed God would call me like he has you; prayed if he did I would take it as a sign I could trust him with my whole life. But I love you too much to pretend. He hasn't called me, Ruth, at least not like you and there is something holding me back ..." He paused as if wishing to say more but restraining himself. "... holding me back from making the kind of decision you've made." He squeezed her hand, wanting her to understand, then tried to close the door on the subject, saying "If God is leading me at all, I'm afraid it's in a far different direction."

A far different direction. Ruth thought he sounded as if he had found God's purpose for his life, but that he wished it were something else. He was leaving something unsaid, something important. For the first time since she had known Jerry she sensed a "no trespassing" sign on part of his life. Reaching up she drew him close, trying to muffle her sobs on his shoulder.

"Nothing has really changed, Ruthie. No matter where we go or what we do we still will love each other, right?"

She nodded her head against his shoulder. "But God even more?"

"Right. But never forget my promise," he said, stroking her hair tenderly.

"You'll always be there for me?"

"Always," he whispered.

CHAPTER 25

JERRY TREKKED THROUGH THE gathering gloom from the Student Union Building directly to the library, found an empty study carrel reserved for graduate students, and flipped on the computer. He shrugged out of his parka and tried to collect his thoughts. Two days secreted away with The Brotherhood had left him an emotional wreck and during the nearly two weeks since, he had struggled as to how best to communicate the nightmare he witnessed. Hellish images kept flashing through his mind as he tried at last to compose his email to Mills. He stared at the screen and willed himself to focus.

The image of Ruth's face, tear-stained, flashed into his mind, but he pushed it away. He had no time for personal regrets. If he were brutally honest with himself, he would have to admit her decision had made his own easier. Love, marriage, children— these had no place where his involvement with The Brotherhood and Mills were leading him. He had no time to reflect on what might have been. He had delayed too long already. Now he had to alert the Agency to what had occurred at the meeting while the horror of it was still fresh.

He shook himself and typed in Mills' secure email address.

Over a thousand miles away, Mills heard the programmed chime announcing an email had arrived on his scrambled, secure server.

Short almost to the point of terseness, the message stirred the hairs on the back of his neck. As a seasoned operative, Mills could almost smell the fear that permeated every word...

"The threat we feared is real and growing, not just to America but to the whole world. Pieces of the puzzle are coming together. They know the agency and the Vatican are on to them. They are capable of anything. Repeat anything—even murder!"

The Vatican? Did that mean Melchisedec?

The gnawing in his gut deepened. He needed a full report from Spencer ASAP.

Jerry stared at the words *your message has been sent* emblazoned across the screen. He knew it had been inadequate, but there was no way he could have communicated the horror in an email. He checked around him. The study area seemed deserted, although he could just make out a dim light in a carrel on the other side of the room.

He turned back to the computer and opened a blank Word document, gathered himself, settled into the chair, and began to type.

Two Years Later

"Sorry, Mr. Spencer, to be giving such late notice, but Dr. Neisen said it was an emergency and that you would understand."

"Thanks for the heads-up, Greta," Jerry replied to the disembodied voice on the other end of the line, "I do. Did he mark in his teaching outlines where he ended his last lecture?"

"Yes, he said he had highlighted where to begin. The outlines for each class are on his desk in his office. I believe you have a key?"

Jerry noticed the usual edge to Greta's voice. A lowly graduate assistant had been granted what twenty years of faithful service had not earned for her—the doctor's trust. Jerry sensed this had been the hurt festering in Greta's mind ever since he and Neisen returned from Hilton Head two years before. Without knowing any of the terrible details of that horrific weekend, she seemed to realize that a bond had developed between them, one with which she could not compete.

Even more reason to be careful, he thought.

"You'll be gone before I come by?" he asked.

"Unless you plan to be here within thirty minutes."

"Can't make it that soon," Jerry replied, relieved he would have the privacy he needed. "Thanks again, Greta," he said. "I'll take care of everything."

The dial tone told him she had moved on to better things.

An emergency. He could think of only one thing that would drag Neisen away from his classes so near the end of a semester—Brotherhood business.

Jerry recalled, just before they left Hilton Head, he heard Abelard tell Neisen he would want him with him when and if he recovered the stone.

Since then there had been only an occasional email from the old man, all essentially saying the same thing: The search for the stone progressed, its whereabouts nearing discovery.

During the last several months, Neisen's demeanor told Jerry these infrequent updates had done little to overcome the professor's growing discouragement over Abelard's apparent lack of success. His morale, however, took a decided upturn when Neisen received a letter from Ruth three weeks ago.

Jerry was not surprised when Neisen told him. She had mentioned her intention to be in touch with the professor in her last letter. What did surprise him was the boost receiving it had given to Neisen's morale.

He glanced at the new picture of Ruth on the shelf above his desk and smiled. A missionary pilot who delivered supplies to the village where she worked had taken it digitally and emailed it to him about ten days before he got her last letter. How time had flown. He glanced again at the smiling face looking back at him. So much had happened since that winter afternoon two years ago when their lives turned in such different directions.

Ruth graduated from Evangel University and immediately enrolled for classes at the Institute of Linguistics in Houston. She finished thirty-nine hours of specialized training in subjects ranging from phonetics to phonology, and several weeks later received an appointment for service with Last Tribe Missions as a Bible translator.

Jerry remembered how happy she had been the day news came of her appointment. She was bubbling with excitement when she called him from Houston.

"Isn't it wonderful the way God confirms things?" she exclaimed.

He acknowledged that it was, thinking fleetingly of his own *calling*.

She had spent the past summer in orientation in Maracaibo, Venezuela, before arriving at her mission station in late August. During that time, she received an introduction to the culture of the Yanoako, the people with whom she would be working for the next several years.

In her letters, she said the tribe had little contact with the outside world until the late fifties. As hunter-gatherers, they once ranged over a large area bordering Venezuela, Brazil, and Peru where, until recently, timber, farming, and mining interests had almost free rein to engage in what euphemistically was called the *development* of Yanoako tribal territories.

In reaction to the coming of outsiders, they retreated farther and farther into the jungle until finally the three countries awakened to the threat this development posed to the tribe's survival and passed laws to protect what was left of their traditional hunting lands. Now, the tribe numbered fewer than twenty thousand, scattered in small villages along several tributaries of the Amazon River.

Ruth's assignment was to work in a village near the junction of the Orinoco and Amazon rivers. Other than a battery operated short-wave radio, her only contact with the outside world would be via a monthly supply plane during the dry season or a trip of several days by canoe to the nearest trading post.

When Neisen announced he had received Ruth's letter, Jerry had a good idea what it concerned. In her last message to him, she said her ability to speak Spanish had been a godsend since the tribe's Shaman also spoke a little. She was able to explain to him the meaning of the words found in John 3:16: "For God so loved the world, that He gave his only begotten Son, that whoever believes in Him should not perish but have everlasting life." As a result, he had become a follower of Jesus and immediately began sharing his newfound faith with the villagers, receiving what Ruth described as "an unexpected response." She didn't tell him what it was except to say she thought Dr. Neisen might have insights that might help her understand what was going on.

One thing for sure—whatever she told him raised his spirits dramatically.

Jerry looked at his watch. *Almost four-thirty.* By the time he got to Neisen's office, Greta should be gone. He put several blank CDs in his laptop case, zipped it, and walked out the door.

He was glad the sun was still shining. Late night visits to Neisen's office were the rule when he was in town but even then, he sometimes had the silly fear Greta was watching from the shadows as he copied Neisen's emails. At other times, he imagined she followed him back to the dorm and watched through the window as he sent them to Mills in Washington.

The other night he had dreamed the shark-ravaged body of Bodien was standing beside his bed, warning him to be careful, when the door burst open and Greta came in with Stiediger's bodyguards.

"Take him away," she yelled, pointing a quivering finger at him.

No sooner had she screamed than he found himself splashing about in the dark waters of Calibogue Sound, then awakened, trembling and in a cold sweat, more aware than ever of the terrible price he would pay if The Brotherhood ever discovered his treachery.

It took him only a few minutes to cross the campus and reach Neisen's office. Just as he thought, the door to the outer office was unlocked, and Greta was long gone. Using his key, he entered Neisen's inner sanctum. Scattered about on his desk was a week's supply of teaching outlines where Greta had tossed them.

He powered up Neisen's computer, highlighted "Saved Mails", and immediately found the message from Abelard. As always, it was short and to the point.

"Come to London immediately. A room is reserved in your name at the Viscount Hotel. Await my call there. I believe I have found it."

After copying it, he cued up Neisen's sent mail file and scanned it until he found the latest one addressed to Abelard. Composed about three weeks before, two words in the body of the message made Jerry's breath catch in his throat. The name leaped off the page: *Ruth Starling*!

Chapter 26

London

As Neisen reached for his briefcase beside the bed, he indulged himself in a moment of well-deserved self-congratulations. The letter from Ruth Starling, his former student, confirmed it.

His initial contact with Starling had been brief—a single course on basic anthropology she had taken under him during her last semester at Evangel. When Neisen mentioned her letter to Spencer, he said they had dated when she was a student and still corresponded, saying, she planned to become a missionary. Checking his records, he found he had given her an A. *Attractive and smart,* he thought when he found Ruth's picture in the yearbook.

He believed the search for the stone was almost over and that his prospects had never been brighter. During the flight to London, that conviction grew and with it, the feeling, at the proper time, he would become Abelard's successor as leader of The Brotherhood.

Age will soon force the old goat to pass his mantle to another, Neisen, always the skillful opportunist, realized as he reached for his brief-case, *And since I am the only member of The Brotherhood asked to join him for the stone's recovery that must mean...*He felt his face tingle with an adrenaline rush ... *that Abelard's chosen me as his heir apparent.*

Unzipping his briefcase, he removed the letter, hardly able to believe the fortunate circumstances that brought it into his hands. If he believed in divine providence, this would have confirmed it.

While the prospect of finding the stone was exciting, a major question remained: What exactly was its use in remaking the world? Neisen felt sure Starling's letter would put The Brotherhood on the trail to finding the answer. He lay down on the wide bed, fluffed up the pillows behind his head, and reread Starling's remarkable message:

Dear Dr. Neisen:

As an undergraduate of Evangel University, I took your introductory anthropology course. I am now working for an evangelical Bible society translating scripture into the language of the Yanoako people here in Venezuela.

Because of my work, several members of the tribe have already become Christians. Though I am happy about these conversions, certain events surrounding them have caused me concern. I am writing hoping you can help me understand what might be triggering these strange experiences. Explaining some of their traditions may help you get a grasp on what I am dealing with.

The Yanoako people believe that long ago the tribe lived deep within the jungle in an area that is now off limits (taboo) to them. Timber cutting, agricultural development and mining have reduced their hunting range each year and driven them deeper into the jungle and nearer to this area they say they cannot enter.

They believe one day their god (gods) will give them permission to enter this taboo area and that there they will discover their reason for their existence. From time to time, anticipating that day, they take what they call "time walks." They burn their villages. Then, taking only what they can carry, they march into the jungle, stopping only to sleep or hunt. They may walk for days, believing by doing this they can reverse time and return to a time when the forest was untouched by outsiders and game was plentiful.

Which brings me to the main point of this letter, Dr. Neisen. As members of the tribe profess belief in Christ, they report having a dream— all, the same dream! With each new convert comes another report of this experience. They tell me that, in the dream, Jesus tells them that after this year's rainy season they are to burn their huts for the last time and go into the taboo territory.

But it seems the dream involves more than Jesus giving them permission to enter the forbidden land. It includes a shared vision of two great "trees of stone" (obelisks?) that mark its border. On these monoliths they describe an engraving that as best as I can tell looks something like this.

Even more amazing, Dr. Neisen, I recognize this symbol! As a child, I read a book entitled *Beyond the Far Horizon* and a particular picture fascinated me. Under it was a caption that read: "Yanoako Shaman sitting on his jaguar bench." Carved into the front of that bench was the same design the converts say they see in their dreams!

The village Shaman has been one of my most attentive pupils and since becoming a Christian, doubly so. When I arrived, he was the first to welcome me by saying he knew I would be coming. When I asked how he knew he replied, "I saw you coming when I journeyed with the jaguar and when I looked into the Stone of Memory." The meaning of "journeyed with the jaguar" eludes me, but the Shaman showed me this Stone of Memory, which he says he uses to help remember the tribe's history.

I asked Akhu (that is the name of the Shaman) if he had a jaguar bench. He said he did, but had put it away shortly after I came to the village since, in his words, "it is no longer necessary." According to him, it is very old, handed down from Shaman to Shaman as long as anyone can remember. I asked him to show it to me and there, carved on its front, was the design I had seen in the picture. When I asked what it meant, he said "it was a mystery none will understand until the tribe enters the taboo land."

Dr. Neisen, I hope you can shed light on what is behind these strange occurrences. The rainy season is almost upon us, and travel then will be almost impossible. I am sending this letter by a man who is leaving in a little while to go to the trading post down river. Enclosed is the address of the trading post. They will hold my letters until I can retrieve them after the rainy season. I hope to hear from you by then concerning any insights you might have into these strange happenings.

Sincerely,

Ruth Starling

The light in the room seemed to dim as Neisen's finger hovered above the drawing Ruth had made in her letter. There was no doubt—it was the same as the one Bodien had discovered in the Vatican archives.

The ringing of the phone broke Neisen's reverie. Reaching, he lifted it from its cradle. "Dr. Abelard," he said excitedly to the presence on the other end of the line.

"The Temple Church, tonight, eleven o'clock. Enter by way of the West Portico. The Norman Doorway will be open. Don't be late."

Neisen held the phone pressed to his ear for nearly a full minute before buzzing announced that Abelard had hung up.

Neisen checked his watch. *Ten fifteen.* He needed to get on the road. From the nightstand, he retrieved a copy of *A Tourist Guide to London*, glad he had the foresight to buy the book. *Damn Abelard*, he thought, muttering in disgust over the man's arrogance. He thumbed through the book's index. *Temple Church.* He found the address and quickly jotted down the directions on a note pad. He knew the tendency of London cabbies to wander about the rabbit-warren lanes of the city with unsuspecting tourists, turning five-pound hops with directions into fifteen-pound journeys without them.

He glanced at his notes. *The church lies just off Fleet Street. Take Waterloo Road to Waterloo Bridge into Lancaster Place, turn left on Strand then right on Mitra Court. The church is on the right.*

Confident he could direct the cabbie, he took the elevator to the lobby. A minute later, he was out the front door, had hailed a cab, and was off into the damp London night. The thunderstorm that raked the city earlier had retreated, leaving behind a misty reminder of its passing.

He was lucky. The driver was a Londoner rather than a Middle Eastern transplant and knew his way around the city. In less than fifteen minutes, the cab stopped on Mitra Court across from Temple Church.

"Shall I wait for you, guv?" the cabbie asked as Neisen reached for his wallet.

"I have no idea how long I'll be."

"A little off the beaten track," the driver observed. "It may be hard to get another cab later."

"Good thinking," Neisen replied, glancing at his watch. *Ten fifty.* "I may be gone for quite a while," he said matter-of-factly. "Just leave the meter running."

"You can count on it, guv," the driver said as Neisen stepped from the cab and walked through the mist toward the church.

He ascended the steps to the West Porch and stood for a moment before the Norman Doorway with its great oak door. Although he would not have been able to find it again without the guidebook, the place was familiar to him. Here he had made his vows to The Brotherhood. In years that followed, he had never doubted the sincerity of his commitment or the rightness of The Brotherhood's cause.

Assured he was alone, he took hold of the massive iron handle, pushed, and was rewarded by a low moaning sound as the door swung inward to reveal the most ancient part of the building.

The Round Church was finished in 1185 and consecrated that same year by Patriarch Heraclias, Bishop of Jerusalem. Modeled after the Church of the Holy Sepulcher in Jerusalem, it served not only for religious services but also as the site for the Knights Templar's most secret rituals. Neisen remembered Abelard had explained this on the night they inducted him into The Brotherhood.

Neisen turned and pushed against the door again. It swung closed with a dull metallic thud that echoed through the vaulted chamber. In the flickering light of a single large candle in the middle of the room, Neisen could see eight floor crypts with lids of Purbeck marble, carved with the effigies of their Templar occupants.

The crypts were arranged along an east-west axis in groups of four, each group parallel with the other. At his initiation into The Brotherhood, Neisen remembered Abelard had escorted him to each of the crypts and symbolically introduced him to the men entombed there. Among them were the Earl of Pembroke, Pembroke's two sons, William and Gilbert, William Marshall, Geoffrey de Mandeville, and the Earl of Essex. At one time, he knew all the names by heart.

"They were all great men," Abelard had said as he gestured toward the crypts. "Seek to match their courage and loyalty to their fraternity, but never forget even the loyal and courageous can be mistaken. Their presence here testifies to their mistake."

Neisen remembered Abelard had walked over and stood beside the Plowmen's monument marking the demarcation between the Round and Middle Church.

"Come here," he said as he looked up and pointed to the six Gothic arches of the Middle Church that swept majestically upward until lost in the shadows above. "Even the architecture testifies to their mistake."

Abelard had taken him by the arm and led him back into the Round Church where he stopped between the quartets of crypts. Neisen remembered what he said then as if it was yesterday.

"These noble men spent their lives looking to heaven for guidance. But Holy Mother Church ..." Abelard lifted his arms and turned full circle as if trying to embrace the edifice, "By its betrayal of their order, unwittingly became our teacher. It taught us not to rely on some transcendent God up there." Abelard pointed a bony finger toward the arches soaring above. "Our brothers' experience taught us that rather than looking to God for help we must look within ourselves for the wisdom to set the world right again."

"Neisen. Over here." It was only a whisper, but the voice was unmistakable.

"Dr. Abelard?" Neisen's voice reached into the darkness beyond the candle's dim glow, probing for a reply.

A pinpoint of light suddenly appeared in the northwest quadrant of the Round Church. He stepped carefully to avoid tripping over crypts as he made his way toward the light. He had almost reached it when it began moving downward. For a moment, it disappeared entirely, leaving Neisen to grope his way along in the darkness.

Stop! Primitive intuition kicked in screaming the word in his mind. He stopped; then, carefully, extending his right foot, he felt for the floor. *Nothing!*

Recalling his earlier visit to the church, he suddenly knew where he was. His foot hovered just above the stairway leading down to the penitential cell.

Abelard had described it on the night of his initiation. "Less than five feet long, with a ceiling so low it's impossible to stand upright."

Neisen asked its purpose.

"To punish those knights who disobeyed their master or broke the rules of the order," Abelard said.

Considering Bodien's grisly death, Neisen reckoned Abelard's punishment for disloyalty had been much less humane than that imposed by their predecessors. Shaking off the thought, he looked down into the stairwell. It was not completely dark at the bottom. A soft glow leaked through a slit in a partially open door.

"Don't just stand there." A voice from beyond the door drifted up the stairway. "Come down here, there's someone I want you to meet."

Abelard... and there is someone with him? But who? Not pausing to reflect further, Neisen found the handrail and felt his way down the short flight of stairs.

At the bottom of the stairwell was a door, hardly high enough for a child to enter, a thin line of light from the room beyond highlighting the crack between it and the jam. Bending down, he opened it and looked inside.

Abelard, his face awash in the golden glow of a candle, sat in a tiny room no bigger than a closet with his back braced against a wall. On the floor beside him, Neisen saw what appeared to be the drawing he had shown the council at Hilton Head.

He could not imagine what the old man had been doing before he arrived until he noticed flecks of white dust covering his dark suit.

"I've broken the seals." Abelard did not look away from the candle as he spoke. "I brought pry bars so we can remove the lid."

What seals? What lid? Neisen's appetite for answers was growing ferocious.

"Come and sit beside me Frederick, there's someone I want you to meet."

Neisen stooped and crawled into the tiny cell. He scanned the cramped space, but it was empty except for the crouching bulk of his former professor.

Abelard's voice took on a ghostly quaver. "I don't believe you've met Walter le Bachelor."

Chapter 27

"He died here, you know, less than a year after De Molay and his friend Ricoldo were executed. They were the only ones…" Abelard's voice trailed away, lost somewhere between the candle's flame and the shadows, flirting with the bleached stonewalls of the cell.

"The only ones?" Neisen's voice was swallowed by the gloom of the tiny cell.

"I found the record you know," Abelard continued. "It was there all the time, right before my eyes—in the journal of the Priory House."

"What was there?"

"The record of their meeting. They arrived in London from opposite directions only two days apart."

"Who?"

"Ricoldo and Walter le Bachelor, the Grand Preceptor of Ireland," Abelard replied as if that would explain everything. His hands moved nervously about on his lap as if feeling for something. "He died here, you know."

"I believe you told me that." Neisen was trying hard to mask his frustration with the old man's verbal meanderings.

"Yes, I did, didn't I? His spirit is still here." He raised his pale hands and let his stubby fingers pluck at invisible strings in the air. "He hovers about, condemned to remain here until…"

His long pauses were grating on Neisen's nerves. "Until when?"

"Until the time rolls round again, of course." Some of the old man's fire crept back into his voice. "They both knew the end was near. Both men had lost faith in the church and knew what others in their order dared not admit, even to themselves."

"And that was?"

"That the Templar's' dream was just that—an unrealistic fantasy. They realized king and pope alike had violated their order's spiritual calling by reducing it to nothing but a military and monetary prop for the Crusades. And at the end to a convenient scapegoat for their own failures.

"You will remember from our session at Hilton Head," Abelard continued, again in his familiar professorial tone, "the treasuries of France, England, and Rome were virtually empty, so naturally, the greedy eyes of King Philip and Clement focused on the Templar's treasury and its vast land holdings. Ricoldo and Bachelor knew it was only a matter of time until both were lost; that their Grand Master, De Molay, was hopelessly naive to think by returning to France and personally defending the order he could salvage its reputation.

"However, one treasure was of greater value than all the other Templar possessions combined—the stone, the so-called mark of Cain. Determined it must not fall into the hands of either pope or king, they decided to hide it away until the day men of wisdom arose who could unlock its secrets and rightly use its powers. Then, as we learned from the scroll that accompanied the stone and as the Gilgamesh epic predicted, time would roll round again, the ancient prophecies would be fulfilled, and Paradise restored."

"He died here you know." Abelard's mind appeared to drift again.

"Yes," Neisen replied softly, a frisson of fear skittering down his spine. Was Abelard losing his mind?

"The Pope and King Philip were sure Ricoldo and Bachelor knew the stone's whereabouts.

Imprisonment and torture awaited Ricoldo after he crossed the channel to join De Molay in France. However, neither could loosen his tongue, so after his execution, Holy Mother Church imprisoned Bachelor here in an effort to starve him into revealing its location.

"Right here," Abelard raised his arms again and let them define the narrow dimensions of the room. "In this small space, where he could neither lie nor stand, our friend slowly starved to death.

"Turn and look behind you." Abelard said abruptly.

As Neisen did, he noticed a small slit in the stone just at eye level. Looking through it, he could see the large candle still burning brightly in the center of the Round Church.

"From time to time I come here to visit with Bachelor," Abelard continued, "and try to imagine what it must have been like to slowly starve to death to the accompaniment of the 'Pegasus,' 'Agnus Dei,' and the echo of voices repeating their 'Pater Nosters' and 'Hail Marys.'

Just think of it, Frederick."

Neisen could almost feel Abelard's hot eyes glaring as he spoke.

"Holy men read aloud from their Bibles and preached their homilies only feet from a man suffering the agonies of the damned!

"When I come here, it reminds me those in the so-called 'holy calling' have no real cures for the ills of society. On the contrary, they are responsible for many of them. All their pious talk about faith, hope, and love, and that claptrap about a coming Kingdom of God is just that—claptrap! Dying by starvation must be pure hell, but to die having to listen to such bilge must have been hell twice heated over!

"I've sat in this position until my limbs are numb." Abelard rubbed his legs then tried to rise. "If you will be so good as to help me…"

Neisen stood as best he could, then took Abelard's arm and helped him to his feet.

"There, that's better," he said as he stepped through the door into the stairwell. "Please take the candle and lead. I will try to follow as quickly as these old bones will let me."

When they reached the top of the stairs, Abelard laid his hand on Neisen's shoulder. "One moment, Frederick," he said as Neisen turned to face him.

"You know, we're not here just to remember the past but to recover a great treasure."

He's finally getting to the point. "I know," he muttered, feeling his heart beat faster.

"Since I believe we are nearing the end of our search for the stone, will you please permit an old man a last indulgence? I think you'll find it interesting."

Not waiting for a reply, he took the candle from Neisen, turned, and walked down the long isle of the Middle Church. Just before reaching the entrance to the narthex, he turned to his right and moved along the wall to the southeast corner. There he stopped and lifted his candle to reveal still another floor crypt on whose marble lid another effigy had been carved.

"As you can see, Frederick, the likeness carved on this lid is not that of a knight but a bishop," Abelard said.

"Whose crypt is it?"

"It is the burial vault of the Patriarch Heraclias, Bishop of Jerusalem. He is said to have dedicated this church in eleven eighty-five. The effigy on the vault implies a church prelate is buried here but that is not the case because church records show that in eighteen hundred and ten the tomb was reopened and the bones of a child were found at the feet of a man's skeleton.

"It is believed the child was, in all probability, William Plantagenet, the infant son of Henry III, said to have been buried in the church in twelve fifty-six. Would you agree it's more reasonable to assume a child might be buried with his father than with a bishop?"

"Yes, but I'm not sure I understand where all this is leading," Neisen said.

"If you'll be patient for another moment, I think you will," Abelard replied. "Our friend Heraclias shared a morbid fear with the ancient Egyptian pharaohs."

"And that was?"

"The desecration of his grave. So, through influence at the highest levels, he arranged during the church's construction to have his burial vault placed beneath its stone floor with the entrance hinged in such a way only someone knowing exactly which stones to press could open it.

"Templar documents reveal this project was so secret the church commissioned artisans from Persia to construct the chamber with their ingenious system of interlocking hinges. During this phase of church construction only the Persians worked on the site, then, when their work was completed, promptly returned home."

"So you're saying the stone and scroll are buried with the Bishop?"

"Exactly," Abelard replied, "I'm sure of it. But here is where the tale really gets interesting."

"More like convoluted, I'd say," Neisen observed.

"If you like," Abelard replied, " but the fact is, after the church was completed, the bishop commissioned an elaborate tomb for himself ... the one you see here."

"With no intention of occupying it?"

"Right on the mark," Abelard said.

"So let me see if I get the picture." Neisen paused a moment to untangle the threads of the story in his mind. "The bishop builds himself a secret tomb, and after the church is finished, he builds himself a visible one."

"That's right, my boy."

Neisen sensed Abelard's excitement mounting.

"But if the bishop dedicated the church in eleven eighty-five, he would certainly have been dead before Henry III's son was buried there in twelve fifty-six. Even allowing that kings might evict bishops and take their tombs, opening it and finding it empty would surely raise questions," Neisen observed.

"Not if only the inner circle of the Templar and their friars knew, and it goes without saying, death as the penalty for revealing the secret would tend to silence the talkative."

"You mean the only ones who witnessed the interment of the bishop, the king, and his son, were Templars?"

"That's correct," Abelard replied. "Only the Templars and friars attached to The Brotherhood here in London. By the way, I have examined the archives of the Priory House, and they reveal the same two friars witnessed the Templars' interment of both the bishop and the king."

Neisen could tell Abelard was relishing building toward the climax of his story.

"You're a bright man, Neisen," he said. "Would you care to guess the names of those two friars?"

The pieces of the puzzle suddenly came together in Neisen's mind.

"Ricoldo Monte Crèche and Walter le Bachelor?"

"Bravo!" Abelard was positively jubilant. "Their friendship was forged as young friars, and then sealed by the secret they shared. But I know their secret," Abelard announced triumphantly as he turned and began walking back toward the Round Church.

"But where…?" Neisen called out from behind him.

In his exuberance, Abelard strode as briskly as someone half his age. "Follow and I will show you," he said without as much as a backward glance.

CHAPTER 28

"IT'S RIGHT HERE." ABELARD fumbled for something inside his coat pocket, retrieved a sheet of paper, and carefully unfolded it. "Let's see if you can read it," he said, handing the paper to Neisen.

In less than a minute, they navigated the aisle of the cathedral and returned to the Round Church where the candle between the quartets of crypts still burned brightly. Neisen moved closer and held the paper to the light. He quickly recognized the same drawing Abelard had shown them at Hilton Head: a circle with a strange drawing above it and eight marks within the circle itself.

Suddenly it hit him—crypts! Standing in the center of the ancient structure, its meaning became obvious to Neisen. Ricoldo had drawn the floor plan of the church with two quartets of crypts in horizontal lines pointing east and west, divided by a central axis.

"Of course," Neisen whispered.

"As you can see," Abelard said, "our friend Father Ricoldo was thoughtful enough to draw the floor plan of Temple Church on the wall of his cell."

"And the marking he placed near the north wall?" Neisen asked.

"The same as that drawn by Beaujeu in his letter to Pope Clement," Abelard replied.

Class dismissed, Neisen thought as Abelard lifted the candle from its stand and set off toward the north wall of the church.

For a few moments, Neisen remained still, transfixed by Abelard's actions. The old man had reached the wall and stood before one of the tall, multi-colored stained glass windows that encircled the lower level of the church. Hundreds of prisms refracted the candlelight, flinging it in dancing bands of colors onto Abelard, the stone floor, walls, and vaulted ceiling.

Though Neisen put no stock in Bible stories, the scene of Moses at the Red Sea came to mind. The whirling kaleidoscope of color about the old man was the fabled pillar of fire and the long candlestick in his hand, the rod of God with which he parted the waters.

"Frederick, if you will kindly hurry." Abelard's voice broke the spell and erased the fanciful images.

Now we can get down to business, Neisen thought, as he walked over and joined him.

"Another crypt is here." Abelard pointed at the floor.

Neisen saw nothing but a rectangular piece of stone that appeared to be of about the same dimensions as the lids of the Knights' crypts. Beside the slab were two crowbars, a hammer, and a chisel. Chips of mortar lay scattered about. He could see a small crack between the lower edge of the stone and the floor. The broken seal explained the dust on Abelard's clothes.

Abelard put the candlestick down and picked up one of the crowbars. "If you don't mind, my boy, I could use some help," he said, nodding toward the other crowbar.

There were no markings on the stone. Neisen remembered *The Visitor's Guide to Temple Church* described it simply as a thirteenth century coffin lid.

Following Abelard's instructions, Neisen inserted his crowbar at the opposite end from where Abelard stood. At the old man's nod, they both pulled up on the bars and the stone began skidding slowly forward.

"During the centuries a legend has grown up surrounding this stone," Abelard wheezed as they inserted their bars and pulled again. This time the sound of stone grinding against stone rewarded their efforts as the lid slid forward several feet.

"According to legend this will be the lid for the crypt reserved for the Grand Master who will someday restore the Templars to their former glory. That day has come!" Abelard's voice was euphoric. "One last pull," he urged, "we're almost there."

Neisen looked at Abelard. The veins in his neck were bulging, his face ashen. "Dr. Abelard, don't you think you should rest a moment?"

How could I ever explain to the authorities the death of the world's leading anthropologist while grave robbing in Temple Church? The thought seized Neisen with momentary panic just as Abelard shouted.

"Heave man!"

This time the stone skidded completely aside, leaving only a dim outline of itself on the stone floor where it had rested undisturbed for centuries.

Though Neisen was not sure what he expected to see, he knew it was not this. The square, smooth-faced stones where the lid had rested were the same as the rest of the church's flooring.

"The Persian workers were skillful at constructing counterbalancing stone hinges." Abelard forced his aged body into a kneeling position as he spoke and was examining the flooring that had been under the stone. Finally, he stopped moving about and carefully dusted a particular block with his hands. "Look at this," he said as Neisen knelt beside him.

All Neisen could see was a small groove, no more than an inch long and a quarter-inch deep near the outer edge of a block.

"Would you say that mark is a natural imperfection or man-made?" Abelard asked.

"A stonecutter's chisel might have slipped," Neisen suggested. To get a better look, he moved to Abelard's right, then knelt again and began feeling along the surface of the floor.

He felt it before he saw it. Moving so the candlelight shone directly on the floor in front of him, he saw what it was. "Here's another mark," he said.

"And another," Abelard replied, pointing to another place on the floor.

"They're too uniform to be simply imperfections in the stone." Neisen observed.

"There's a design here somewhere." Abelard slowly stood to his feet and, for at least a minute, appeared deep in thought as he looked at the floor around him. "North, south, east, west..." he said, more to himself than to Neisen. "Let's have a look, just there."

He moved south of Neisen about eight stones' width from the north wall and pointed down. Neisen rose from his knees and joined him. In the candlelight, he saw it, just where Abelard seemed to believe it would be—a fourth groove.

"North, south, east, west," Abelard muttered again. "Let's try connecting the marks."

"If we connect them there can only be two possible designs," Neisen volunteered. With the toe of his shoe, he traced an imaginary line. First, from north to east, then east to south, to west, then back to north again. "A diamond shape," he said.

With his toe, he traced two new lines between the marks, the first from north to south, the other from east to west. "Now we have a cross," he observed. "One of two possible designs," he said with finality, "a diamond or a cross."

"Let's try the cross," Abelard said as he knelt down again where the two lines intersected.

Neisen watched with fascination as the old man began counting the stones. "One, two, three, four... One, two, three. These marks define an area four blocks from north to south and three from east to west," he said.

"And the significance of that?"

"If we allow twelve inches for each stone that would be thirty-six by forty-eight inches. Plenty of room for a small entrance. Let's see if we can find the combination."

Abelard pressed on the stone where the lines intersected. Nothing happened.

"Let's eliminate all the possibilities," he said, pressing each of the marked stones in order. Still, nothing.

"Try pressing several stones at the same time," Neisen suggested. Abelard nodded. Moving out from the intersection of the lines, they began pressing down on several stones at once. The only result was a growing feeling on Neisen's part that if the stones formed a hinged door there might not be time to find its key.

He looked at his watch. *Two o'clock.* Abelard said the custodians always arrived at five. That should have given them plenty of time to finish their business. But at this rate?

"Let's try putting ourselves in the place of the designers," Abelard said. "What if the Persians built a failsafe into the system, designed in such a way that one man acting alone couldn't open the crypt?"

"I'm not sure I follow," Neisen responded. "What difference would it make if it took two men rather than one to open it? I don't see—"

"All the difference in the world," Abelard interrupted him. "If it had to be opened by more than one, those opening it illegally would risk disclosure. I do not know what the penalty for desecrating the tomb of a bishop might have been, but being drawn and quartered comes to mind."

"So let's suppose you're right," Neisen said. "If two men were needed to open it, how would they do it?"

As if preferring the company of his own thoughts, Abelard dropped his head for a moment. "Their weight... Of course, that's it!" He did not attempt to hide his excitement. "Two men would have to apply their weight on different stones, at the same time."

"Okay," Neisen said, trying to follow. "Where would they stand?"

"I think they would have stood as far apart as possible."

He moved and planted his feet on the stone marking the northern point of the line. "You stand over there." Abelard pointed to the mark four blocks to the south. Neisen walked over and was about to step on the stone.

"Be ready to jump back," Abelard warned. "I have no idea how this thing may work," he said, just as Neisen cautiously put his feet on the other block.

For a moment, nothing happened. Then Neisen felt the ancient stones shudder as though suddenly awakened from a long sleep. From somewhere deep in the bowels of the church came the low, grinding sound of stone against stone. The west edge of the blocks began to slowly drop away as their east edge started to rise.

"Quick! Get off!" There was near panic in Abelard's voice.

"All clear," Neisen answered as he stepped quickly from the tilting blocks and joined Abelard at a safe distance.

"Somehow the underpinning for the floor is being withdrawn," Abelard said. "That's why one edge is falling and the other is rising."

The process continued until the east edge of the floor had tilted upward to about a forty-five degree angle. Then the whole slab began to slide backward; slowly at first, it gained momentum as the slab's weight exerted downward pressure. The process which began so slowly, ended quickly in a shower of dust as more than a thousand pounds of stone blocks slid with a grinding crash into the bowels of the building.

Neisen stood dumfounded, staring at the opening. Then, he looked across at his old mentor and grinned. "I don't guess we'll be closing the door when we leave," he said with a laugh.

Abelard completely missed the irony. "Ricoldo and Bachelor closed it," he said as he moved to the edge of the pit and looked down into the darkness.

Chapter 29

"This will be more helpful now." From somewhere Abelard produced a flashlight and shone it into the cavity. About a foot below the surface of the floor, Neisen could see stone steps leading downward. At the bottom, he made out what looked like a small antechamber similar to the one leading to the penitential cell.

Abelard let the light play on the portion of the entrance just below floor level. As it did, Neisen got some idea of what mechanical processes had been at work to cause the stone slab to disappear. By the use of an ingenious track, the sub- floor had pulled back. He could see its outer edge slightly recessed into the wall of the entrance opposite the steps.

On the other side, Neisen saw a slit. It was constructed at a forty-five degree angle with the floor and was slightly wider and deeper. Neisen realized, by standing on the right floor blocks, they had activated a mechanism causing the supporting floor to pull back. As it did the floor above began to tilt until it aligned with the slit, then ... away it slid, like launching a ship. *Amazing engineering*, Neisen could not help but marvel.

There was no time for him to search for the mechanism that accomplished this wonder since Abelard had already eased himself into the opening and begun shuffling down the short flight of stairs. The man amazed Neisen. He had appeared old when Neisen first met him nearly thirty years ago. He had to be near ninety and grossly overweight; however, his enthusiasm for the search was obviously overriding his physical limitations.

"No time to dawdle." With his next step, Abelard disappeared into the hole. "Come on, my boy," he called, "we're almost there."

Neisen retrieved the candle and followed down the steps. There were twelve of them. With some quick arithmetic, he figured about an eight-inch drop for each step meant they were about nine feet beneath the floor of the church.

Abelard had already moved from the stairwell to the anteroom beyond when Neisen reached the bottom of the stairs. "Come quickly!" he shouted.

Rushing into the room, Neisen found the old man standing before a recess cut into the far wall, the beam of his flashlight focused on a skull. More than a skull, he realized, as Abelard's light swept the recess; an entire skeleton with the tattered rags of what obviously had been a burial shroud clinging to its bones. On one bony finger, Neisen saw an ornate golden ring, and around the neck hung a large golden cross.

"Heraclias," Abelard whispered, as if speaking louder might awaken him.

"But where is the stone and scroll?"

Abelard shot the light around the tiny chamber. "They're not here."

"Not here! They've got to be here!" Neisen's voice grew frantic. If true, this would be a death sentence to The Brotherhood's dreams. They had worked so long, come so far and spilled so much blood through the centuries, it was unthinkable it would all end here—in an empty tomb!

"I tell you it's not here, Neisen." Abelard again let his light play about the small room.

"Empty…" Abelard's voice shook like that of the old man he was, as he leaned against the wall, and slowly slipped to the floor.

"Dr. Abelard!" Neisen set his candle aside, bent and retrieved the flashlight that had dropped from the professor's hand. He let its light play over the old man's crumpled body. Abelard's head drooped forward, his chin resting on his chest, but he was still breathing. His vacant eyes, however, told Neisen his teacher had retreated beyond the reach of any more disappointments.

He focused the light on the skeleton again. *The scroll and the stone must be here.* His mind raced. *It has to be!* He swept the room again with the flashlight. The walls of the tomb were bare plaster except for a few places where it had broken away to reveal the brick underneath. *If I were concealing something here and wanted it found someday by the right people, where would I hide it?* He looked at his watch again: *three forty-five.* He had to think!

He focused his light on the niche again. "The person I wanted to find the stone would have to be familiar with the sign," he muttered to himself. "Therefore, I would…what? Think!"

Suddenly it came to him. He would mark its hiding place with the sign. But the walls were bare.

He played the light again on the skeleton of Heraclius. The gold cross around the neck and the ornate ring on his finger shimmered in the light. *The ring!* The revelation, like sunrise, lit his mind. *The ring! Of course! It has to be!* A Bishop's ring was a plain gold band. Even from a distance, he could see this one had a design cut into its face.

The light trembled in his hand as he reached down and removed the ring from the skeletal finger. He gasped as he held it to the light. There, graven in its face – the sign! His heart pounded.

Ricoldo and Bachelor had put the ring on the dead man's finger to mark the hiding place!

Carefully, he pushed the bones aside and wiped away remnants of the shroud beneath them. The ledge was common brick and had not been plastered over. In the light, he saw slight indentations on several of the bricks. *They have been removed, and then replaced,* he realized.

He needed something with which to pry, and all Abelard's tools were on the floor of the chapel.

"I'll be right back," Neisen said, as he let his light fall again on Abelard's vacant face.

Bounding up the steps, he found the hammer and chisel then returned to the crypt where Abelard still sat slumped against the wall beside the candle.

A few strokes and Neisen had driven his chisel into a crack and pried loose one of the bricks. It was easy then to remove several others around it. For a moment, he let the beam of his flashlight play around the edges of the small opening, dreading to look inside for fear of the ultimate disappointment. When he finally mustered the courage to shine his light into the hole, he almost wept with relief.

Less than an arm's length away lay two objects. One stood on end and came to within six inches of the top of the hole, another smaller object nestled beside it.

"Abelard, I've found them!" he shouted, grasping the scroll and drawing it from its hiding place. He was so riveted on what he was doing he did not see Abelard lift his head. "A leather pouch...I can see it at the bottom of the hole. It's the stone! It's got to be." He reached his arm in and withdrew it. The prize at last in his hand, he turned and was startled to see Abelard had raised his head, his eyes following his every move. "Professor, I've found it!" Neisen shouted again.

Far back in Abelard's mind where his disappointment now resided, he heard Neisen's announcement. Like an adrenaline rush, it spiked his body with new strength and jerked him back to reality. "We must be going," he said, extending his hand.

Neisen grasped it and hauled the old man to his feet, amazed at his recuperative powers.

"The custodians…" Abelard muttered.

"I know." Neisen looked at his watch again. "It's four fifteen. They will be here in less than an hour."

"There's no time to close the crypt," Abelard said.

"No need." An idea of how to cover their tracks was already taking shape in Neisen's mind. "How did you get here?" he asked.

"One of the Brothers drove me. He's parked a block over."

"Good," Neisen looked at the candle. It had almost melted away. "There's just enough time. You stay here; the candle will last until I get back."

Abelard nodded as Neisen bounded up the stairs.

As he exited the west door of the church, he could see the cab still parked across the narrow lane. A street lamp silhouetted the shadowy form of the driver inside, his head tilted against the back of the seat. *Asleep*, Neisen realized, as he knocked lightly on the window. There was no response so Neisen knocked again more forcefully. This time the cabbie raised his head and looked about groggily before spotting Neisen standing by the window.

"Guv, is that you?" the man asked as he lowered the glass.

"Yes," Neisen replied, making a quick appraisal of the man: middle-aged, overweight, perhaps slightly drunk as evidenced by his bloodshot eyes and the half-empty bottle on the seat beside him.

"Where to, guv? The hotel?" The driver brushed back his hair and reached over the seat to open the back door.

"Not yet." Neisen tried to make his voice sound as relaxed as possible. "First, I need your help. The Temple Church there is undergoing major restoration." The cabbie regarded Neisen with dull eyes, nodding knowingly.

"In the process of the restoration renovators discovered a burial chamber beneath the building. My associate and I have been commissioned to examine the chamber and assess its archeological significance before work in the area can continue. I'm sure you appreciate how important it is that antiquities are preserved."

The cab driver nodded again.

"I'm afraid my colleague has injured his back or something. He cannot manage the stairs. He's a rather large man. Can you help me?"

"Maybe we should just call for an ambulance, eh? I'm not in the best…"

"There's an extra ten pounds in it for your trouble." Neisen took a large wad of bills from his pocket. "Of course, that would be in addition to a generous tip."

The cabbie's face lit up like neon as his eyes devoured the bills in Neisen's hand. "Why didn't you say so in the first place, guv?" He opened his door and started toward the church.

He followed Neisen through the west entrance just as he flipped on his flashlight.

"They're rewiring the building, and the power's been turned off. We've had to resort to candles and this flashlight," he said over his shoulder.

"No problem, guv. Lead on."

Neisen was glad he had the presence of mind to extinguish the large candle on his way out of the church. A few moments later, they reached the north wall. Stopping, he shone the beam of light into the hole. "The stairs to the vault are there," he said.

Drawn by the vision of a fat tip, the cabbie moved ahead of Neisen in the direction of the beam.

Neisen knew the workers would soon be arriving. He envisioned their gaping into the hole, descending the stairs, and finding the scattered bones. They would rush to a phone and call the police. But Neisen needed them to see it as more than simple vandalism – a robbery gone badly, a falling out among thieves. Anything to divert suspicion from the monumental importance of his discovery.

"I don't see no stairs." The driver's voice jerked Neisen's attention back to the immediate job at hand.

"There," he said, allowing his light to brush the upper edge of the stairwell. "My associate's down there."

The cabbie saw the opening and moved to peer over the edge into the inky darkness below. "If you could shine the light a little this way—"

"Right," Neisen purred behind him as he shoved the man over the lip of the hole.

The cabbie screamed as his body pitched forward, and his chin connected with the ledge opposite the stairs. The ancient church echoed with the crack of his neck, then the thud of dead flesh hitting stone at the bottom of the stairs…then…silence.

"Neisen? What the hell's happening?" Abelard's voice sounded far away and frightened. Looking down the stairwell Neisen could see the faint glow of the candle.

"I'm coming," he said as he made his way down the stairs, stepping over the cabbie's body, sprawled like a broken offering on the ancient stones.

Neisen did not need to feel for a pulse. The eyes stared at nothing. Turning, he watched Abelard haul himself to the stairwell entrance.

"I see helping to dispatch Bodien whetted your taste for blood." Abelard said as Neisen walked past him into the burial crypt.

Neisen felt the old man's eyes watching as he carefully replaced the bricks hiding the secret chamber, then removed the cross from the skeleton and scattered the bones about. Picking up the hammer and chisel, he wiped them clean of prints then returned to the stairwell where he pressed the cross into the cab driver's outstretched hand.

"Don't forget to wipe our prints off the candlesticks and the crowbars," Abelard reminded.

"I won't," Neisen said as he felt to make sure the ring was in his pocket.

"*Petty Thief Dies While Vandalizing Church*," Abelard quipped. "I can see the headlines now. You surprise me, Frederick. I'm impressed with your ingenuity."

"Let's get out of here. We can check out our find when we get to the hotel. You will be coming with me, I presume?"

"Yes, of course," Abelard said.

Because of Abelard's frail condition it took them longer to clear the church and walk the two blocks to his car than Neisen would have liked. As they walked, he could tell the old man had not fully recovered from his seizure because he continued to rub his forehead and mutter about a headache.

"A good breakfast will put you right," Neisen said, straining to hear the singsong whine of police sirens.

By the time they reached the car, the gray half-light in the east signaled the approach of morning.

"Viscount Hotel," Abelard said to the driver, who had slipped from behind the wheel and opened the door for them.

Abelard lay back, panting on the way back to the hotel. The stimulant of discovery had worn off and he remained silent until they reached Neisen's suite.

"Would you like me to order you some breakfast?" He did not wait for Abelard to reply before dialing room service.

"A small glass of orange juice and some dry toast would be nice," Abelard said absently.

Breakfast ordered, Neisen returned to their business. "Let's take a look at our treasure."

"Neisen untied the leather thongs of the pouch and retrieved the stone.

It was larger than he expected. About three inches long and perhaps half as wide, it was set in a gold border on which had been engraved the intertwining tails of snakes. A raised design was graven on the stone like that drawn by Beaujeu and scratched by Father Ricoldo on the wall of his cell.

Holding it up to the light, Neisen stared in awe as rainbow bands of luminescence washed over its surface. As he gazed into it, he felt he was staring through a window on the universe as galaxies of stars danced and sparkled against the blackness of its depths. Mesmerized, he watched as they coalesced into a single whirlpool of light that suddenly broke free of the stone, spun into the room, and drew him down ... down.

"Dear God!" Neisen's cry of alarm erupted like hot lava.

Never had he invoked the name of God in such a penitent way. In the past, he had always cloaked any reference to the Deity in cynicism. But now...

"Give it to me!" Abelard's command was an invisible hand, jerking him back to reality through a spinning nebula of stars. "Now!" Abelard bellowed.

Neisen felt his mind break free of the stone's attraction as he placed it in his teacher's trembling hand.

Abelard clutched it tightly for several moments as though savoring its possession, then opened his fingers.

"Oh, my God!"

The expression Neisen saw on the old man's face gave the word "terror" a new and even more terrible meaning.

"Abelard!" Neisen shouted.

There was no response. He grasped Abelard's rigid arm, but except for the erratic rise and fall of his chest, there was no movement.

Is it my imagination, or is the light in the room growing dimmer? Neisen looked about for some point of reference. From the sitting area, he could see into the bedroom. Lit moments ago, it was now bathed in darkness as a malignant vapor crept into the sitting room. Although the sun should be up, no light shone through the windows. He looked across the room at Abelard – frozen in place, head down, eyes fixed on the stone. The darkness was swallowing him as well.

Again, Neisen tried to rouse him, but his efforts proved futile. *Wherever he is, he can't hear me.*

The darkness was almost total now. The lighter shadow that was Abelard, now barely distinguishable from the pitch-blackness around him.

Reaching, Neisen frantically snatched the stone from Abelard's hand, and still trembling, raised the old man's chin from his chest.

"Oh, God!" It was Neisen now, who screamed in terror.

Abelard's eyes! God in heaven ... Abelard's eyes! His eyes, like the stone, were projecting a maelstrom of fiery iridescence, windows through which Neisen dared not look, but did, then cried out as giant hands reached from the darkness, gathered up galaxies of stars, and flung them into the swelling whirlpool of light.

The waiter's knock at the door propelled him back to his familiar world. Reaching down, he felt beside his chair for the leather bag and quickly replaced the stone.

Later he tried to convince himself lack of sleep, coupled with an overactive imagination, was responsible for a hallucination, choosing to ignore the fact that the moment he plunged the stone into the darkness of the bag, the light returned.

Abelard, however, did not see it. All signs of life were gone from his eyes and the blank fixed stare of a catatonic had replaced it.

"Call a doctor quickly," Neisen shouted to the startled waiter as he opened the door, "I think my friend has suffered a stroke."

CHAPTER 30

IN THE WINTER DARKNESS, the Aleuts struggled to winch a large crab trap from the shallow bay bordering Rat Island. As the trap broke the surface, a light as bright as the sun rose over neighboring Semichi Island and sped across the narrow gulf toward the startled men. There was no time to understand its source, only a millisecond for the thought to register that their trap was full of crabs.

In another millisecond, they were beyond the need to understand anything as the cyclonic blast of wind arrived, tore their small boat from its mooring and sent it to the bottom of the bay.

All eyes were on the door as the President and CIA Director Conner Mills came into the room. The President's face was ashen as he walked to the conference table, found his place, and sank wearily into a chair. The members of the National Security Council followed suit.

"Thank you for getting here so quickly," the President said. His voice quivered slightly, and for a moment, he fumbled with the folder before him as if having difficulty opening it.

From across the table the Chairman of the Joint Chiefs eyed the President thoughtfully, and what he saw worried him. Normally ramrod straight, he slumped forward in his chair, his eyes fixed on the folder. Whatever it was he had to tell them, the Chairman knew must be bad.

The President finally lifted his eyes. "Gentlemen," he said, "at ten o'clock this morning, we received the following communication by e-mail. The CIA believes its route came via more than a dozen intermediate points around the world, making its origin almost impossible to trace. The message speaks for itself," he said as he retrieved a paper from the folder and began to read.

"By now, you are aware that at nine-thirty Washington time today a thermonuclear incident occurred at your ballistic base on Semichi Island in the Aleutians.

"If our demands are not met, this is only the first of many such incidents. Be advised, we have accessed the arming, targeting, and detonation codes of all long and intermediate-range missiles in the nuclear arsenals of the United States, Great Britain, France, Germany, Israel, and the Russian Federation."

"They wouldn't dare!" The Chairman of the Joint Chiefs hit the table with his fist and half rose out of his chair. "It's not possible!"

A babble of voices erupted as heads swiveled toward CIA Director Mills who sat stone -faced and silent at the far end of the table.

When the emotional storm subsided, the President continued reading.

"Should you seek to retaliate by launching your missiles at any group or nation suspected of issuing this ultimatum, be advised they have been retargeted to fall on your own cities. Also, all missiles have been reprogrammed to detonate on their launching pads if any effort is made to alter their targeting programs."

Outrage and disbelief gradually gave way to reflection as some at the table remembered that only a few years ago Mills had warned them of this very possibility.

"Gentlemen," the President said, "please. There is more."

The room grew quiet as he continued in a calm, almost detached voice. Several members exchanged glances, unsure how to interpret their Chief's demeanor.

"'Low-yield nuclear devices have also been placed in the major cities of your respective countries. Should you not comply with our demands within one hundred and twenty days, we are prepared to destroy a city for each day of delay.'"

"What in God's name do they want?" The Chairman of the Joint Chiefs banged his fist on the table again.

"Let the President finish," Mills said.

"Our preliminary demands are these," the President continued. "One. That you declare Israel illegitimate and recognize the Palestine Liberation Organization as the sole legal representative of the people of Palestine. Two. That you nullify all treaties and other trade agreements with the so-called nation of Israel. Three. That you withdraw all troops, planes, and ships from forward staging areas in the Middle East, Japan, and Korea. Four. That all defense treaties with Japan, Korea, and Formosa be declared null and void.

"Again, these demands must be carried out in one hundred and twenty days. Other demands reflective of the new geopolitical realities will follow shortly. Seeking to negotiate will be futile."

The President put down the paper as a funereal silence settled over the room, and everyone retreated into their own thoughts.

The Secretary of Defense finally spoke. "How's the ultimatum signed?"

"It isn't," the President replied.

The Chairman of the Joint Chiefs exploded again. "Then who in hell are we supposed to deal with? I don't see—"

"General, you don't have to see!" the President shot back. "The realities of the problem exist whether you see them or not. As for dealing with anyone, it seems they've made it clear they don't intend to deal."

"We at State have certainly been left out of the loop." Secretary of State Ellen Jorganson shot a sharp glance at the CIA director.

Mills ignored her. "It's obvious who's behind this. We have known for fifteen years such a possibility existed."

"Then why didn't NSA and your agency do something?" The Secretary of the Treasury's tone conveyed the frustration they all felt as he swiveled in his chair and faced Mills.

"You of all people should know the answer to that." Mills felt the sting of the treasury secretary's remark and did not try to hide it. "Congress has appropriated less and less to the agency each year since the end of the cold war. They have been blind to the danger."

"Conner, you said it's obvious who's behind the ultimatum," the President said. "Explain to the others what you mean."

"The demands are a dead giveaway," Mills replied. "For instance, who is galled over our protection of Formosa?"

"China," several muttered.

"And who wants sole rights to Palestine?"

"The Palestinians of course," Jorganson answered, punctuating her impatience with the rhythmic tapping of her pen on the polished tabletop.

Again, Mills ignored her. "By the way, who wants to see every pro-Western Arab leader toppled?" Not waiting for a reply, he answered his own question. "The Muslim fundamentalists," he said. "That is the picture as I see it. I'm sure NSA will confirm our conclusions."

Mills looked down the table at Herb Farnsworth, Director of the National Security Agency.

"I'll confirm Connor's assessment and then some," Farnsworth said, taking Mills' cue. "We know the Chinese have wanted to break out of their Eastern box for centuries. They see themselves as having been cheated and exploited by the West since their first contact with Marco Polo."

"And their territorial ambitions extend beyond Formosa, the Kurils, and that small strip bordering Russia," the President said.

"Absolutely, sir," Farnsworth replied. "They want to control all Southeast Asia, especially Siberia, in order to exploit its resources and to provide space for their exploding population."

"And the Chinese are exploiting Muslim ambition for religious dominance in the world," Mills replied.

"Exactly," Farnsworth interjected. "The fundamentalists are their foot soldiers. The Chinese probably supplied the computer know-how to break our missile codes and the fissionable material for any nuclear weapons they may have."

"So we're at war," the President said, "and our adversary is a coalition of all our enemies."

"But we can't prove it," the Secretary of State added grimly. "And even if we could..."

The unstated question hung in the air of the Situation Room. The President finally voiced it.

"So what do we do?" He looked at his watch. "It's almost noon. We now have less than a hundred and twenty days." His weary eyes swept the faces of his advisors. None met his gaze directly.

"We have to try and buy some time," The Secretary of State finally murmured, as if to herself.

"How?" the President asked.

Secretary Jorganson's eyes darted around the table, searching for the understanding face of someone willing to voice the only obvious answer. Finding none, she finally said, "By acceding to their demands."

A cacophony of protesting voices was hushed as the President raised his hand. "Give in to terrorists, Ellen? Is that your solution?"

"It would only be a temporary expedient, Mr. President," she said, her tone one of reason and conciliation. "A hundred and twenty days is not enough time to find—"

"Not on my watch," he interrupted, his anger barely controlled.

Connor Mills gazed back at the President, struck by how the man had aged in just a matter of a few hours. However, if the terrorist threat was not enough, there was the message Mills had gotten from his agent in The Brotherhood. It suggested an even more dangerous peril to the nation's security might be lurking over the horizon.

Mills had practically memorized the message he had received from Spencer. *"Neisen has found the stone, and it is in his possession. He believes its powers are real and that the key to unlocking them lies in a remote part of the Amazon jungle."*

Somehow, a Bible translator working in the region was involved, and Spencer said he and Neisen were traveling to meet up with her there as soon as the rainy season ended. He promised to keep Mills informed.

His mind drifted back to the heated discussion now raging around the huge table in the Situation Room. When he was a boy, he remembered his father would quote a verse from the Bible when things went wrong, something about there always being enough evil to go around.

CHAPTER 31

NEISEN SWITCHED ON HIS office computer and clicked to his mail account. The excitement he felt in London had withered somewhat under the hot blast of Erick Stiediger's presence. The two men had never liked each other, but the haughty German was necessary, especially in light of Abelard's stroke.

Neisen called him in Bonn immediately after depositing the old man in the hospital. In less than four hours, Stiediger was in Neisen's hotel suite listening as he related all that had happened the previous night as well as the contents of Ruth Starling's letter.

Neisen had removed the stone only briefly from its pouch when Stiediger asked to see it. "It behaves strangely when exposed to the light," he said, adding he thought it wise to know more about it before examining it more closely. Though he was sure his explanation did not fully satisfy Stiediger's curiosity, it did seem to pacify him, at least for the moment.

Not being in on the stone's discovery had obviously bruised his ego, and Neisen tried to soothe it by asking him to take the scroll and get it translated as soon as possible. "It may give us the answer to the stone's purpose," he said.

Neisen returned to America with the stone and had since been preparing for his journey to the Amazon. He fumed about weather delays in that godforsaken part of the world, but knew he had no choice but to wait.

The intercom buzzed, and he snatched up the phone.

"A Mr. Stiediger for you," Greta said. Neisen punched the button without replying.

"You have the translation?" he asked without preamble.

"You will have a complete copy in your hands soon," Stiediger said. "It was written in Aramaic and not difficult to translate at all." He paused for a moment. "Unfortunately, most of it is just a rehash of material we already have from other sources." Again, he let a beat of silence lengthen. "Except for the prophecy."

"A prophecy?" Neisen could hear the rustle of papers on the other end of the line as Stiediger searched for something.

"Ah, here it is," he finally said, "an exact quote."

"'Before all things are restored, the stone will seek out a people to return it to its source.'"

"That's it?" Neisen could not mask his disappointment.

"That's it," the thick German voice replied emphatically. "No explanation of the stone's purpose or how to use it at all. However, we have business that is just as important. Is your line safe?"

"If you mean secure, yes, it is."

"Good," he replied curtly.

"What could be as important as the business at hand?" Neisen asked.

"What happened yesterday," Stiediger replied.

"What do you mean? What happened yesterday?"

"It seems we don't have long to discover the stone's purpose if we're to stave off Armageddon, my friend." There was no longer the slightest hint of haughtiness in Stiediger's voice.

"Quit screwing around, Stiediger. What are you talking about?"

"My sources in Bonn say a terrorist threat has been made against all the Western governments. If their demands are not met in four months, they have threatened to begin wiping out our major cities with nuclear weapons."

Neisen was speechless. He stared into the mouthpiece of his phone.

"The Chancellor tells my sources your President will be making a token response to these demands in hopes of buying time. The assessment here is that when the terrorists realize the governments are stalling, they'll begin setting off their bombs before the deadline."

"This makes absolutely no sense. Why haven't we heard about this? What are the Western powers doing about it?" Neisen hardly knew where to begin. He had at least a million more questions.

"Leaders here in Germany have already begun the orderly evacuation of critical services to underground shelters near Berchtesgaden. My informants say your President and his cabinet are going to your command and control center at Cheyenne Mountain in Colorado. Your other critical government personnel will be scattered at underground sites in Virginia, West Virginia, and the Smokey Mountains."

"Don't they think all this sudden movement will set off national panics?" Neisen could envision the interstates of the country clogged with autos as the large cities tried to disgorge millions of people at once.

"There'll be the usual speculation from the press," Stiediger said, "but I'm told Western defense establishments have a boiler plate plan for such an emergency. They think it will give temporary cover and hold down panic. Tomorrow, Western leaders will hold a joint press conference via satellite announcing the launching of Operation Hard Hat. They will announce this is a security training exercise whose purpose is to test our ability to disperse military command and control and other critical government functions rapidly."

"Won't that provoke a response from whoever has his hand on the trigger?" Neisen asked, still having trouble believing he was having this conversation.

"Probably not immediately," Stiediger replied. "Your President, in coordination with other Western leaders, plans to begin a cosmetic response to the ultimatum starting tomorrow. Several of your aircraft carriers on standby in the Persian Gulf will be recalled for refitting. He will also announce a five-thousand-man reduction in your military stationed along the DMZ in South Korea, saying this is being done in light of improving relations with North Korea."

"And he thinks these moves will buy them time to get out of town?"

"They hope so," Stiediger replied, "and by the way, Brotherhood members have been alerted, and I'm sure are already beginning to scatter."

"What about Abelard?"

"Resilient as always," Stiediger said. "Our people in London are saying he still can't walk but has regained his speech and left the hospital. When I hang up, I am sending a plane to take him to my country estate in Scotland."

"That should put him outside of harm's way," Neisen thought aloud.

"I hope so. We certainly need him, especially now."

Really, Neisen thought, smiling.

"This will probably be our last contact before you leave for the Amazon," Stiediger continued. "You must be gone before all this madness goes down. At most, you have a matter of a few weeks. It goes without saying The Brotherhood is depending on your success."

"Of course." Neisen felt the same power rush he'd felt in London when he took possession of the stone. "Thank you, Stiediger, for the warning. Good luck."

A dial tone told him their conversation was over.

Neisen returned to his computer, put the curser on compose, and stroked a key. He typed in the address of the New Tribes Mission office in Caracas. Rainy season or not, he and Spencer needed to get out of the United States before the whole world blew up.

Chapter 32

RUTH'S FLIGHT FROM BOLIVAR to the Yanoako village over a year ago had been cramped but uneventful. Packing gear and supplies in the small four- seater, adequate for at least six months, had been daunting but doable once the pilot showed her how.

However, the smoothness of the flight did not calm her pounding heart as the pilot began his corkscrew approach to the landing site on a sand bar near the river, and she saw the village for the first time.

The plane had hardly taxied to a stop before a gaggle of naked little children descended on it, their eager hands reaching out to touch the pale-skinned woman and receive what she might give them as she got out.

Ruth was glad Dr. Francisco Lopez, a Christian friend she met while visiting a church in Maracaibo, had helped prepare the village for her arrival. A Last Tribe missionary preceded her to gain permission from the village Elders for her to enter the village. However, Dr. Lopez had been the most help in arranging for her arrival; arrangements that included a new hut freshly built for her by the tribe.

Dr. Lopez was not only a dedicated Christian, but also an official with Venezuela's National Water Resources Commission and as such made periodic visits down river on the Orinoco checking water levels. On these visits, he had come to know the Shaman of this Yanoako village and more, become a trusted friend. It was this friendship and his government connections that led to Last Tribe Mission's invitation to be the first outsiders ever to gain permission for a missionary to live among them.

"Bring candy for the children, fish hooks, line and tobacco for the men, and a bolt or two of colorful cloth for the women. An exchange of gifts always precedes a stranger's entrance into their villages," Dr. Lopez advised.

He was right. The candy placed in eager outstretched hands not only produced shouts of excitement from the children, but timid half-smiles from their mothers as well ... half-smiles that erupted into laughter and giggles when Ruth presented them with the bolts of cloth.

Realizing the men had not joined the women and children in greeting her, but stood in a group apart, she remarked to the pilot that they seemed standoffish.

"Not standoffish Miss Starling, just dignified," the seasoned pilot, familiar with tribal ways replied. "They're waiting for you to come to them."

She had just started walking toward them when the tallest of the group suddenly broke from the others and ran toward her with outstretched arms.

"What the ..." The startled pilot had not finished expressing his surprise before the man reached Ruth and embraced her.

"I am Akhu," he said in imperfect Spanish.

Ruth was grateful she had taken it as a minor in college because she understood him perfectly.

"And you ..." He backed away and smiled as he took her measure. "You are the beautiful pale-skinned woman of my visions."

Then, embracing her again, he whispered, "You have kept your promise."

The pilot was speechless, unable to comprehend this strange reception by the Shaman of the tribe. Finally he blurted out, "I know he knew you were coming Miss Starling, but he acts as if you're a long lost friend."

"We were long lost friends, but lost no longer," she replied, placing her hand on Akhu's shoulder.

Translating for the Shaman what she said to the pilot produced still another hug, then, taking her gently by the arm, he led her to where the other men were standing.

"This is the little sister of my vision," he said. "She has come to teach us the way to the land of our beginning."

Though Ruth could not yet understand their tongue, each man's embrace told her there was no need for fishhooks and tobacco to gain their trust. Akhu's visions had opened the door for her to share God's message and her own vision as a child had prepared her heart to enter this strange new jungle world.

Ruth twisted in the cocoon-folds of her hammock. In her dream, her eyes followed rows of empty seats that stretched toward the front of Lone Oak church. To her left and right were more unfilled pews, their rich varnish gleaming warmly in the sunlight shining through the windows. For some reason, the church's emptiness did not seem strange but only reinforced the feeling God had chosen this time and place to do private business with her.

Suddenly, a crescendo of reedy notes broke the silence, and she was startled to see Minnie Flowers sitting on the organ bench. A cascade of yellow crocuses spilled from the top of the organ cabinet and down both sides. *I didn't know Miss Minnie could play the organ.* The old woman's hands swept over the keys. She lifted one to wave without seeming to miss a note. Through the windows, Ruth saw a sea of golden wheat and a shimmering wake marking the passing of a horse and rider moving through it toward the church.

In a moment, Ruth saw the rider's face clearly. *Timmy!* It couldn't be! Her little brother was only a memory from childhood, yet here he was, all four-feet-three of him, Stetson and all, just as she remembered. And he was riding Gypsy—right up to the church door.

He dismounted, and now he was coming inside. She could hardly contain her amazement. Her eyes followed him as he walked confidently down the aisle and toward the pulpit.

"Come up here, Timmy, and lead us in an offertory hymn." Pastor Travis suddenly appeared and gestured to the boy to join him on the platform.

The pastor's invitation produced an instant change in Tim's appearance. He was still the little boy of Ruth's memories, but now he wore a shepherd's robe, just like the one her mother had made him for the Christmas pageant.

Miss Flowers began to play "Jesus Loves Me" as Timmy mounted the platform, and then turned to the congregation of one.

"Come on, everybody, let's sing," he shouted with the same enthusiasm he had demonstrated on the night of the pageant.

Jesus loves me this I know, for the Bible tells me so...

At first only she and Timmy were singing, but soon she was aware that an invisible choir had joined them.

"Will the ushers please come forward to receive the morning offering as we sing the last verse?" Timmy said.

Jesus loves me, he who died, heaven's gates to open wide...

As Ruth sang, she sensed others had entered the church and were coming down the aisle behind her. She heard their voices joining in the song before she saw them. Their words sounded strange but the melody was the same.

He will wipe away our sins...

Her heart jumped when she saw them. Four brown-skinned men, naked except for their loincloths, walked somberly toward the communion table at the front of the church.

Let his little ones come in...

Yes, Jesus loves me. The Bible tells me so.

As the song ended, Timmy stepped back from the pulpit and the pastor took his place.

"Akhu, please lead us in the offertory prayer," he said.

A broad-shouldered man, whose regal bearing set him apart from the others, lifted his face toward heaven and began to pray. Ruth could not understand his words, but his spirit was transparent. She felt certain he was pleading with God for his people.

When he finished, she watched with apprehension as the four men began moving up the aisle again. Each stopped where she sat and held out his plate to her. But every time she tried to put in a bill, each man quickly drew back his plate with a sob.

"They don't want your money, Ruth." Pastor Travis had left the platform and was standing beside her. "They want you to give them something more precious than that."

The scene changed as quickly as it began. She was no longer in the church, but standing at the edge of a dark forest. The four brown-skinned men were also there and had started down a trail into the forest. They gestured for her to follow.

For the first time since her dream began, she was afraid.

"You should be afraid," a voice hissed from the shadows. "No one knows where you are, Ruth. There is no one who can help you. You are all alone."

"No, you're not!" A familiar voice caused her to turn. Jerry!

"Remember my promise, Ruthie," he said, breaking into a smile as bright as sunrise. "I'll always be there when you need me. Always."

"Jerry, I need you now!" she cried.

"Not yet, love, but soon you will…" As if painted on a canvas of gossamer threads, his image dissolved in the sunlight breaking through the canopy of trees. "Soon…soon…" his voice trailed away to a whisper and was lost in the breeze that rustled the leaves about her.

"Jerry! Jerry, wait!" she cried.

The chatter of monkeys jerked her from her fitful sleep, her lips still forming Jerry's name as she opened her eyes and saw Akhu, his body framed in sunlight, standing in the doorway of her hut.

"You were troubled as you slept little sister. You kept calling a name."

"Jerry?" Ruth's eyes brimmed with tears.

Akhu nodded. "Is he someone you fear little sister?"

"No, Akhu, he's a dear, dear friend. I dreamed he was here with us."

"Some of my people also dreamed again last night." His somber face grew sadder still. "The same dream as before."

Ruth did not respond. How many times in the last several months had he brought her the same report, she wondered. A dozen? Fifty? Each time he stood patiently waiting for an explanation. An explanation she could not give.

"I don't understand it, Akhu, at least not yet," she finally said, certain her admission would bring the same response as always.

"When the god above all others chooses, you will, little sister," he replied before he turned and walked out of the hut.

I hope so, she thought, and prayed again that soon she would hear from Dr. Neisen. She felt desperate to unravel the mystery and somehow knew time to do so was running out, that the dreams were harbingers of some event yet to unfold.

CHAPTER 33

THE COVER STORY WAS holding, but just barely. Late news reports made it apparent to the President that, as usual, Washington had underestimated the media's sixth sense for deception. It had been little more than a week since he, the Joint Chiefs, and their executive staffs, had arrived at Cheyenne Mountain, and already word had leaked out they were here. The press was in a feeding frenzy, fueling speculation around the world that "Operation Hard Hat" was more than just another NATO training exercise.

The tranquilizing effect of the joint press conference held by Western governments at the beginning of the crisis had been short lived. News articles on his desk told him the press was again fully awake and feverishly digging for the story they sensed hidden behind the NATO announcement.

They were running out of time. The President knew he had to do something quickly, although he did not have a clue what it might be. He rested his head in his hands as his eyes scanned the latest press releases:

Dateline: Moscow

Reliable sources here report the suspension of train, truck, and plane schedules in and out of Moscow. It is widely believed this action is in response to NATO security exercises announced in Brussels on Wednesday. Large numbers of planes carrying civilian and military personnel are reported taking off from Moscow's Domodedovo International Airport, and convoys of trucks are clogging highways leading toward the Ural Mountains, fueling speculation a crisis is imminent.

Dateline: Tel Aviv

Israeli schools stand vacant today following the unexpected transporting of thousands of the nation's children to what government officials are calling 'more secure areas'. A source close to the prime minister tells WNS this action is in conjunction with current NATO security exercises in order to test the nation's readiness for quick evacuation in the event of an emergency. Our source also claims this transport of children by the government took parents by complete surprise.

"The buses that usually bring our children home after school never arrived today," one distraught mother said. "It was only after I called the school that I learned the government had taken them away."

WNS has also learned the government fears widespread demonstrations in the aftermath of this unprecedented action. Militant Jewish groups who believe terrorist threats have made this action necessary are reported to be committing reprisals against the Palestinian population.

Dateline: Jerusalem

Jerusalem's Chief Rabbi urged those of other faiths, in his words, "to join your Jewish brothers and sisters and pray to God for mercy." He called on the crowd gathered outside the Knesset to "fall on your knees before the Almighty," then read II Chronicles 26:12, which says: "Oh God, wilt thou not judge them? For we have no might against this great company that cometh against us; neither know we what to do: but our eyes are upon thee."

WNS has learned this demonstration was in response to what the government is calling an emergency relocation exercise. It says the action is part of an ongoing NATO project, but it is fueling the fears of many Israelis that a catastrophe is imminent. Speculation as to its nature ranges from the possible collision of the earth with an asteroid to a nuclear attack by Muslim extremists.

"Where's the blasted button?" The President fumbled nervously for the intercom switch, found it, and snapped, "Get Holbrook in here! Now!"

"Yes, Mr. President." His secretary fought to remain calm as she frantically searched for the Secretary of Energy's extention. *Everything's chaotic—files scattered, people misplaced.* She felt her weak grasp on control slipping away. Her raw nerves quivered in sync with the gathering storm, just like those of everyone else at Cheyenne Mountain.

She found the secretary's extension and buzzed it.

"He's on his way, Mr. President," she announced a moment later.

President Stewart willed himself to speak softly to the woman who had been his right hand since the day he was inaugurated. "Thank you, Hazel."

Operation Hard Hat required the movement of members of the executive branch to Cheyenne Mountain near Colorado Springs, and the relocation of the legislative and judicial branches to shelters prepared for just such an emergency in the hills of Virginia, West Virginia, and North Carolina. The Vice President was responsible for working out the logistics for the move. To date he reported the relocation of over twenty thousand government employees and their dependents, all in less than a week. And that did not include those declared "critical national resources," people such as doctors, nurses, and scientists.

There was a knock and Stewart's door opened.

"Mr. President, the Secretary is here."

Harry Holbrook stepped into the room as Hazel closed the door behind him.

The two men had no need for greetings. They had been friends since their days together in Congress. Harry was that rare bird in Washington, a political insider who was not a lawyer. He had been a scientist working for the government's Sandia Lab before deciding to run for public office. At the President's urging, he left the House of Representatives to head the National Energy Agency.

"The cat's out of the bag, Harry. The whole damn thing is coming unraveled. I figure we have less than a week to come up with some answers before the world finds out it is on the verge of incineration. The Israelis are already guessing we're under some sort of nuclear threat and are battening down their hatches for Armageddon."

"I see," the secretary said thoughtfully.

"What do your people have for me?"

"Nothing definite, I'm afraid," Holbrook replied, "but we are working on a possibility."

"Tell me."

Holbrook heard desperation in the President's voice and wished he had better news. "Do you remember those computer whiz kids that hacked their way into the IRS files several years ago?"

The President nodded.

"We convinced Justice it would be a shame to waste that kind of talent making license plates."

"Yes," Stewart replied. "We gave them the choice of jail or working for us. They chose the latter. We pay them quite well, as I recall."

"Well, they think there may be a way to disarm our missiles without setting them off," Holbrook said. "Not the suitcase jobs the Arabs or whoever may have planted. Just the missiles."

"That would be a start. How?"

Holbrook heard the lift in the President's voice and prayed he wasn't giving his old friend false hope.

"I'm a scientist, John, but I don't pretend to understand the exotic world of computers at that level," Holbrook replied. "They tell us it might be possible to create a binary mirror image of the detonation code, whatever that means."

"How soon will you be able to test their theory?" The President stood as he spoke.

"Next Friday at the earliest, but I'll need your authorization for the test."

"You have it. What else?"

"I just want to be certain you understand what you're authorizing." Holbrook paused and studied the bleary eyes and washed-out face of the President.

"OK Harry. Give me the downside, short and sweet."

"Sir, if the test fails, you will be condoning a nuclear detonation that could be the beginning of the end for all of us."

Chapter 34

Ruth rose from her small crude desk, her body and mind demanding a break from the tedious task of translating scripture into the Yanoako language. Though frustrated by her inability to make sense of the tribe's dreams, she was comforted in knowing the rainy season would soon be ending. Except for occasional light showers, the rains had almost stopped, and already the river was edging back into its banks. Soon the men would be going down-river to the trading posts to pick up supplies and four months' worth of her letters.

In her short time with the Yanoako, Ruth had discovered the rainy season was the hardest. Sloshing about in ankle-deep red mud and never feeling dry was bad enough but cut off from her family and friends made the incessant rain doubly depressing.

When she felt sorry for herself, she would remember what a teacher in language school had said: *there will be times when only the absolute certainty God has called you will keep you on the mission field.*

She glanced at her watch and approached her precious radio transmitter on the small table the men had made for her. Two o'clock was the appointed time to contact Father Alfonso. She sent up a silent prayer that he had heard from Caracas and another that her radio, her only lifeline to the outside world during the rainy season, still had battery power enough to transmit and receive.

She switched it on, relieved when it came alive with static, which meant the batteries were holding out. Because replacements would be impossible to obtain until the men's trip to the trading post, she limited her transmissions to one a day, except in an emergency. Her one tenuous connection to the outside world was too precious to jeopardize.

As it was, the transmitter's range was limited, reaching only as far as Platanal where the Jesuit mission had a tower high enough to send and receive signals over the Sierrada Pacaraima Mountains that lay between the Orinoco River and the city of Bolivar. When she needed to contact mission headquarters in Caracas, Father Alfonso relayed her messages.

It had been nearly two weeks since she received word from Hugh Brumble, the mission's representative in Caracas, that Dr. Neisen had received her letter and was eager to visit her station as soon as possible. With the rainy season ending early, she saw no reason why he should delay.

Ruth pressed the send button on her mike.

"Starling calling Platanal. Father Alfonso, do you copy?" She hoped her voice did not betray the gnawing impatience that grew stronger each day. *Neisen should be here. What was he waiting for?* She knew it was not just Neisen's delay stoking her feeling of urgency and keeping her stomach in knots. It was also the visions—hers and Akhu's, and now the dreams of the new Christians and the other night's dream of Lone Oak Church, Timmy, the tribesmen, and Jerry.

Before the other night, she had not dreamt of Jerry in a long time. She had come to terms with her decision and the likelihood her calling meant giving up the man she loved. Marriage. Children. Yet his face had been so vivid in the dream, his voice just as she remembered it. *"I'll be there when you need me."* His words were a promise still echoing in her mind when Father Alfonso's voice replied to her call.

"Copy you five by five."

"How's the weather there?" Ruth asked, beginning with her standard opener. She relished these brief moments of conversation with the Priest.

"Sunny for several days, my dear. The river's going down. Before long there won't be enough water for a decent Baptist baptism."

She heard him laugh at his little tease.

Father Alfonso was always a pick-me-up. He had been the Priest in residence at Platanal for nearly fifteen years and had long since come to terms with his isolation during the rainy season. Even the most dismal day did not seem to dampen his sunny disposition.

"I copy you, Father," she laughed into the mike before remembering to release her send button.

"Glad to put some sunshine in your day, dear girl," he said. "Are you ready for the rest of the news?"

Ruth's heart skipped several beats before she answered, "Absolutely."

"Your people in Bolivar have sent word this Dr. Neisen of yours will be on his way in a few days. I told them from where I'm sitting, conditions for landing near the river should be ideal in a week or less. How do things look on your end?"

"About the same, I'd say. I noticed yesterday the river had already gone down enough to expose a long sand bar near the village that looks perfect for a landing site."

A week! Maybe a little longer. Ruth could hardly contain her excitement. "Tell them I look forward to seeing Dr. Neisen as soon as he can get here."

"I'll do that," he replied. "Oh, and by the way, I almost forgot. Your people also said the doctor will be bringing a colleague with him, if you have no objection."

Her mind raced. *The dream... Could it be?*

"Did they say who?"

"His graduate assistant. A young man named Jerry Spencer I believe."

Joy washed over her as she willed herself to calm before pressing the send button. "Tell Caracas that will be just fine," she heard herself say and signed off. Crossing the hut, she fell into her hammock, closed her eyes and again remembered Jerry's promise. In spite of belief in her calling and determination to bring the Word to the Yanoako at all costs, she could not keep her heart from swelling in anticipation of their reunion.

Jerry is coming! She let the tears slide down her cheeks unchecked. *He is keeping his promise.*

Several thousands of miles away, Neisen checked his email. The news from the queerly named Hugh Brumble at the mission's headquarters in Venezuela could not be better.

"Miss Starling has been contacted and has given the go-ahead," Brumble reported.

The Pilots Missionary Fellowship, who would be supplying the chopper, felt confident they could be ready in a matter of days based on the latest weather forecasts. The requested donation of two thousand dollars was a pittance since all the expenses of the trip would be borne by The Brotherhood.

Neisen smiled with satisfaction as he replied to the email. He agreed that the terms were reasonable and that he would transfer the funds immediately. He would advise Brumble of his exact arrival date as soon as arrangements were completed. It was all coming together. In a matter of days, he would have the answers to questions that had plagued The Brotherhood for centuries and it was he, Frederick Neisen who would get the credit.

Savoring his impending success, he picked up the phone to tell Spencer to get his bags packed.

Chapter 35

"My computer whiz kids rate our chance of success at better than 80 percent. Both NSA and the CIA concur, and it is their assessment this is the only viable option. The Israeli missiles appear to be clean."

As Holbrook spoke, the President studied the map of the world electronically generated on the glass-paneled wall in front of his desk. Blinking red diamonds pinpointed the location of every intercontinental missile in America's nuclear arsenal.

My prayers have been answered. The President gave silent acknowledgment to the Deity's part in the unfolding events, as he picked up the phone. "Get me the Prime Minister of Israel," he ordered.

His counterpart picked up immediately. The possibility that Israeli missiles might have been reprogrammed to rain down death on his tiny country had aged the man noticeably since being told of the ultimatum.

"Mr. Prime Minister." The President willed his voice to register calmness. "Our assessments are that your missiles are clean."

He listened intently.

"I know it is not a sure thing, but it is better than we had any right to expect. I also feel encouraged that your Mossad confirms our assessment."

He caught Holbrook's eye and managed a weak smile.

"Yes, Mr. Prime Minister, I agree. The Palestinians would never knowingly agree to such a plan if all they stood to inherit for their trouble were a radioactive graveyard.

"There's another bit of important news. Our computer people believe they have come up with a way to reprogram our missiles without triggering a detonation."

The President listened, his face again grave.

"Yes, that's right." Once more, he looked across his desk at Holbrook. "Our people say the chances are better than even we can successfully reprogram."

Holbrook saw impatience wash over the President's face as he listened to the prime minister, who was famous for his long-winded diatribes on the threat of Islam to both Judaism and Christianity.

"Of course you're right," the President managed to interject. "If we can regain our deterrent capability... That's right; it will take some of the steam out of their ultimatum. They will have to think twice about bombing one of our cities."

The President squared his shoulders and took control of the conversation. "The primary reason I called is, as I said, our computer people are at least eighty percent sure we can reprogram, but..." He paused again. "The thing is we need a clean missile of relatively low yield in a remote area on which to test our theory." He glanced again at Holbrook. "Your southern desert seems the logical place."

He waited, and then nodded vigorously. "Yes, I know there's a risk, but the Negev offers the safest environment. Our assessment is that we and the other major players in NATO will be the big losers if we fail to reprogram. If the missile should detonate, whoever jumbled its brains will know we are trying to countermand their program and will probably warn us to stop by setting off a nuclear device in one of our cities."

For several moments, the President listened quietly. "I understand," he finally said. "You can be assured of our complete cooperation. When the crisis is over, we will move immediately to help you upgrade your nuclear deterrent."

"Yes, I agree." He gave a positive nod to Holbrook. "I'm sure this will draw our two nations closer together, Mr. Prime Minister. Rest assured, a suitable way will be found to express our appreciation for your government's cooperation." The President nodded to his unseen counterpart. "Yes, it is indeed in God's hands, Mr. Prime Minister. We can only pray. Shalom."

"We've got the green light." The President eased wearily from his chair and walked around his desk to where Holbrook was standing.

Holbrook noticed how the strain of the last few weeks had chiseled itself on the President's face as he took his old friend's hand and shook it.

"Harry, we're behind in the game," the President said. "It's the bottom of the ninth, two outs, the bases are loaded and you're up to bat. For God's sake, knock it out of the park."

"Here's the plan." At the Israeli command center in the Negev desert, one of Holbrook's computer programmers drew two rectangles on the chalkboard in the briefing room. "We have a good idea of how our missiles have been reprogrammed," he said, pointing to the two rectangles. "Think of their programs as having two doors. The first we'll call the activate/deactivate door."

He marked A/D on the first rectangle.

"The second is the targeting and detonation doorway." He scribbled T/D across the second rectangle.

"The most important thing to understand is that the two doors are interlocked. When the A/D door opens, the T/D door will go either into standby or automatic mode. In order to avoid a nuclear accident all NATO missiles are programmed to go into standby mode before initiating a launch."

"You said *are* programmed, but the programs have been changed." It was Solomon Levy, the Commander of Israeli strategic defense forces, who spoke.

"Yes, sir, they have," the engineer answered. "After breaking into our computers, the hackers reprogrammed the missiles. When powered up, they will go into automatic launch sequence. For safety reasons each missile has an overriding thirty-second delay built into the system if a malfunction is detected. In a word, launch, detonation, and targeting programs are reprogrammable but the thirty-second delay in the launch sequence is not."

"Why not simply key in a code countermanding the launch order?" Solomon Levy asked, interrupting the engineer and turning to face Holbrook.

"That's a major part of our problem, Solomon," Holbrook replied. "If we try to cancel a launch, the hackers have warned that the missiles are reprogrammed to explode on their pads."

"Worse yet," the engineer interjected, "if the launch is allowed to continue, the missiles have been retargeted to fall on our own cities."

"Do you think the hackers have a code to kill the launch?" Levi asked.

"Probably," the engineer answered.

"But there's no way we could get the code short of giving in to their demands," a youngish looking American general volunteered.

"Even then you wouldn't get the code." Levi shook his head in frustration. "We Jews have had a long and painful experience of dealing with the Arabs. If the Palestinians and the Islamic fundamentalists are involved in this threat, rest assured giving in to their demands will solve nothing, but will only lead to more demands."

"So we're damned if we do and damned if we don't," someone at the rear of the room said in exasperation as several muttered their agreement.

"Gentlemen, let's not throw in the towel just yet," Holbrook interjected. "My engineer here may have found a way around our problem." He nodded to the man, giving him the floor again.

"All ballistic missiles have a lock-down sequence built into their systems," he explained. "In the event of a power surge or electronic failure, they are programmed to shut down until repairs are made."

"So, once the launch sequence has started just how do you propose to shut the missile down?" the young looking general asked.

"During the thirty-second delay, we propose to download a virus into the system we hope will fool the missile's program into thinking an electronic failure has occurred."

"Could you be more specific?"

"Certainly," the engineer replied. "Now that we're sure your missile," he nodded at Levi, "has not been reprogrammed, we propose to change its program ourselves to one corresponding to that of the hackers."

There was a collective gasp.

"You mean you're going to change the program so that the missile goes into automatic launch mode when powered up?" Levi's voice was shaking with frustration, and with a look implying he thought the idea insane, turned to Holbrook. "Is the man serious?" he asked.

"Let us explain," Holbrook replied patiently.

"Yes, let me explain why we plan to do this," the engineer continued. "After the launch sequence begins, we will have thirty seconds to download the virus into the missile's brain and fool it into thinking there's been a malfunction."

He paused and looked uncertainly at Holbrook before continuing. "Here's where it gets sticky," he said. "To avoid collateral damage, we will also have to program the missile to explode on the pad if the virus fails to fool the computer."

"Only thirty seconds to give it a nervous breakdown," someone muttered under his breath. "It isn't much time."

Holbrook sensed the others were having visions of a mushroom cloud rising over the desert and tried to shift their attention to the practicality of testing the theory in the Negev.

"This location is the primary reason the President requested permission to conduct the test here," he said. "It is farther from any major cities than any of our missiles, and the prevailing winds aloft should insure little or no fallout on major population centers."

"But only thirty seconds," someone repeated.

Levi looked squarely at the engineer. "What if you fail?"

"My friend and I..." The engineer pointed to a young man sitting near the door. "We'll have to pay for our mistake," he said softly.

"And you're confident enough to risk your lives?" Levi pressed.

"We're confident we have no choice but to try." The engineer smiled at his friend who had stood as if anxious to leave the command center. "Right, Jim?"

"Right," Jim replied.

The command center fell silent as each man in the room retreated into himself, searching for courage like that showed by the two engineers.

Levi finally found his voice and spoke for the group. "Gentlemen," he said soberly, "we have no choice but to try what our friend has suggested. Are we agreed?" A murmur of assents swept the room as Levi stood and shook hands with the engineer. "We greatly admire your courage," he said clasping their hands warmly.

After handshakes all around, Holbrook, Levi, and the others followed the engineers to their Hummer parked outside the command center.

"You'll be in our prayers," Holbrook said to the engineers as he laid a hand on one of their shoulders.

"Thanks," he replied as he settled behind the steering wheel. "We'll need them."

The group watched as the Hummer moved out into the desert, becoming smaller and smaller until finally it was just a dot on the distant horizon, leaving behind only a trail of dust to mark its passing.

CHAPTER 36

ALL HAD BEEN DONE that could be done. The Israeli missile's brain now conformed to the engineer's best understanding of how the terrorists had reprogrammed its NATO counterparts. With its targeting data scrubbed, the nuclear warhead would explode thirty seconds after the launch sequence ended unless the virus did its work. As a final action, the engineers set the sequence to automatic. The next time the activation door opened there would be no closing it.

The engineers pushed away from their consoles, stood and walked to the door of the bunker and stepped outside. The desert air was cool, a welcome relief from the oppressive heat of the day.

"The stars look close enough to touch," one said as he looked at the sky. Neither was anxious to test their theory. There would be time enough for that. For now, both felt the need to soak up the desert's stillness and to let their eyes feast on something bigger than themselves or any of the world's problems.

"Look." One pointed to the almost full moon overhead. "Just moments ago it was the color of burnished silver. Now it's blood red."

A stiff breeze began to blow.

"The wind's kicking up the sand and refracting the light," the other replied.

"Well, the wind's not causing that." His friend pointed toward the eastern horizon.

"Wow, I see it," he gasped.

To the east, the stars had formed into clusters that were slowly spinning across the sky. As they watched, the first made its transit and disappeared over the western horizon just as new constellations rose in the east.

"I wonder if it's a sign," one said.

"I guess we'll know in a few minutes," the other answered wearily as he inhaled one last breath of the sweet night air and walked slowly back into the bunker.

The engineer at the first console took a deep breath. "Nine," he said. "Confirm."

There was a heart-stopping pause. Then both men announced almost in unison, "Missile deactivated."

The security people were right. The Israeli missile is clean, Holbrook thought as he watched the test via a TV monitor in the Israeli command center. Now, if only their engineers are right as well.

"Seven…six…five…four …" The engineer at the master console glanced at his companion across the room. "Prepare to download the virus," he said as the other man slipped a silver disk into a slot on his console.

"Here we go," he said. "Three…two…"

"One," they said in unison and pushed their launch buttons.

"Launch sequence activated," the first engineer reported.

Computer screens on both consoles came alive with displays of declining numbers. The thirty-second delay had begun its countdown.

"Download the virus on my mark. Five, four, three, two, one, now!" he shouted.

Again, both pressed a button on their consoles.

"Downloading complete," one confirmed, as the display continued counting off the seconds.

"Twenty-five. Twenty-four. Twenty-three. Twenty-two…"

One man counted the seconds aloud while the other watched his screen for the three words that would announce their reprieve from certain death: "Missile Locked Down."

Not taking his eyes off the screen, one of the men felt for his wallet and retrieved a picture of his family. From the corner of his eye, he saw the grinning face of a towheaded boy holding a baseball glove and a little blue-eyed girl smiling directly at him. Behind them stood the dark-haired beauty that had been his wife for nearly fifteen years. *Please, God,* he prayed.

"Twenty. Nineteen. Eighteen…"

Still, there was nothing but numbers tumbling across the screen.

At the count of fifteen, dull metallic thuds announced restraining latches on the missile had disengaged.

"Eleven. Ten. Nine." The disembodied voice droned on.

Oh, God, there's not going to be enough time. One of the men began to pray the only prayer he knew by heart. "Our Father who art in heaven…"

"Five. Four. Three."

"Thy Kingdom come…"

The screen suddenly went dark, and then the message of deliverance began spelling itself out. "MISS…"

Dear God, it's working, one of engineers thought as he looked into the blue eyes of his little girl.

"…ILE…"

"Two. One."

His last memory? The smiling face of his little girl just before his assent into the vortex of the spinning stars.

The news could not be worse. Word had just reached Conner Mills that the thirty-second delay programmed into the Israeli missile had not been long enough for the virus to do its work. Seismographs around the world had recorded the failure, and now there would be hell to pay. He was sure the terrorists already knew they had tried to override their program, and he shuddered at the vision of orange fireballs and mushroom clouds rising over the great cities of the West.

There was a knock at the door.

"Enter." Mills looked up from his desk as a young petty officer came in.

"Sir, an encrypted email has just been received addressed to "sponsor what if."

Spencer. "I'll take care of it," he replied.

As the officer left the room, Mills turned on his computer and opened the message.

He recalled some ancient sage observed the importance of a matter is determined by how simply it is stated. Spencer's email proved the truth of the aphorism.

"Leaving tomorrow for the Amazon with Neisen," it said. *"Neisen has the stone and is taking it with us. He thinks the Yanoako Indians may hold the key to unlocking its power. I will keep you informed."*

Chapter 37

"Something's up, dear girl, something big."

Ruth was sure she heard concern in Father Alfonso's voice rather than his usual tone of good cheer when she made her daily radio check.

"Maybe the isolation is finally getting the best of me," he said before Ruth could speak. "The hurry-up visit by your professor to this backwater place, especially at this particular time, seems strange."

There was a moment of dead air.

Ruth's voice finally filled the void. "You're not worried about me, are you?"

"Not really. It's just that…"

"What?

"Like I said, it just seems strange."

"If you remember, I asked the professor to come," she replied as anxiety nibbled at her mind.

"I know. It's just that I've been hearing things."

"What things?" Anxiety had stopped nibbling and was gnawing.

"I didn't want to alarm you, dear girl. The rainy season's depressing enough without me conjuring up a thunderstorm."

"What things, Father Alfonso?"

"Reports on the short wave. I didn't want to worry you unnecessarily."

"You already have," she shot back in exasperation.

"I'm sorry," he answered weakly. "I'm hearing reports that many Western leaders are taking cover. They're calling it a NATO security exercise, but from what I hear in the news, people aren't buying that explanation."

"What do they think is going on?"

"I'm not sure. Some doomsayers think they're battening down the hatches for nuclear war or some such awful thing."

"And you think Dr. Neisen and Jerry's coming has something to do with—"

"I really don't know," Alfonso interrupted. "I probably shouldn't have said anything. Like I said, it's their coming at this particular time that bothers me."

There was more dead air.

"Just be a careful, dear girl," he finally said.

"I'll try," Ruth whispered and signed off.

The news was growing worse by the hour. Ever since NATO had announced their supposed security exercises, fear fueled by the media that the world might be on the brink of a catastrophe had grown exponentially.

Neisen and Jerry Spencer huddled with dozens of others around monitors in the American Airlines international departure area of the Dallas-Ft. Worth airport.

Jerry was not only watching the continuous bulletins, but Neisen's reaction to them. The man's sense of urgency seemed to be growing in a direct ratio to the bad news coming out of Israel.

"We must get to the Amazon before it's too late," Jerry heard him mutter to himself with each news update.

"We go live to Harry Kramer in Tel Aviv," an anchor in New York announced.

Neisen leaned forward in his chair, straining to hear over the din of PA announcements.

A disheveled and obviously nervous reporter appeared on the screen. "It was just announced tremors felt across this tiny nation at approximately 7:30 last night were the result of the accidental detonation of a ballistic missile in Israel's southern desert. Sources close to the Ministry of Defense tell CRN a computer malfunction was responsible for the accident. These same sources emphasize fallout from the blast is expected to be small and confined largely to unpopulated desert areas.

"The blast heightens concern growing here since the evacuation of Israeli children that a disaster is imminent. In the meantime, demands are growing for the deportation of all Palestinians from Israel for what many in the Knesset describe as 'their continuing provocations.'"

The reporter paused and seemed to be getting a cue through his earpiece before continuing.

"I am being told Sandy Jamerson is outside the Knesset in Jerusalem where another explosion has just been reported. Sandy? What can you tell us?"

For several seconds the screen was awash in out-of-focus images as a camera operator scrambled to find his subject.

"This is Sandy Jameson near the Knesset," an obviously excited young woman said as she finally came into focus. "Just moments ago an emergency session of the Knesset was interrupted by an explosion that rocked the city."

She turned toward an elderly man who had joined her on camera.

"Sir, you are a member of the Knesset?"

"That's right."

"Can you tell us what happened?"

The old man's voice was trembling with rage. "I just got off the phone," he said nervously, as if trying to relate all he knew in a single breath, "with a friend in the Old City. He says the blast was in that area and that a number of buildings have collapsed and many were killed. All I can tell you is that we will have our revenge. I must go."

He turned from the camera and joined others who were heading for their cars.

"That's all I know from here, Harry." There was another pause but this time the camera stayed focused on the young woman who was nodding as she received more information through her earpiece. "Yes, I understand," she said to someone off camera. "Harry," she finally said as she refocused on the television camera, "I'm being told that right now a reporter with World News Service is in a helicopter over the Old City. We should receive a live feed from him in about ten seconds."

For a moment, Neisen's eyes left the screen and swept the waiting area. Like an infectious disease, anxiety and fear was spreading. Its symptoms were visible on every face. *I must act soon,* Neisen thought, feeling the onslaught of the contagion himself, *or it will be too late.*

Once again, the monitor came alive with a flurry of snowy, out-of-focus images. "Oh my God!" someone was heard shouting off camera.

As the picture came into focus, a collective gasp erupted from those gathered around the monitor. What others in the terminal saw was bad enough, but what Neisen saw was even more horrifying. The scroll predicted terrible birth pangs would precede the earth's restoration. In his mind's eye, he saw its forerunner on the screen, a scene his father had vividly described in a sermon before he lost his faith. *Above the city of Jerusalem rode a rider on a pale horse, its bridle dripping blood, and in the shadow of its passing the smoking rubble of what had been the golden domed Al-Aqsa mosque.*

As the scroll predicted, the time was coming round again, Neisen realized as he watched the future playing out in fast forward in his vision superimposed on the television screen.

He was repelled by his vision of the world he saw coming, unless he could unlock the secret of the stone in time.

"We're receiving real-time images from our satellite over their western border."

The briefing officer highlighted the area on a large illumined map at the front of the hastily assembled situation room nearly half a mile beneath Cheyenne Mountain.

"Switch to real-time transmission," he said to a technician sitting at a nearby console. At his order, the map dissolved, instantly replaced by hundreds of tiny black squares.

"Magnify," he ordered. The squares vanished and a large single square appeared.

"Are those tents?" the President asked.

"Yes, Mr. President," the briefing officer replied. "We estimate ten thousand troops are bivouacked in that area."

"Reverse magnification," the officer ordered.

An image of hundreds of black squares reappeared.

"We believe there are at least ten thousand of these tent cities in this area alone," he said.

The President shook his head in disbelief as he looked at Harry Holbrook and his military advisers seated across from him. "Do you mean to tell me they have prepared shelter and logistic support for a million men at this location? Impossible!" He slapped his desk for emphasis. "That's nearly as many as the NATO armies combined."

"Mr. President, the picture doesn't lie," a military advisor interjected, "and you've only seen the first one."

"There's more?" Stewart felt his heart pounding, and his head ached terribly as he recoiled into his chair.

"Several hundred more I'm afraid," the briefing officer replied before giving an order to display the next picture.

As it came into focus, the President could see it was a carbon copy of the first. "Are you telling me these tent cities are preparing to receive…?"

The pounding pain in his head was too strong for him to finish the thought.

"Not just to receive, Mr. President, but to dispatch," the briefing officer explained.

Holbrook moved to the President's side. "The CIA reports all reservists have been called to active duty," he said. "All commercial transportation in the country has been halted. Trains, planes, trucks, practically everything with wheels has been commandeered to carry military personnel and supplies to these receiving areas."

"Next image," the briefing officer said, anticipating the need for more visual proof.

This time the President needed no one to tell him what he was seeing: a large railroad-switching yard filled with flatcars loaded with long cylindrical objects whose outlines were clearly visible under their covers. "Missiles?" he whispered.

"Short-range, yes, sir," the officer replied. "Radiation patterns picked up by our satellite sensors tell us they're nuclear lights. "

"Isn't that a euphemism for neutron bombs?" The President reached and loosened his collar then clasped his sweaty palms together.

"Right, Mr. President," Holbrook interjected. "No radioactive contamination, no destruction of assets, a controlled kill radius."

"The weapon of choice, if you're going to field an army for an offensive," the briefing officer added.

"They're taking no pains to hide any of this from us, are they?" the President said, more to himself than the others. The photos had erased any lingering doubts in his mind. He was sure now he knew who was behind the nuclear blackmail.

"They know we can't retaliate," Holbrook said quietly. "Based on our best intelligence, the Chinese are fielding an army of two hundred million men and preparing to invade the Middle East within the next two weeks."

At that moment, the President of the United States clutched his head and collapsed into his chair. Holbrook was the first to reach him. He shouted for a doctor, but the fixed stare of his old friend announced that something irreversible had short-circuited in his brain. President John Stewart no longer was troubled by the disintegration of the world he had known or by anything else.

Holbrook held the limp body in his arms and wondered if perhaps the President was not the lucky one.

CHAPTER 38

NEISEN LOOKED AT HIS watch: one forty-five. In less than an hour, they should be landing in Caracas. Hugh Brumble said it was just a short walk beyond customs to the gate where they were to catch the four o'clock flight to Bolivar. There was no way they could reach the Yanoako village before nightfall, so they would have to wait until the following morning.

He felt in his inside coat pocket for the pouch containing the stone. Every moment of delay lessened their chances of getting there before... In his mind's eye, he saw the face of a clock, its hour hand spinning around. Time was running out to undo the Creator's mistakes, he thought, as he clutched the pouch tightly.

Pilot Missionary Fellowship had told Brumble the most convenient time for them to fly to the Yanoako village would be toward the end of the week. Neisen's doubling of their requested donation, however, had apparently made the weather much less of an issue. Brumble and PMF signed on to their earlier travel schedule without protest.

Jerry had said almost nothing since they boarded the plane in Dallas. Like most other passengers, he was listening intently on his headset to the international news.

Unlike earlier in the terminal, Neisen now ignored the constant updates. What difference did the news make anyway? If the assessment of The Brotherhood's man in the White House is true, things will only get worse until the "restoration."

Restoration. That word, like a pebble in a stream, had tumbled around inside his mind since he first read Stiediger's translation of the scroll.

"The word is hard to translate," the German said, "and it lends itself to several shades of meaning including balancing, realigning, or mending. It can even denote a reunion."

Taken in context, it seemed the writer envisioned a point in time when the distant past and the present would somehow overlap, and as the scroll described, the time would roll round again.

"I believe what the scroll is telling us," Stiediger said, "is that when this overlapping of past and present occurs, the stone will play a part in somehow bridging the gap between the present world and the perfect one that existed in the beginning."

For want of a better term, the scroll had turned out to be a *To Whom It May Concern* kind of document. According to Stiediger's translation, it predicted that throughout the ages the stone would only fall into the hands of those ordained to carry it toward this restoration.

Neisen fingered the hard edge of the stone in his pocket and silently quoted another passage from the scroll:

Know, child of dust, that for your allotted time, you are the stone's hands and feet to carry it toward the moment when the time rolls round again. It is your Urim and Thummin, the light that will guide you to the perfection you seek.

Neisen quickly dismissed as an absurdity the possibility these words might refer to the very mission he was on, yet the scroll's last words haunted him.

Fret not about the stone's purpose. It is enough you are its hands and feet. Those chosen to use it are unknown by earth's mighty. It will be they who will open the door. Follow them.

Follow whom? Where? He jumped as Jerry nudged him out of his reflection.

"Dr. Neisen, you've got to hear this," he said, as cries erupted in the cabin.

Neisen jerked a pair of earphones from the seat pocket and turned on his radio.

"Awful! Oh, dear God..." The newswoman's voice became incoherent, and for several moments, there was nothing but dead air. Then Neisen heard someone in the background say, "Get Fred on the mike! Quick!"

Again, more dead air, followed in a few moments by someone nervously saying, "We are experiencing technical difficulties. One moment please."

Finally, a male voice, obviously struggling to sound calm, announced, "This is John Keller in Atlanta. International News Service is reporting that a tremendous explosion has just rocked the city of Albuquerque, New Mexico. News is sketchy, but our affiliate KCOK in Santa Fe reports the blast produced shocks there and that a giant plume of smoke is visible in the direction of Albuquerque. We'll give you more news as soon as it becomes available."

There was another pause, long enough for Neisen, Spencer, and everyone else on the plane to envision the lovely city of Albuquerque reduced to a rubble-filled, nuclear wasteland.

"Has all been arranged?" Shadows hovered about the old man on the bed, as he spoke.

"The drug did its work as expected." Eric Stiediger walked over to Abelard's bedside. "The US President is now comatose; and, as prescribed by their Constitution, our man holds the reins of power. At mid-morning our time, he will issue an Executive Order bringing the United States into alignment with our plans.

"Oh yes," he added, almost as an afterthought, "the accidental detonation of a nuclear missile in southern Israel has forced the Muslim fundamentalists and their Chinese patrons to make good on their threats."

"Where?" Abelard asked.

"Albuquerque, New Mexico has ceased to exist," Stiediger replied dryly.

Abelard gave no hint of surprise. "Are we on schedule in Israel?" he asked.

"Our operatives in the Jewish Department of Antiquities have completed their mission. High-tech explosives planted in passages under the Al-Aqsa mosque detonated about five hours ago. Nothing remains but a crater."

"Good, good," Abelard chuckled. "The Jews will be blamed. The Palestinians will launch another wave of suicide missions; Israel will attack in force to crush them once and for all, and—"

"And that will be all the provocation China needs to come to the Palestinians' defense and their excuse to take over the Middle East oil fields," Stiediger interjected.

"And our nuclear device? What about it?"

"It's on its way," Stiediger reported. "Two of our men have it and should be trying to cross the Russian/Chinese border in less than two hours."

"Unsuccessfully, I'm sure." Abelard looked at the German and flashed a twisted smile. Since his stroke had paralyzed the right side of his face, his lower lip sagged, exposing even more prominently his pointed yellowed teeth.

"Absolutely unsuccessful," Stiediger replied stiffly. "The men's descriptions and the danger they pose have been leaked to Chinese security. They will be stopped at the border, and the bomb will be found."

"And they will confess?" Abelard reached for a tissue and wiped away the drool oozing from his half-open mouth.

"Quickly, I am sure. The Chinese have ways of making death a pleasant prospect. The plan for a Russian/American nuclear stealth attack on China will be fully exposed," Stiediger said.

"I presume the Chinese will respond indirectly?"

"Through their fundamentalist friends," Stiediger replied. "A dirty bomb will explode in central Moscow sometime tomorrow."

"Good. You have lived up to your reputation," Abelard said. "Our cast of characters is on stage, and soon the curtain will rise on the last act. China, the Western nations, Israel, and the Muslims should be at one another's throats in a matter of days."

"Then it will be time for us to step forward." Stiediger's stiffness melted, and for the first time he sounded excited.

"With the stone," Abelard said, as he turned and looked through the window. The wind was whipping a late snow into miniature tornadoes that danced and bobbed among the lights ringing the manor.

"Neisen expects to arrive with his assistant at the Yanoako village later today," Stiediger volunteered. "He's nearing the end of his search."

"And ours," Abelard replied softly, again flashing a twisted smile.

The old man looked through the window again and let his eyes sweep the blackness bordering the lights outside.

"There is a word," Abelard said dreamily, more to himself than to Stiediger.

"What word is that?" Stiediger cocked his head as he looked at Abelard.

"One translated from the scroll. The one you said you used when you spoke to Neisen about the stone's purpose."

"Restoration?"

"Yes, that's it. Restoration." Abelard inspected his distorted reflection in the window. Inky pits where eyes should be stared back at him from a sallow, bloodless, face. "It must come in time for me," he said.

CHAPTER 39

Mʀ. Vɪᴄᴇ Pʀᴇsɪᴅᴇɴᴛ ʏᴏᴜ'ᴠᴇ got to speak to the nation now!"

In the situation room, a chorus of voices all clamored for attention at once.

Vice President Sheldon Andrews kept his finger on the pulse of Middle America and knew its leader's expressions of spirituality in times of national crisis played well. He also knew Americans were a sympathetic people; that his appearing deeply grieved over the loss of the President would garner support.

The people's sympathy, coupled with the attack on Albuquerque and the need to protect national security, would seal their support for the Executive Order he would be announcing.

Though appealing to any kind of deity sickened him, Andrews' instincts told him this was the time to do so as he slumped into a chair. "Oh, God," he said just loud enough that those nearest him could hear, "help us. Help *me*!"

The babble of voices grew louder by the moment. "Please!" Andrews shouted, then lowered his voice and folded his hands together. "If you must talk, talk to God. He is the only one who can help us now. Just let me think!"

The Vice President's outburst sealed his advisors' lips and wrapped the room in silence.

Finally, he raised his head and let his eyes sweep those gathered around him. Several of the secretaries wept openly, while their bosses at the conference table stared helplessly into space. *Pathetic weaklings,* he thought. *Indecisive and dependent people like you make The Brotherhood necessary.* He shuffled some papers before him. *We will act to undo the mistakes of the past—if only there is enough time.*

He checked his watch. Neisen should be nearing Caracas. If he believed in such superstitious claptrap, he would be praying for his colleague's success right now. Had he not felt all eyes on him, Andrews would have laughed at the absurdity of the idea. *The Brotherhood's plan needs no supernatural assistance.* He forced his face into a look of somber concern and studied the Executive Order on the desk before him.

"Please fasten your seat belts, and return your seats to their full and upright positions." For a moment, the voice of a flight attendant broke into the channel carrying the news. "We will be landing shortly in Caracas."

Since CRN first announced the explosion at Albuquerque, Neisen had given the news his full attention. It was still sketchy, with no survivors of the blast found as yet to interview.

Landing instructions given, the pilot cleared the channel, and Jerry heard the reporter speaking again.

"As a news organization, we are still in the unenviable position of having announced a tragic event without being able to furnish any specific details."

There was more dead air, and then the newscaster's voice came through the headphones again. "Excuse me," he said solemnly, "but I have just been informed that Vice President Andrews will be speaking to the nation from Colorado Springs momentarily."

Speculation from a panel of commentators followed the announcement as to whether or not the Vice President would be able to furnish more information on the explosion. Suddenly, the President's press secretary interrupted their dialogue.

"Ladies and gentlemen" he said solemnly, "the Vice President of the United States."

The tone of Andrews' well modulated voice was intended to convey both resolution and sadness. "My fellow Americans," he began, "I speak to you at a doubly difficult time in our nation's history."

The flight attendants stopped their preparation for landing and, like all the others on board, gave his words their full attention.

"Only a few hours ago, our beloved President suffered a severe medical episode rendering him unable to continue leading our country. As the Constitution dictates, this tragedy requires I assume the helm of government. Compounding this calamity has been the report of a nuclear explosion in Albuquerque, New Mexico."

Neisen glanced at the reaction of those about him. Andrews was playing his part well, conveying both sadness and confidence.

"The Albuquerque blast has been confirmed by both reconnaissance satellites and land-based radiation monitoring stations. All communication with the city is cut off.

"It is my sad duty to inform you that our satellites reveal devastation on a scale equal to that inflicted on Nagasaki and Hiroshima during the Second World War."

A collective gasp erupted in the cabin. Neisen had difficulty suppressing a smile as he watched the flight attendants in the aisle embrace and begin to weep.

"At this time," the Vice President continued, "we do not know whether this was a deliberate act or a tragic accident. Until we do, and in order to protect the security of the United States, I have just declared a national emergency and signed the following Executive Order, which carries the force of law and includes the following provisions:

"One: A dusk to dawn curfew is declared in cities with populations of fifty thousand or more. The only exceptions will be for work-related and medical reasons.

"Two: Travel will be limited to a fifty-mile radius of one's home. Again, the only exception will be for work-related or for medical reasons.

"Three: Congress, both the House and Senate, and the Judiciary will stand adjourned for the duration of the emergency.

"Four: Trial by jury is suspended and replaced by military tribunals. These tribunals will have authority to hold suspected criminals without formal charge until disposition of their cases.

"Five: To prevent hoarding, price gouging, and other economic crimes, I have instructed the Agriculture, Energy, and Treasury Departments to prepare a system of rationing to be in place within two weeks. This will ensure equity in food and energy distribution and provide a mechanism for the regulation of all financial transactions.

"Six: To avoid the spread of undue panic due to rumor or speculation, all public meetings will be strictly monitored. Each church, synagogue, or other places of public worship will be limited to one religious service weekly on its particular holy day.

"Seven: A Division of Media Responsibility within the Department of Education will be staffed and operational within one month. After that, DMR will clear all print, radio, and television news prior to its publication or announcement. Any violation of this provision will result in the immediate forfeiture of broadcast licenses and confiscation of physical properties owned by any media outlet.

"Eight: Those found violating any part of this Executive Order will be subject to immediate arrest."

Jerry's mind reeled at the implications of what he just heard. By Executive Order, the Vice President stripped away some of America's most cherished freedoms, and all in less than five minutes! It was doubly amazing when he fell back on standard Presidential boilerplate for the conclusion of his speech.

"Thank you, my fellow Americans," he said in a warm, fatherly way, "for your complete cooperation in this grave hour in our nation's history. God bless you and the United States of America."

After a short pause the newscaster was back, his voice registering the same shock Jerry felt as he tried to verbalize the implication of what he just heard. Just then, the pilot interrupted the reporter's stunned disbelief with an announcement of his own.

"Well, folks," he said, "this is no Executive Order, but I suggest that while your crew lands this plane, you spend some time talking to your God. I imagine all of us have things we need to tell Him." He paused for a beat "And I'm sure He has a few things to say to us as well."

Neisen winced at the pilot's pious platitudes and could not help noticing Spencer had bowed his head and closed his eyes. He wondered if the boy was going soft on him. Not that it would change the big picture. He smiled when he thought of Andrews' Executive Order and the course correction history was about to make. The harsh new laws were right out of The Brotherhood's playbook, broadcast, he was sure, with only slight variations, throughout the Western world.

Without thinking, he reached again for the hard outline of the stone.

"Presidential press secretary Michael Farnsworth, in a rare early morning press conference, has just announced that an estimated two hundred thousand persons have been killed or injured in a nuclear blast that rocked Albuquerque yesterday. Though a freak accident has not been ruled out entirely, he said it appears likely the tragedy was the work of terrorists."

All eyes in the Pilot Missionary Fellowship office were on CRN International. Neisen and Jerry had planned to fly out of Bolivar for the Yanoako village at six thirty, but like everyone on the PMF staff, they had become caught up in the drama playing out on television.

"We need to be airborne by eight o'clock at the latest," the pilot told Neisen during a commercial break. "It's my rule never to let night catch me over the jungle."

"Right," Neisen replied as the commercial ended and the camera focused again on the newscaster.

"In a related story," he said, "China has just announced it will lodge an official protest today with the United Nations for what it calls an act of terrorism against the Chinese people by the NATO/Russian axis.

"China News Service reports two men identified by authorities as NATO/Russian agents were intercepted at the Russian/Chinese border today carrying what was described as a small nuclear device. It says they have confessed to being under orders to detonate the device in the capital. Had they been successful, authorities believe the resulting death toll could have been in the hundreds of thousands. Both NATO and Russia have denied these charges and issued the following statement: 'Charges NATO and the Russia Federation have engaged in terrorism against the People's Republic of China by attempting to smuggle a nuclear device into their country are false. Because of the massive military buildup by China along its western border, such an allegation only serves to worsen already strained relations between NATO and the People's Republic.'

"Elsewhere," the reporter continued, "representatives of the European Union have been meeting since seven a.m. London time today for what is being called an emergency preparedness session. The meeting, convened in the wake of the Albuquerque disaster, is fueling speculation European cities may be on the terrorists' target list. Our correspondent, Elisa Combs, is outside Common Market headquarters in Brussels where the meeting has just broken up and brings us this report."

"Declaring 'extraordinarily dangerous times demand stringent measures,' representatives of the European Union have just voted to recommend to their respective governments suspension of personal liberties deemed, in the words of their news release, 'inconsistent with public welfare.'

"When fully fleshed out, it is believed these regulations will duplicate those contained in an Executive Order issued by the Vice President of the United States yesterday. The rather lengthy statement concludes on a positive note, pledging to restore all personal freedoms as soon as the crisis is over. This is Elisa Combs in Brussels returning you to CRN in New York."

"This is as good a time as any for us to be on our way," the pilot said as he got up and started for the lounge door.

"I agree," Neisen said and nodded to Spencer as he picked up his bag.

Ten minutes later the helicopter was airborne. In five more, it had cleared the ring of shanties bordering Bolivar and was winging over an unbroken expanse of green toward the Brazilian border. Neisen pressed the soft-sided leather brief case in his lap and again traced with his finger the outline of the stone inside. *Soon,* he thought, *soon.*

Glancing over his shoulder into the back seat, he saw Jerry had converted one of their bags into a pillow and was already asleep. He, too, was exhausted. He let his head fall back on the seat's rest and closed his eyes as bone-numbing weariness swept over him. Just before drifting off to sleep, he remembered another line from the scroll, memorable because it captured his sense of place in the unfolding events.

"Each man is a runner," it said, referring to those who, throughout history, had carried the stone toward its goal. Neisen imagined himself clutching it and running toward his vision of Paradise. But he was not just another member of the relay team that had brought the stone out of its many hiding places. No! He was the last one, the one who would cross the finish line! *Running...running...* He dreamed of getting nearer with each heartbeat to the goal. *Running...running.*

"You'll want to hear this." The pilot's hand on his shoulder jostled Neisen from his nap as he took off his headset and handed it to him. "It's traffic control in Bolivar," he said, as if that would explain everything.

Neisen listened for a moment. "I don't understand Spanish that well," he said, handing the headset back to the pilot. "What is he saying?"

"That all international flights from Caracas to the US, Europe, and the Middle East are canceled indefinitely because of the latest bombing."

"You mean in Albuquerque?"

"No, this time it's Brussels," the pilot answered, never taking his eye off the horizon in the distance.

CHAPTER 40

RECENT EVENTS HAD MADE Dr. Neisen's counsel doubly urgent, yet Ruth felt relief that he and Jerry would not be arriving until early afternoon. She needed the time to collect her thoughts after the strange happenings last night.

At about four a.m., she was awakened by shouts of villagers outside her hut. One of the women rushed inside, pulled back the mosquito netting above her cot, and shook her as she said excitedly, "Teacher, come quickly!"

Ruth felt herself pulled none too gently to her feet, had slipped quickly into a pair of jeans and blouse and gone outside to the ceremonial area where, seemingly everyone in the village had gathered. She spotted Akhu immediately. Like all the others, he was staring unblinking into the night sky.

"What's happening?" she said groggily as she stumbled up beside him.

"Look up, little sister." His eyes did not shift from the sky as she let her own follow his lead.

"Oh." She exhaled in wonder, as the people began singing in harmonious counterpoint. "Oh, my."

"Little sister, the time has come to make our journey," Akhu said quietly.

Without being certain exactly what he meant, she murmured, "I know."

She and the villagers remained in the courtyard looking at the sky until dawn erased their vision. Then, without a word, she and Akhu went to their huts, and the others returned to the long house.

Sitting now at her desk, Ruth felt as if she had just awakened from a dream, one so otherworldly that words could not describe it. *But I have to try.* She picked up her pen, opened her journal and began to write, her words running an uneven race with her vision birthed in the night sky.

"The only assurance that what I describe was not a dream," she scribbled, "is the unusual stillness still hanging over the village.

"By now, the men should be in the jungle hunting, and the women and children in the garden, but all is still quiet. Even the howler monkeys that usually announce each sunrise seem infected with silence.

"Without a word, the tribe left the ceremonial courtyard at dawn. Akhu and I came to our huts, the others to their hammocks in the long house. It was as if everyone wanted to be alone with their thoughts as they prepared for whatever is coming.

"The predawn gathering seemed spontaneous; each person seemingly awakened by an internal alarm and drawn outside.

"Akhu believes it is time to make the journey about which he and the other new Christians have been dreaming.

"I just found two scriptures I think best describe what we saw in the night sky. The first, Revelation 6:14 which says: 'The heavens departed as a scroll when it is rolled together.' The other,

Isaiah 34:4 seems to expand on the first and says, 'All the hosts of heaven will be dissolved, and the heavens will be rolled together as a scroll.' There are no better words to describe what I saw.

"When I looked up, I could not see a single star. However, just above the tree line surrounding the village, I observed a ring of them, slowly rising and rotating around the dark sky overhead. I am sure if I had been on my folks' nearly treeless farm in Texas and could have seen all four horizon's clearly, I would have witnessed rings within rings of stars orbiting the dark sky overhead.

"As I watched, more rings appeared above the trees and as they did, the circle of darkness grew smaller. "Finally, just before first light, a tunnel-like core of darkness overhead was clearly defined by millions of stars slowly circling around it.

"Word has reached me that Dr. Neisen and Jerry have been delayed in Bolivar but should be arriving in just a little while. It is possible I will not need Dr. Neisen to explain the dreams as I first thought. They may explain themselves. I am closing my journal with the feeling this may be my last entry. I believe that tunnel outlined by the stars leads somewhere. Soon, I expect, I'll discover where."

She closed her journal and sat staring out at nothing, wondering what the omen in the sky portended. She hoped that, whatever came, she would face it with faith and courage. She whispered a prayer for guidance and asked for blessings and care for Jerry and for her parents so many thousands of miles away.

Frank Starling closed his eyes, as a soft sigh escaped his hard set lips.

The weather report was grim. An expected cold front was coming farther south than first predicted before making a turn to the east. If it kept on that track, it would bring fallout from Albuquerque directly over the farm. The latest government advisory said the radiation over West Texas should not reach critical levels. Nevertheless, people were being encouraged to remain indoors, preferably in a sealed room, for at least twenty-four hours after the front's arrival in order to avoid as much dust as possible.

Frank knew the government was trying to be as low key about the disaster as possible, but it was not working. Runs on grocery stores in Lubbock had stripped canned goods and bottled water from the shelves in a matter of hours. Plastic sheeting suitable for sealing windows and doors had disappeared soon after. Several expectant mothers in the church called Diana expressing fears, that due to radiation, their babies might be born deformed.

Anticipating future censorship, broadcasters filled the airwaves with news reports and commentary non-stop.

He and Diana stared in disbelief at the first pictures coming out of Brussels where nearly half a million people were reported killed with another million seriously injured.

It was obvious to Frank the so-called NATO training exercise had been the Western governments' cover for a potential catastrophe. Now the unthinkable had happened, and the people had learned the truth, leading to the exodus of millions now clogging highways out of major European cities.

Things in the United States were no better. Washington was already a ghost town. Interstates had choked on traffic disgorged from New York, Los Angles, Houston, Chicago, Atlanta, and dozens of other cities as panic took hold.

The Dow Jones, which topped out just above twelve thousand before the nuclear accident in Israel, had fallen over four thousand points before trading was suspended. Reports circulated across America of runs on the banks, that under emergency powers given by the government, were limiting withdrawals to five hundred dollars in any twenty-four-hour period.

Frank stepped out on the front porch and looked west where he could see clouds, like the vanguard of an approaching army, gathering for the cold front's assault on the plains.

Brother Travis had called the congregation together for a special prayer service last night and the building was packed. He told the congregation to enjoy the fellowship while they could because holding evening meetings would soon be a violation of the law.

"I believe the Lord's coming soon," he said. "But before He does, we are going to have our faith tested. If you are not sure you're ready to meet Him, now is the time to make certain." Then, he gave the most impassioned invitation Frank had ever heard, and the people responded as if awaking from a coma, coming forward by the dozens to affirm their faith in Christ or to renew their commitments to Him.

From the porch, Frank could see the front gate. Again he remembered how Ruth waited there for the bus to take her to school for the first time and sensed again the sadness he felt then at the prospect that one day God would take her beyond his care.

"*Beyond your care, but never beyond mine,*" he remembered a voice saying in his mind as he watched the bus kick up a cloud of dust then disappear into the distance. The voice was so clear, it seemed someone behind him had spoken, and he remembered turning to see who it was, only to realize no one was there; the only sound disturbing the silence, the squeak of the porch swing swaying gently in the breeze.

That was the first time God spoke to him. The second was just last night.

After the service, everyone gathered on the parking lot to watch an awesome whirlpool of stars. From every direction, ring after ring of them rose above the horizons then slowly rotated around the darkness overhead. In the reverential awe that had silenced everyone, Frank heard God whisper, "You have always feared for Ruth and what the future held for her. Fear no more my son. I have chosen her to lead you and the others through the darkness to the light."

Frank knew in his heart the Pastor was right. Tough times were coming for Christians, as well as the rest of the world. He raised his head and looked again toward the dark clouds boiling in the west. He felt the weight of fear lift from his sagging shoulders as he reaffirmed his faith that no matter what might come, he knew God would see them through the coming storm.

CHAPTER 41

BY THE TIME THE helicopter touched down, news of worsening world conditions made it obvious to Neisen time could not be wasted trying to unravel the mystery behind the Yanoakos' dreams.

After stepping from the helicopter, there had only been time enough for Neisen to shake Ruth's hand and for Jerry to kiss her before the village Elders took them to Akhu's hut. On the way, Ruth expressed surprise Akhu insisted the three visit him at the same time.

"Normally he meets outsiders one-on-one," she said. "Bringing you together may mean he feels like I do."

"And how's that, Miss Starling?" They had reached the door of Akhu's hut when Neisen turned and eyed Ruth questioningly.

"That there is no time to observe social custom."

Akhu's black eyes appraised Neisen and Jerry as they entered and with a nod acknowledged Ruth's introduction.

"We leave on our journey tonight," he announced, then, without further explanation, turned and addressed Ruth directly. "You, little sister will be going with us."

"Yes, of course," she replied without hesitation.

"And you..." Akhu's black eyes sought out Neisen and Jerry. "You may come if you wish."

Akhu continued to stare stoically at Neisen, who smiled and nodded as Ruth translated his invitation.

"Yes, certainly, but the day is half over. Would it not be better if we waited until morning? Until we can see where—"

With a sweep of his hand, Akhu cut him off. "Shi will give us all the light we need for our journey."

Ruth saw the hint of a smile on his face as he waited for her to translate. *He remembers the Bible story*, she thought.

In translating the Gospel of John, she had chosen the word "Shi" as the Yanoako word that best expressed God as Father, Son, and Holy Spirit. She taught them the God of the Bible was not a god above other gods, but the only true God who revealed himself as a father, a son, and a spirit.

One night as they shared an evening meal, she told the tribe the story of Israel's long journey through the wilderness. Since the idea of a desert was foreign to their experience, she described it as a jungle. "Ahs" of amazement punctuated the story when she described the parting of the Red Sea and told how Moses brought forth water from a rock. As she related Israel's long journey through the jungle, one of the older boys interrupted with a question.

"But teacher," he asked, "If the jungle was not the tribe's home, how did they find their way through it?"

Their eyes grew wide when she described Shi sending a cloud by day and a fire at night to guide them.

Just as they were about to leave the hut, Neisen took Ruth's arm. "Before we go, Miss. Starling, there's something I want to show the Shaman."

Surprised, Ruth glanced at Jerry, who nodded his agreement.

Be kind enough to translate for me," Neisen said, as they turned and faced Akhu. Without ceremony, Neisen seated himself on one of the two benches near the entrance of the hut.

Ruth tried to cover this breach of Yanoako etiquette by smiling and waiting for Akhu to sit on the other bench before settling beside him.

"Akhu," Neisen began, "I have come from a great distance to seek your guidance and wisdom."

While Ruth translated the blatant flattery, Neisen pulled the pouch from inside his jacket pocket. Removing the stone, he handed it ceremoniously to the Shaman.

Akhu's response was everything Neisen had hoped.

"The mark of Shi!" His expression of annoyance at Neisen's rudeness instantly morphed into one of astonishment. For a fleeting moment, his fingers reverentially touched the stone's design then drew back as he held out a hand to Neisen.

"He wants you to give him the bag," Ruth said.

Neisen passed it to Akhu, who replaced the stone, rose, and walked over to another low bench covered with an animal skin. Removing the hide, he picked it up and brought it to the hut's entrance where the trio still sat.

Wordlessly, he pointed to the intricate carving on the front of the bench. "The mark of Shi," he finally said as he approached Neisen and laid a weathered hand on his shoulder. "You have not chosen Shi," he said solemnly, "but Shi has chosen you. You have been his feet to bring the stone to me."

As Ruth struggled to translate, Neisen looked up, riveted by Akhu's black eyes. "He has chosen you," the leader of the Yanoako said again, "to have a part in making all things new."

"*New* isn't quite right," she said, searching for the right english word. "Bring together? Or maybe, restore?"

Akhu pointed toward the jungle and looked at Neisen intently as if reading his most secret thoughts. "Your destiny lies there," he said.

Turning, he glanced at Ruth then looked back at Jerry. "Your destiny," he announced, "like ours, lies with little sister here and Father Shi in the land of our beginning."

He must have seen Jerry's expression of wonderment because he rose from the bench and walked over to where he sat as Ruth continued to try to translate, "On our journey," he said, "you will understand what it means to trust Father Shi with all your heart." As he said this, he reached and gently patted Jerry on the chest.

A light suddenly came on in Jerry's mind as he realized this primitive man just pinpointed the source of his own difficulty trusting Christ.

I have tried to make faith in Christ an intellectual exercise, one carefully reasoned out before I made a commitment. However, Akhu just called God "Father." That's what I've been missing all these years! I have no more need to have all my questions answered before I trust Christ than I did before I trusted my dad. I have had everything about faith backwards. I have wanted to understand before I trusted rather than simply trusting, knowing understanding would follow. I have so intellectualized faith I have missed its simplicity; failed to see its faith that sets the table and intellect that enjoys the meal...

Neisen was not thinking about faith in God or anything resembling it. He did realize, however, that Akhu was echoing the scroll when he spoke of someone carrying the amulet forward through the ages toward the restoration. *This is going to be simpler than I imagined.* He nodded at Jerry knowingly as Ruth finished translating. *He thinks I am here on God's business. All I have to do is let him lead me to the stone's final destination, and then show me how to use it.*

Akhu signaled their visit was over by rising, but when Neisen reached to retrieve the stone, the Shaman shook his head in displeasure and said something to Ruth.

"What did he say?" Neisen asked, feeling a tinge of anxiety for the first time since entering the village.

"He says it was yours to carry, and now it is his to use," Ruth replied.

"I see." Neisen did not look at Akhu but could feel him watching for his reaction. "When can I expect to get it back?"

She quickly translated his question and just as quickly gave Akhu's reply. "He won't return it. When the journey is over, he will give it to the one who made it."

Jerry felt tension building in the air and was relieved when, instead of displaying anger, he saw a look of surprise on Neisen's face.

Let the old fool hold on to it, Neisen thought. *As long as he takes me with him, and I learn how use it...* He touched the bulge of the pistol in the shoulder holster under his left arm. Unable to carry a firearm on the commercial plane, Neisen had relied on a member of The Brotherhood in Bolivar to deliver it to his hotel room before his arrival. The gun was reassuring as he flashed Akhu a smile. *I'll get it back when your usefulness is over, you old savage.*

"What was that all about?" Ruth asked as they started across the ceremonial area toward her hut. She spoke to Neisen but looked at Jerry for confirmation. "I thought I was the one who asked you to come and help me understand this dream thing, and now Akhu says you came to bring him a stone?"

Before Neisen could answer, Jerry said the first thing that popped into his head. "It will soon be clear, Ruth. For now, you need to trust us."

Neisen glared at him, obviously resenting his intrusion into the conversation.

Ruth stared directly at Jerry. "I do trust you," she replied, surprised that for the first time in her memory, he called her "Ruth."

As they approached the door of her hut, she turned to Neisen. "Is there anything else you need to tell me Professor, or should I expect more surprises?"

That horrible night on Calibogue Sound flashed in Jerry's mind. He knew how ruthless Neisen could be when crossed and signaled caution with a shake of his head but Ruth's full attention was now on Neisen as she waited for an answer.

"It's really quite simple, Miss Starling."

Neisen's ability to mask his true feelings under a veneer of charm amazed Jerry.

"As Jerry may have told you, I have worked on many archeological digs in Israel. Several years ago, an associate and I discovered the stone which you just saw," he lied.

Neisen paused to measure the effect his explanation might be having. Ruth simply stared and waited.

"When I saw the picture of the Shaman you sent Jerry—the carved designs on his bench and their similarity to that on the stone—when your letter came inviting me to come, I—"

"You saw an opportunity to satisfy your intellectual curiosity," Ruth interrupted. "At the expense of these people?"

"No! I mean yes, of course, that was part of it. But I also hoped I could help you understand the meaning of the dreams. I wanted to try to kill two birds with one stone. Help you, but also see if I could discover how the design came to appear in two such widely separated cultures.

Trying to dilute suspicions, he became professorial.

"I was intrigued by the possibility this might support the contention by some geologists that Africa and South America were at one time a single continent.

"The old earth theorists believe the separation happened long before man appeared. Some believe, however, the earth is relatively young and that this separation might have occurred after man emerged and cultures began to develop."

"So you're suggesting the Yanoako may share a gene pool with some Middle Eastern tribe?" Ruth's voice had softened, obviously caught up in what he was saying.

"They may have shared not only a gene pool but certain oral histories that in the case of one tribe, Jews to be precise, were later written down."

"Things like the Bible's story of creation."

"Exactly," Neisen replied. "You told me the Yanoako have an oral history of creation that in a very general way reflects the Biblical account."

"So, what about the dreams?" Ruth asked. "They believe they are preparing them to enter this taboo territory in the jungle. Where do they fit in?"

"Perhaps their dreams are more evidence supporting the theory of racial memory," Jerry suggested.

"Exactly," Neisen responded.

"So let me see if I understand," Ruth said. "A genetic timer was set in the brains of the Yanoako eons ago to be activated when it was time for them to make their journey into the taboo territory?

"Possibly," Neisen replied.

"What's the significance of the fact the dreams began after their conversions?" Jerry asked, anticipating Ruth's next question.

Neisen hated to give Jerry credit for thinking of something he had not considered. However, it was a pertinent question and one that challenged him to speculate further.

"It's possible that before the Creator left man to find his own way, he encoded into his forming brain the genetic material responsible for specific responses to various thoughts, emotions or situations. We know, for instance, that fear triggers either fight or flight and that love can trigger anything from sexual desire to sacrifice."

"What about faith?" Ruth had the feeling she was on the verge of a great discovery. "Isn't it possible that faith, once planted in certain people, may trigger—"

"Dreams!"

Neisen nodded knowingly.

"Dreams that tell the Yanoako it's time to go to the forbidden place and learn the reason Shi placed them here," Ruth said under her breath.

"What?" Neisen asked.

"Oh nothing really, it's just…"

"What?" he pressed.

"Akhu says that in the forbidden territory they will learn the reason for their existence."

There was a long pause.

"Do you think that is possible?" Ruth asked, almost to herself. "To know, for certain, why we have been put here?"

Jerry cast a nervous glace at Neisen, anticipating his reply.

"Perhaps we'll all find out tonight," he finally said.

Chapter 42

Beyond earth's sun and the heavens' galaxies of suns, beyond the wall of ice and the mighty deep whose depths are beyond measuring, there was singing in the third heaven. The Time had come round again!

Darkness blanketed the jungle, muffling every sound. By ones, twos, and threes, from the youngest to the oldest, the Yanoako assembled in the ceremonial area. No one spoke. They brought no weapons, no provisions, only themselves and their faith in the invisible God who commanded that tonight they make their journey into the forbidden land.

Jerry stood beside Ruth at the edge of the gathering, glad Neisen had not finished dressing when he left the hut. His delay gave him his first opportunity to be alone with Ruth since arriving at mid-day.

Like last night, rings of stars had begun rising above the trees surrounding the village then rotating around the core of darkness overhead. Overwhelmed by the unfolding scene, she and Jerry stood holding hands and said nothing for several minutes.

"Ruth." Jerry spoke without taking his eyes off the swirling stars. "Can I tell you something, something I'm just now admitting to myself?"

Ruth looked at Jerry's shadowy profile highlighted by the back-drop of stars. "Sure, if I can ask you something, too."

Jerry shifted his gaze to Ruth's upturned face. "It sounds crazy," he began, as if feeling in the dark for the right words. "The last thing I want to do is sound super religious, because you know I'm not."

Ruth heard the struggle in his voice.

"Today when Akhu spoke of God as his Father, I finally understood what I'd missed all these years. I've played a seeing is believing game with God, waiting for Him to answer all my questions before I trusted Him. Akhu helped me see believing is seeing."

He paused as if waiting for Ruth's confirmation.

Instead, she simply squeezed his hand, not wanting to distract from what she knew was a sacred moment.

Finally, he blurted out a conviction he could not contain any longer. "Ruth, I see something I've never seen before."

"What is it Jerry?"

"Out of contact you probably don't know all the disasters that are shaking the world; bomb blasts killing millions, our freedom lost, financial collapse, people in a panic heading for the hills."

"I've only heard a little, but what is it you see?"

"I believe with all this happening, Jesus is coming soon."

Ruth's heart leaped. *Thank you, Lord,* she prayed silently, *for answering my prayers.* She squeezed Jerry's hand even tighter. "I do, too," she whispered as she sought his eyes and kissed him with a passion, until now, reserved for a calling greater than life itself.

"I don't mean soon, like twenty or fifty years from now or after we have seen and done everything and squeezed life so dry we're ready to discard it anyway."

Jerry's eyes probed Ruth's for understanding. He drew her even closer and whispered, "I mean soon, Ruth, like real soon, like any moment."

"Jerry," she replied, "last night as I watched the spinning stars I had the same feeling, one I realized had been growing in my mind for nearly a year." Tears reflected the starlight making her face appear to glow as she spoke.

"A feeling like we're caught in a swift current…about to be carried over a giant waterfall?" he murmured.

"Exactly. I think Father Alfonso, the Catholic Priest who keeps in radio contact with me, feels it too. On the radio yesterday, he said he believes anxiety is giving the Western world a nervous breakdown."

"It'll get worse before it gets better." Again, Jerry remembered the terrible scene on Calibogue Sound, the horror of Abelard's transformation.

"Remember all the plans we had to visit faraway places together?" he asked..

"This may be our first and last faraway place," Ruth said as her eyes swept the heavens now ablaze with a whirlpool of stars that clearly outlined the mighty deep at its center.

At that moment, only God knew that as Jerry and Ruth held each other close, the sun, whether overhead or hidden by darkness, like a flickering candle, was suddenly extinguished. But had they known, how could they have comprehended the power that plucked it from the heavens or the hands that folded space in such a way so that everywhere on earth everyone saw the same swirling rings of stars, the same gaping mouth of darkness.

"Aren't you afraid of snake bites?"

Ruth and Jerry had not noticed when Neisen joined them at the edge of the crowd.

"Hardly ready for a trek through the jungle," he observed, pointing at their walking shoes and bare ankles.

"This is all I have," Ruth replied. "But look at the Yanoako. We're a lot better protected than they are. I notice you came well prepared," she added dryly, giving Neisen a quick once-over. Calf-high boots, heavy-duck hiking pants, a safari hat, shirt and jacket. *He certainly has it all together,* she thought, noticing that Jerry was also eyeing the professor's Indiana Jones get-up as well.

An Elder approached and whispered, "Teacher, Akhu calls." He gestured toward Jerry and Neisen. "All of you."

"Are you ready for our journey?" Ruth asked holding out her hand to Jerry.

"As long as you're with me," he said, giving her that boyish grin she remembered.

Neither noticed Neisen's face cloud as he fell in behind them.

The tribe parted as the Elder guided them to the ceremonial area where Akhu stood waiting. Only his height made him distinguishable from the hundred or more who crowded the small space.

As they broke clear of the inner circle, Neisen saw the stone clutched in Akhu's hand.

"Little sister," he said as Ruth walked up beside him, "Shi calls, and now we must follow."

For the first time since Ruth had known him, she heard emotion in his voice.

"Your people have waited a long time, haven't they?" she asked gently.

"So long," he replied with a sigh.

Like the other men, he wore only his loincloth Ruth saw there were no ceremonial markings on his body and even his precious Stone of Memory was absent from around his neck, replaced now by Neisen's talisman he clutched in his hand. The other men's bodies were as his; no feathered halos on their heads or quills in their lips, even the small fetish bags many wore around their necks were gone.

Akhu read her questioning look and gestured toward those around him. "We go to Father Shi just as we came into the world … with nothing." Then he looked directly at her. "Now pray for us, little sister."

Jerry did not understand her words, but as Ruth and the others about them bowed their heads, their meaning became clear.

"The Lord is my shepherd…I shall not want…he makes me lie down in green pastures…" Though her words were in the Yanoako tongue, their cadence told him she was probably quoting the Twenty-third Psalm.

Suddenly he realized he understood perfectly what Ruth was saying. The realization came as a high voltage jolt to his spirit, bringing even more assurance he was exactly where God wanted him to be.

"He leads me beside still waters. He restores my soul. He leads me in the path of righteousness for his name's sake. Even though I walk through the valley of the shadow of death, I will fear no evil."

The words reinforced Jerry's with a newfound faith in Christ. *We are about to go through a valley not into a box canyon,* he realized, *along a path leading to something, to Someone, wonderful! And, if death overtakes us on the way? It will only be a passing shadow.* "*…and we will dwell in the house of the Lord forever.*"

As Ruth finished praying, Jerry opened his eyes. The Yanoako were pointing to the stars.

The stars! Ruth, Neisen, and Jerry gasped, unable to find words. No longer a swirling whirlpool, they had reformed into a blazing, comet-like hand pointing eastward.

To the house of the Lord! The look of rapture on Ruth's face told Jerry the same thought had seized her.

Neisen had not taken his eyes off Akhu while Ruth was praying. He watched the hand in which he clutched the stone and saw him raise it toward the stars as she finished. Though his action produced no feeling of physical movement, Neisen had an immediate sense of dislocation.

Jerry felt it too. He looked across the courtyard toward the huts. They were gone. He turned toward the forest and as he did, it dissolved before his eyes. Looking down, he realized even the ground beneath him had vanished. Except for an awareness of Ruth and the others nearby, he felt completely detached from everything physical.

"Look!" Ruth's shout of rapturous wonderment broke the silence engulfing them as she pointed again toward the heavens.

The stars had reformed again into a corridor of shimmering lights that were no longer far away but almost close enough to touch.

"Our pillar of fire," Ruth said joyfully. In the starlight, she saw Akhu, too, was smiling.

For Neisen, Ruth's words and his feeling of detachment from the physical world were having a different effect. His security rested on men and things. Their loss created an immediate sense of unease that, like dark waves, lapped at the underpinning of his confidence. He reached inside his jacket and caressed the pistol in his shoulder holster. The cold steel was a comfort, something solid, something real he could still touch.

Without any sensation of movement, the earth tilted, and they glided silently through the corridor of stars.

CHAPTER 43

IN CHEYENNE MOUNTAIN, ALL radio contact with the outside world had been lost. Except for one of the giant television monitors in the command and control center, all displayed the same ominous words: "transmission terminated." The one exception was a live feed from a satellite on a station a hundred and twenty miles above the earth.

"The word from upstairs," a technician reported to the duty officer, "is that, except for that satellite's transmissions, the world topside is as dark as our monitors. "To be expected," the duty officer said as he looked at his watch. "It's one a.m."

"But past seven in London. Our last contact from there before transmission was lost a few minutes ago said it was dark there as well," another technician added.

"Then we're really flying blind," the duty officer said.

"Except for that." The second technician pointed again to the single monitor now displaying South America in a warm glow."

"What's the source of that light," the duty officer asked? "It's certainly not the sun at this hour."

"Not at any hour" the first technician said, shaking his head in confusion. "All we can tell you sir is that it seems to be emanating from somewhere there." With his control, he highlighted an area near the junction of the Orinoco and Amazon rivers. "Watch closely and you will see that the luminescence is spreading.

It was, the duty officer realized. Since they started watching the monitor, it had spread to the Atlantic on the east and the Andes on the west, to southern Mexico on the north to southern Brazil on the south.

"Take a look at this." Another man handed the duty officer an eight by ten photo of the area. "This is a picture we captured on the bird's last pass over the area about an hour ago. Notice the areas that are absent of trees and vegetation?"

"Yes. What's that supposed to mean?"

"Those splotches are areas of the jungle that were clear cut for timber then planted for crops until the soil lost its fertility. Now it's essentially areas of clay or, as some call it, dead earth."

"I see," the duty officer said "but this can't be true," he exclaimed as he arrowed the satellite imagery on the screen.

Where only dead earth was visible on the bird's last pass, a blanket of green now covered everything.

"It can't be, but sir it is," the technician said. "Except for this narrow belt just here." He pointed to a small gray area surrounded by a forest of green between the Orinoco River in southeastern Venezuela and Guiana. "Everywhere but here the dead earth seems to have healed itself!"

None of the travelers knew how long their silent journey lasted. With no sun to rise or set, no hunger or weariness to feel, reckoning time was impossible. The corridor seemed a timeless void between two worlds, one that was passing away...one that would soon appear.

Their insubstantial journey ended as suddenly as it began as they again felt the earth beneath their feet. Neisen was the first to feel it through his heavy fang- proof boots. He was also the first to see the pillars looming out of the half-light, like spears of stone, threatening the heavens.

"Wait, my son," Akhu called out, as Neisen rushed toward the columns. "Do not act in haste."

Neisen had not heard him, but even if he had, his words would have had no effect. By the time he reached the columns, he was far ahead of the others. Even in the dim light, he could make out the design—the same as on the amulet except for one glaring difference: *not raised, like on the stone, but engraved.* He recalled words from a sermon his father preached when he still believed the promises of scripture: "*Through Adam's sin paradise was locked away, but Christ is the key to finding it again.*"

The key! The stone's design—raised. The sign on the columns, engraved...so that one will fit the other! If he had believed his voice would carry across the abyss between the living and the dead, he would have shouted to his father, "Dad, I've found it, the key that unlocks the gate to Paradise. One he knew would be his on his own terms rather than those of the Christians' precious Christ!"

Even as a young man, he dreamed of such a place. Now his dreams had come true and the destiny for which he had prepared was about to be fulfilled.

With a trembling finger, he probed the indentation on the pillar. *The stone, inserted just here, is the key—to everything.*

The others were still too far away to see the sleek jaguar that suddenly materialized from the shadows. "You have discovered your birthright at last, I see," the beast said.

"My birthright?" Though initially startled, Neisen did not hesitate to talk with the giant cat.

"Certainly. Don't you remember the teachings of your order?" the jaguar purred.

"You know of The Brotherhood." Neisen registered surprise.

"Why shouldn't I? After all, it was I who created it, and I who have preserved and enriched it through the centuries."

"You? I...I don't understand." A shiver of fear made Neisen's voice quiver.

"I created The Brotherhood to rescue the stone from those who would misuse its powers for their own selfish ends," the creature said. "Don't let this form deceive you." With a paw, he touched the corner of his head. "This is the guise I assume when I walk among the Yanoako. But I have inhabited many other bodies; many hosts, desiring what I can give, have welcomed me as their guest. One you know quite well, in fact. I believe he was your mentor. He has been my frequent home."

Neisen swallowed hard. "Abelard?"

"None other," the cat purred. "It was I, in fact, who inspired him to invite you into The Brotherhood. He has been quite helpful over the years. But it is you, Neisen, whom I have chosen to lead mankind to the fulfillment of its destiny."

Neisen felt his heart beating wildly in his chest. All the years—the study, the sacrifice. Could his reward be as close as this strange beast, now crouching beside him and speaking as an Oxford don, suggested? He forced himself to speak calmly.

"And that destiny is…?"

"The attainment of knowledge and immortality," the cat said as it turned its great head and glared in the direction of the approaching figures.

"You will soon have all knowledge and an eternity to enjoy it," the beast said as it raised itself on its back legs and caressed the sign on the monolith with its paw. "Here is the lock, now get the key!" the jaguar growled as it turned from the column and melted again into the shadows.

By the time Akhu and the others reached him, Neisen could barely suppress the blinding, overwhelming need for the stone the creature's words had spawned in him.

"You should have waited." Akhu's flinty voice made Ruth flinch. She had never heard him speak so harshly. Sensing her distress, he turned to her. "Little sister, we are not alone in this place."

In a few moments, the rest of the tribe had reached the pillars and gathered around Akhu. Jerry realized his feeling of detachment from the physical world was now completely gone and seemed to be from Ruth and the others as well. For the first time, he studied their surroundings. Beneath the bright corridor of stars lay a scene of complete desolation, no sign of any living thing—neither tree, bush, nor stream, not even a sprig of grass.

"It is as the man and woman described it long ago," Akhu said solemnly. "They came this far and spoke of these stones." He reached and reverently touched one. "They mark the boundary of the taboo land."

"It's not taboo any longer." Ruth pointed down the corridor of stars that disappeared like a silver ribbon into the distance, directly into the murky darkness of the forbidden land beyond the columns.

Akhu gestured them forward. "It is not good we linger here." He touched Ruth's arm and began walking.

"Not just yet." Neisen strode menacingly toward Akhu, his hand reaching for his revolver. "I would be obliged, Miss Starling, if you would tell him to give me the stone."

"What?" Ruth stepped back, startled by Neisen's abrupt change of manner.

"Tell him to give me the stone!" he shouted.

"Dr. Neisen, please." Jerry held out a tentative hand. "This isn't right, and you know it. Give me—"

Neisen whirled. "Shut up, you sniveling coward! You have no true heart for The Brotherhood or for what is required. I should have seen it on the boat when we took care of that prying Priest." He pointed the gun at Ruth." If you value her life, stay out of this." The muzzle swiveled back and forth between the Ruth and Akhu. "Now tell him to give me the stone."

Without waiting for Ruth to comply, Neisen reached out with his free hand and grabbed Akhu's wrist. The old man twisted away and clutched the stone more tightly to his chest.

"I've lied and sweated and killed for it my whole life, you ignorant savage. Give it to me!"

Tired of resistance, Neisen fired.

Akhu stared into the crazed eyes of the white man, who, like many others, had raped his land and slaughtered his people. A sad acceptance spread across his wrinkled face and he seemed not to notice the blood flowing from the ugly wound in his side as he sank slowly to the ground.

In a heartbeat, Neisen was on him, prying the stone from his clenched fist.

"Mine!" he shouted triumphantly as he retrieved the stone and pushed his way through the horrified natives toward the pillars.

Torn from the horror that for several moments kept him frozen in place in disbelief, Jerry rushed after him. "Neisen, in God's name!"

"God has nothing to do with it, you fool. Get out of the way or die!" he screamed.

"But there's still time to turn back," Jerry shouted after the crazed man. "What if you're wrong? What if you're just being used?"

Jerry did not see Ruth until it was too late to stop her. Panting, she raced ahead and planted herself between the columns and Neisen.

"Please, Dr. Neisen," she screamed, "put down the gun before someone gets killed!"

"That will be you, missionary, unless you get the hell out of my way." "No!" Jerry cried and charged, grabbing desperately for Neisen's gun hand.

"Die," Neisen shouted as his shot at Ruth went wild.

The explosion and Ruth's screams echoed off the towering stones as Jerry crumpled to the ground.

Chapter 44

Neisen raced to the pillar and pressed the raised design on the stone into the engraving on the pillar, shouting as he did, "I declare this the first day of the New Age!"

For what seemed an eternity, nothing happened. Neisen stood, arms upraised, like a king awaiting his coronation.

Then, from somewhere far away, a single trumpet sounded, and Neisen looked up. The stars had reformed again into a whirlpool of light encircling the dark abyss...but now it was slowly descending.

A second trumpet sounded, so near, the force of its blast rocked the earth beneath his feet. In moment, there was a third, then a fourth, then another, and another, and another until an antiphonal chorus of trumpets filled the sky, all blowing in cadence with the chasm that continued slowly to descend.

Then, a cacophony of screams and curses, even louder than the trumpets, erupted from the depths of the chasm's darkness, that merging with them, created such a bedlam of dissonance, the Yanoakos covered their ears and fell to the earth in terror.

Ruth crawled to Jerry. Wrapping her arms around him, she buried her face in his chest. Her mind, staggering under a weight of horror, sensed evil's distilled essence was being sucked into the stygian darkness at the whirlpool's core.

At the end however, as the swirling vortex slowly settled over Neisen and the pillars, only he finally understood what he had unleashed or what had been his destiny from the beginning.

Jerry and Ruth, spared at the end the horror of hearing Neisen's insane screams and pleas for mercy or watching as the jaguar ripped out his throat and dragged his thrashing body into the maw of the whirlpool, could only gaze speechless, as the tunnel retreated into the sky to become again a distant void, surrounded by the spinning stars.

Only God, whose nature is both love and justice, knew the dark whirlpool had not descended for Neisen alone. His destiny was to open the gate to final judgment—to set the whirlpool churning on its damning course around the world, free at last to swallow the godless and their hopes for a paradise without Him.

It surged into Abelard's room on a North Sea gale. He saw its approach and cried out in disappointment and frustration. Beyond all sense of guilt, he did not beg for mercy, but simply yielded his leprous life to the cold embrace of darkness, knowing there remained no other place for him.

The whirling darkness also appeared above the desk of Vice President Andrews. It was the last thing he saw just before putting the gun in his mouth and pulling the trigger. Taloned paws, reaching from the abyss was his first horrific vision as he leaped into eternity.

The ground where the columns had stood was bare of evidence they had ever existed.

Frederick Neisen, however, was another matter. The stone, lying where he dropped it, testified he had been among the living only moments ago. But neither he nor hell could possess the stone for long. That honor and duty had been reserved for Ruth and Akhu.

Reverently, she bent down and picked it up. As she held it toward the heavens, words came unbidden to her lips. "Oh God, be our Urim and Thummim, our light to Paradise," she prayed as the corridor of stars reformed before them.

Using a sleeping mat a tribesman had brought, two of the men laid the unconscious Akhu upon the pallet and gently picked it up. One of the women had packed his wound with a piece of material torn from her garment. Thankfully, the bleeding had stopped.

Neisen's second bullet had gone through the fleshy part of Jerry's upper leg and had left a clean wound. Using the sleeves of his shirt, Ruth quickly made a tourniquet. Braced between two of the men, he joined her and the others as they began walking down the corridor of stars into the forbidden land.

Chapter 45

ALMOST IMMEDIATELY, THEY BEGAN to notice a change in the landscape. Waves of luminance washed over everything as the gray, sterile desert that surrounded the pillars slowly gave way to a scattering of green bushes.

Life! Ruth thought.

Finally, trees appeared. Dwarfish at first, they grew larger as they continued deeper into the land. At last, they came to a stream. In the Amazon, all the streams run muddy, but Ruth could see this one was clear. On impulse, she bent, cupped her hand, and drank, sighing at the sweetness of the water. She picked a broad leaf from a nearby bush, rolled it up to collect some water, and carried it to Akhu.

Once they crossed the shallow stream, things changed dramatically. The forest thickened.

"Ruth, do you notice anything peculiar about this place?" Jerry asked, his eyes scanning their surroundings.

"Only that it's very beautiful."

"But have you ever seen a forest without any underbrush? Or broken limbs or dead leaves?"

"You're right. None since we crossed the river. Strange."

"And something else."

"What?"

"The whole forest looks manicured, like the grounds of an English country estate. It's as if someone's constantly taking care of the place."

As he spoke, they crested the brow of a low hill and saw a valley stretching out below whose elysian fields beckoned them with haunting beauty. They saw it clearly, because like everything else, the light was changing. Inner luminescence had completely replaced the half-light of the stars and seemed to radiate from everything.

"Ruth, try casting a shadow."

Ruth looked at Jerry quizzically as she held out her hand in front of a tree. Nothing. She held it close to the ground but still no shadow. Finally, she put it near Jerry's face and exclaimed, "I see one here."

"I think it's because we're different," Jerry replied. "We have no internal light. At least not yet."

"Maybe soon," she whispered wistfully.

She had no idea where her insight and feeling of anticipation came from, only certain of its rightness as she feasted her senses on the green freshness of the trees and plants, the sweetness of the air, the untouched purity of this place that shimmered as if bathed in a shower of sparkling light.

At the bottom of the hill, two rows of stately trees marked the boundaries of a grassy path leading to the center of the valley. Pausing, they looked down the avenue toward a bank of fog in the distance. Though no hint of a breeze, it slowly lifted, curtain-like, to reveal a solitary tree.

Far larger than any they had ever seen, it was its shape that captured their attention. Some thirty feet above the ground, its trunk divided into two identical sections whose branches appeared as large as sequoias and continued upward in perfect parallel another hundred feet. There, as if by design, they separated and curved out and down in graceful arches toward the earth in perfectly balanced symmetry.

"The tree! Like the sign on the stone," Ruth whispered in awe.

"It is the mark of Shi," someone said behind them.

Ruth and Jerry both turned, startled to see Akhu standing tall and erect.

Ruth rushed to his side. "You shouldn't be walking! Your wound—" She stopped abruptly when Akhu pointed to his side.

All the blood and the gaping hole had disappeared. Astonished, she watched as even the faint pink scar marking the bullet's entrance faded away.

"And you, my son?" Akhu gestured to Jerry's leg.

The two men supporting Jerry stepped away as Akhu gently removed the tourniquet from his leg.

Like his own, the wound had healed completely.

Ruth's eyes were captured by Akhu's face, where his deep wrinkles were melting like snow in a spring thaw.

"I have one last duty to perform, little sister," Akhu said resolutely. "Not just for my people, but for all the others Shi has chosen. It is His will that I do this thing."

Gently he took the stone from Ruth's hand and set off up the pathway toward the giant tree. Jerry, now walking as if a bullet had never torn through his body, took Ruth's hand as they followed Akhu whose bearing and stride had become that of the warrior he might have been.

As they drew nearer to the tree, they heard singing that was spreading down the long avenue from tree to tree like ripples on a still pond until it seemed every branch vibrated with the melody.

Ruth surveyed the Edenic scene, feeling her spirit yield to the music's call to worship, just as it broke free of the garden to spread its doxology of praise around the world.

She felt her soul fly upward on its message. Faster and faster, farther and farther. Beyond a billion stars, beyond billions of galaxies of stars, beyond space whose distances the minds of men could not conceive. Her soul thrilled as the music of the invisible choir breached the wall of ice, vaulted the great deep, and filled the Sanctuary of the Third Heaven. It was there in her spirit, she joined with the angelic chorus and all creation in singing praises to Christ who was making all things new.

"You are worthy" they sang, "to take the book and to open the seals thereof, for you were slain and have redeemed us to God by your blood out of every kindred, tongue and people and nation. And have made us unto our God, Kings and Priests: and we shall reign upon the earth…worthy is the Lamb that was slain to receive power and wisdom and riches and strength and honor and glory and blessing."

The song faded, and Ruth was aware that she, Jerry and Akhu had reached the tree as reverential silence settled over everything.

"We've entered the Holy of Holies," Ruth whispered to Jerry as they watched old Akhu, now young again, approach the trunk of the tree and kneel.

"He's looking for something," Jerry said.

After a moment, Akhu stood and held a small stone block in his hand, which, when he turned it over, revealed its significance. Etched deep into its face was the engraved sign of Shi, identical to that carved on the amulet he carried.

"The stone cut without hands," Ruth whispered, remembering the Prophet Daniel's description of Christ.

Spellbound, they watched as Akhu raised his face toward heaven, his lips moving silently in prayer. Then, gently he inserted the amulet into the block's indention.

The effect was instant. Just beyond the great tree, the stone columns that had marked the border of the taboo land suddenly materialized. Out of the warm light spilling between them, Ruth and Jerry saw Timmy, Miss Flowers, their parents, and Father Bodien all running toward them to the accompaniment of the same beautiful singing they had heard as they approached the tree.

As the music swelled, each knew within their soul that the mighty deep between God and his children had been bridged by the smiling man who now stepped from between the columns; a man, though never having seen, they knew with an inner certainty born of faith. Faith that now accepted his invitation to draw near – faith, having given way to sight, rejoiced in his words of greeting when he said, "Welcome home, my children, to the place I've prepared for you. Welcome home to Paradise."

Time had rolled round again.

Made in the USA
San Bernardino, CA
22 April 2015